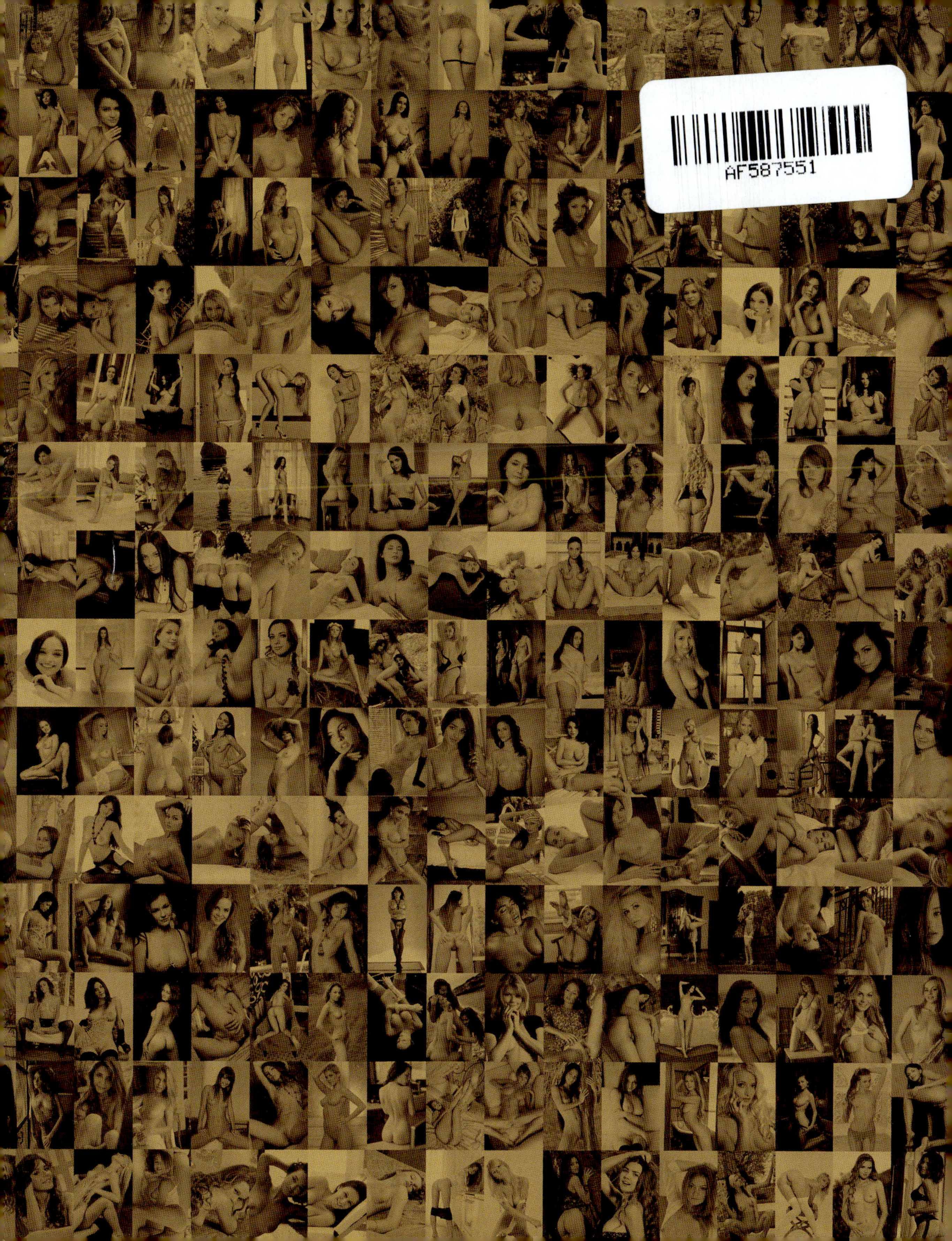

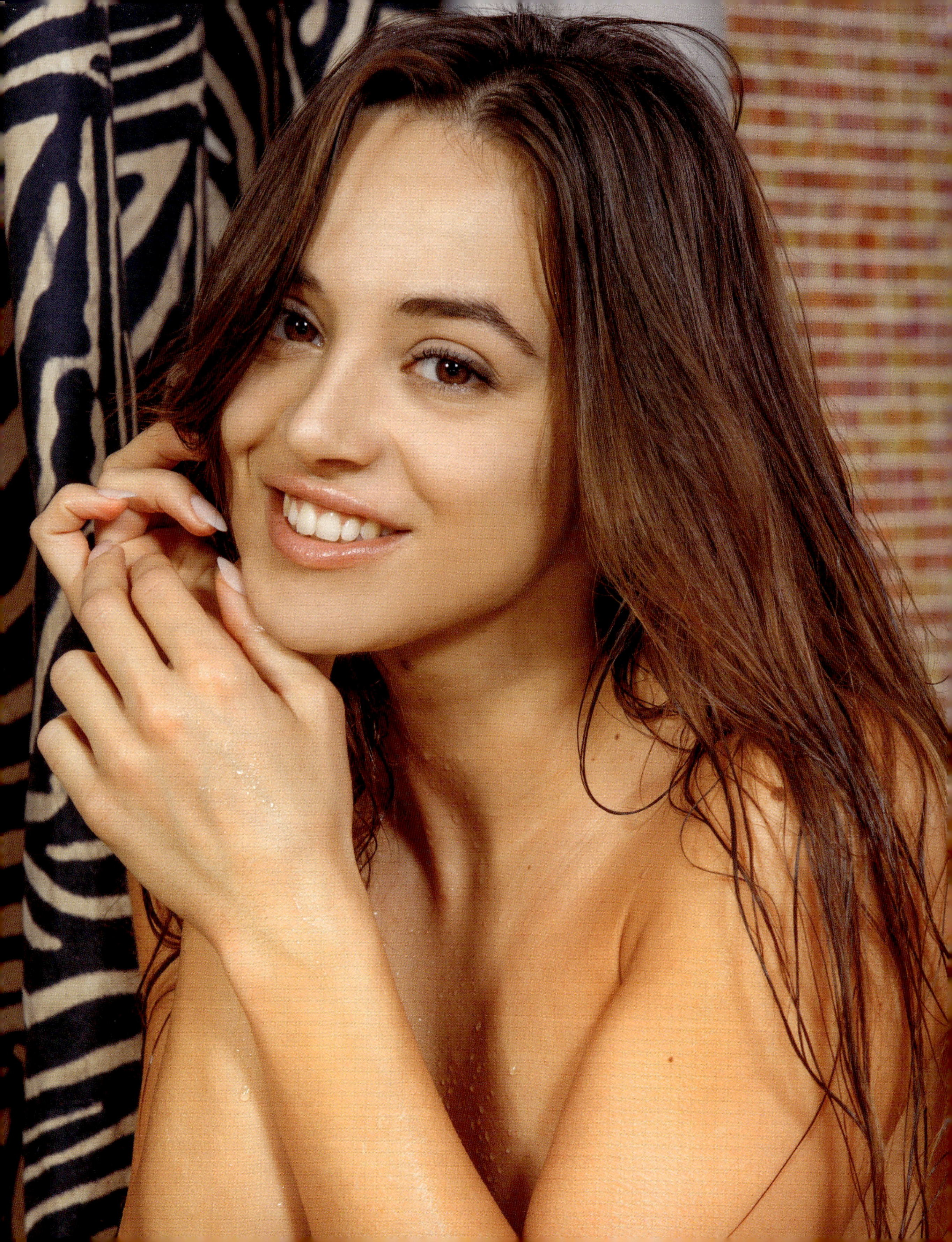

TOP MODELS OF

METART.COM

WHERE FLAWLESS BEAUTY MEETS ART

# DOMINIKA A

COLLECTED AND EDITED BY ISABELLA CATALINA

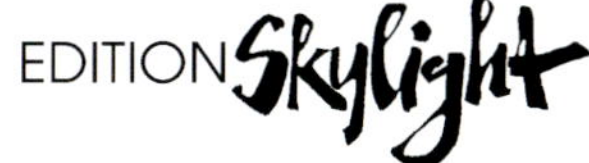

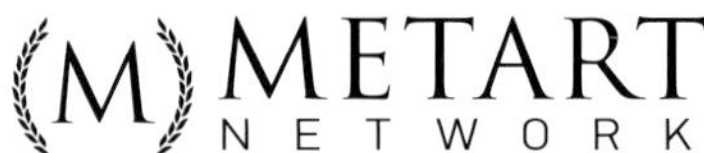




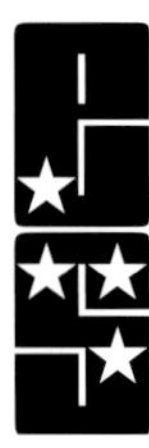

2. Auflage 2024
1. Auflage 2021


EDITION SKYLIGHT
Rosengartenstrasse 13B
CH-8608 Bubikon / Zürich
Switzerland
info@edition-skylight.com
www.edition-skylight.com

ISBN 978-3-03766-679-1



Bibliographic information published by Die Deutsche Bibliothek
Die Deutsche Bibliothek lists this publication in the
Deutsche Nationalbibliografie; detailed bibliographic data
are available in the Internet at http://dnb.ddb.de.

Printed in Czech Republik

# SENSUAL BEAUTY DOMINIKA A

**Gorgeous brunette Dominika A** has movie star looks and an exhibitionist nature. One of Metart's most popular erotic nude models, the sultry Czech sweetheart is sheer physical perfection, with golden tanned skin, a peachy bottom, perky breasts with dark nipples, and puffy labia that spread open into an enticing butterfly. A flirtatious extrovert with a radiant smile and a passionate expression in her soulful brown eyes that is sure to seduce you, she makes no secret of her powerful sensuality and her pleasure in sharing it with the world. She made her Metart debut over a decade ago at the age of 24, and she seems to become more beautiful with every passing year, whether gloriously naked on an exotic beach or dressed up in sexy lingerie and heels to show off her long, athletic legs. No wonder her devoted fans call her *Dominikaaaaaaaah!*

**Die brunette Dominika A** sieht aus wie ein Filmsternchen und besitzt eine gehörige Portion Exhibitionismus. Als eines der populärsten Models bei Metart besticht dieser tschechische Schatz mit einem perfekten Körper, braungebrannter goldener Haut, einem wohlgeformten Hintern und vorwitzigen Brüsten. Ihre Schamlippen von ungeahnter Form öffnen sich wie ein grosser Schmetterling, so etwas Aufregendes sieht selbst der erfahrene Geniesser nicht alle Tage. Die stets flirtende Extrovertierte mit dem strahlenden Lächeln zeigt ihre hitzige Sinnlichkeit der ganzen Welt. Sie startete ihr Debut bei Metart vor 10 Jahren im Alter von 24 und Sie wird immer begehrenswerter. Egal, ob Sie nackt an einem Südseestrand ihren Körper streckt, in sexy Wäsche oder nur in hohen Stöckelschuhen ihre langen Beine zeigt, die Fans stöhnen *Dominikaaaaaaaah!*

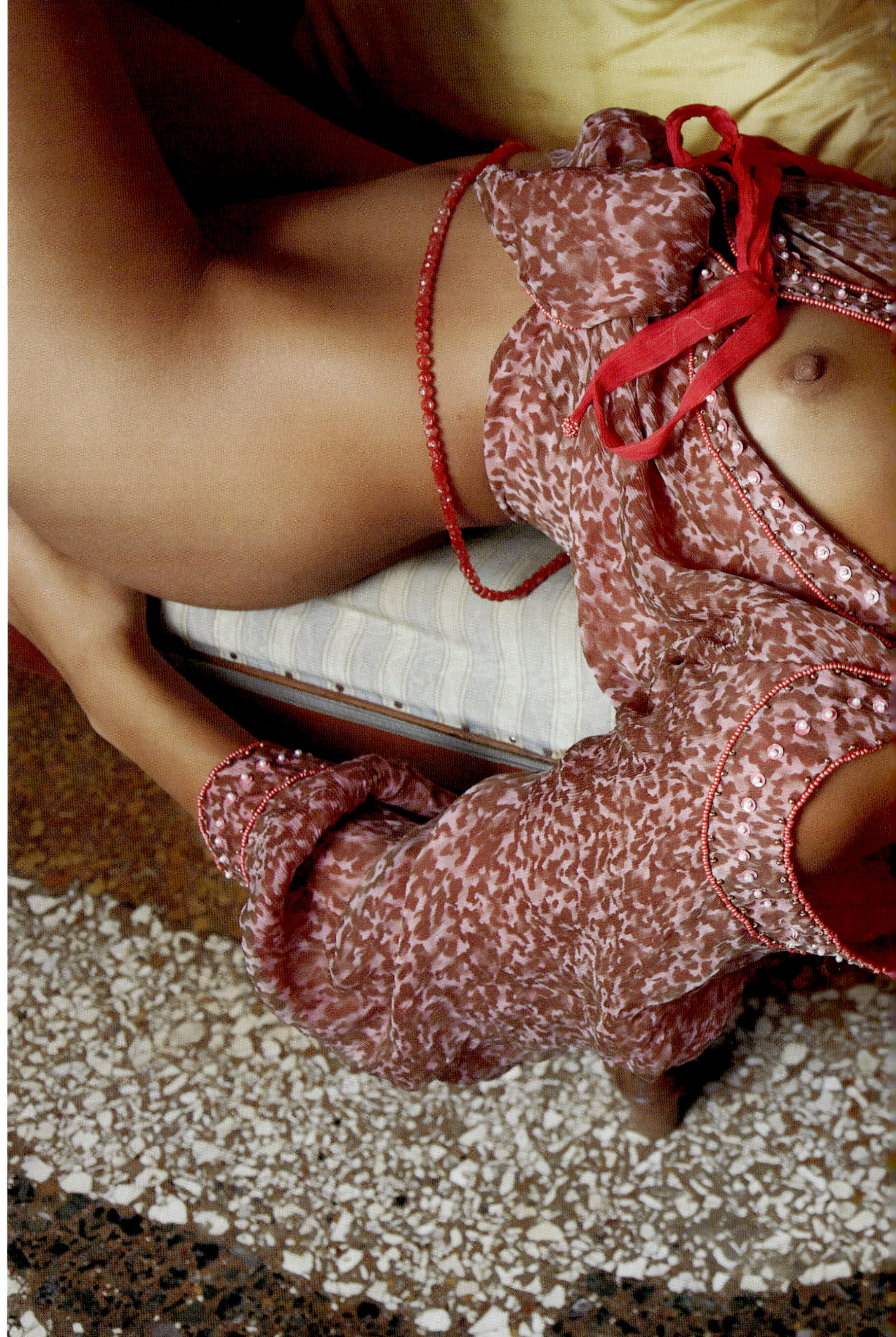

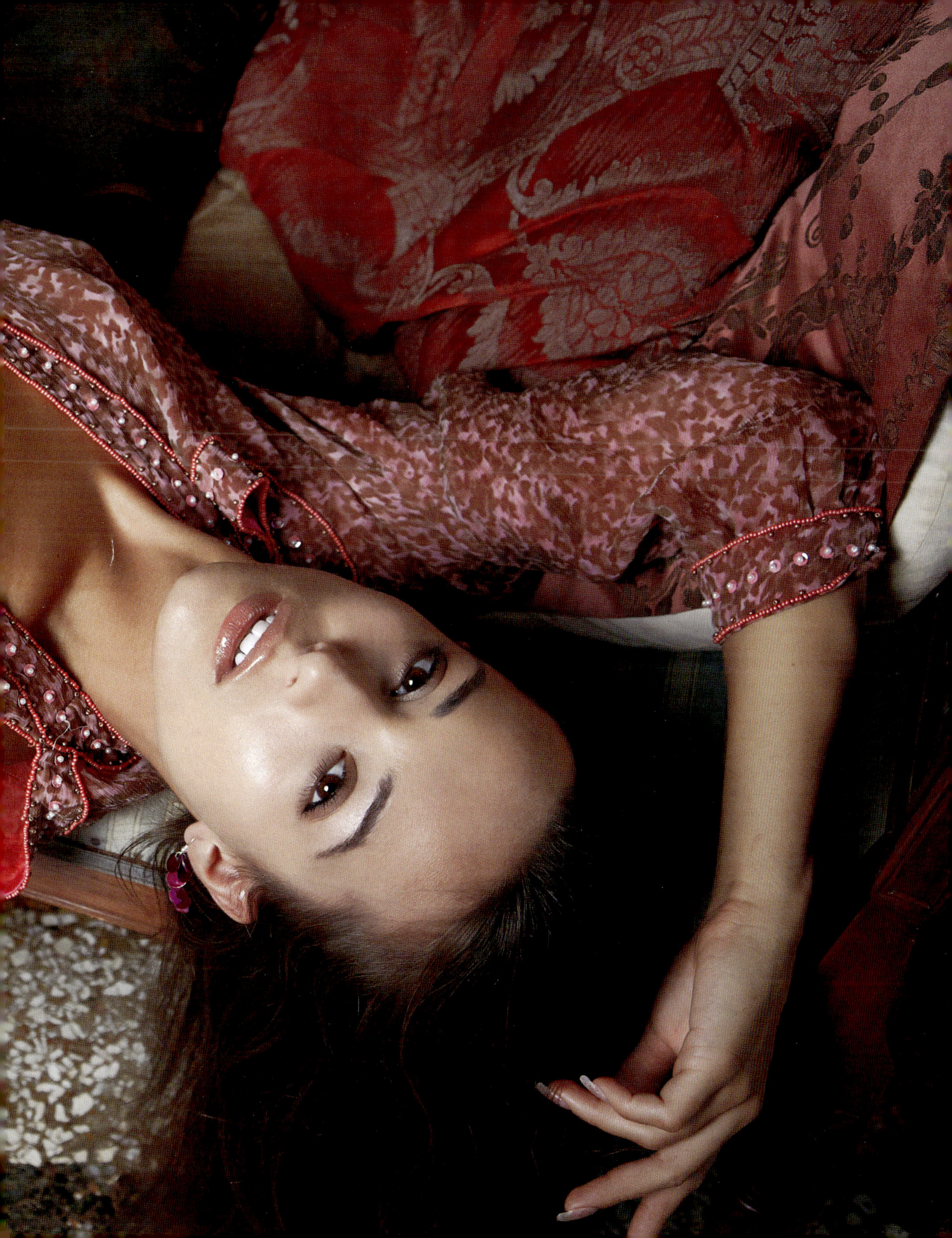

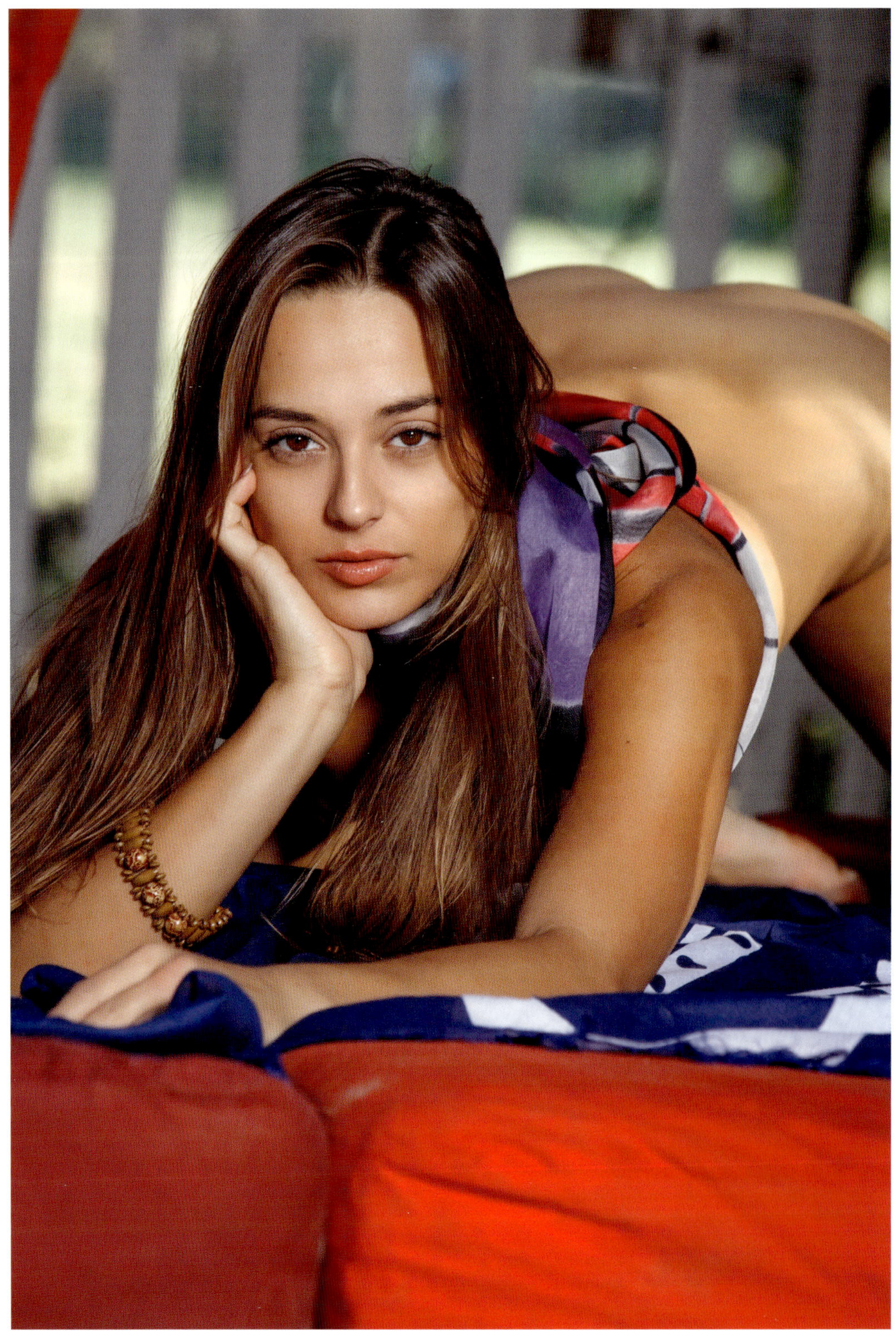

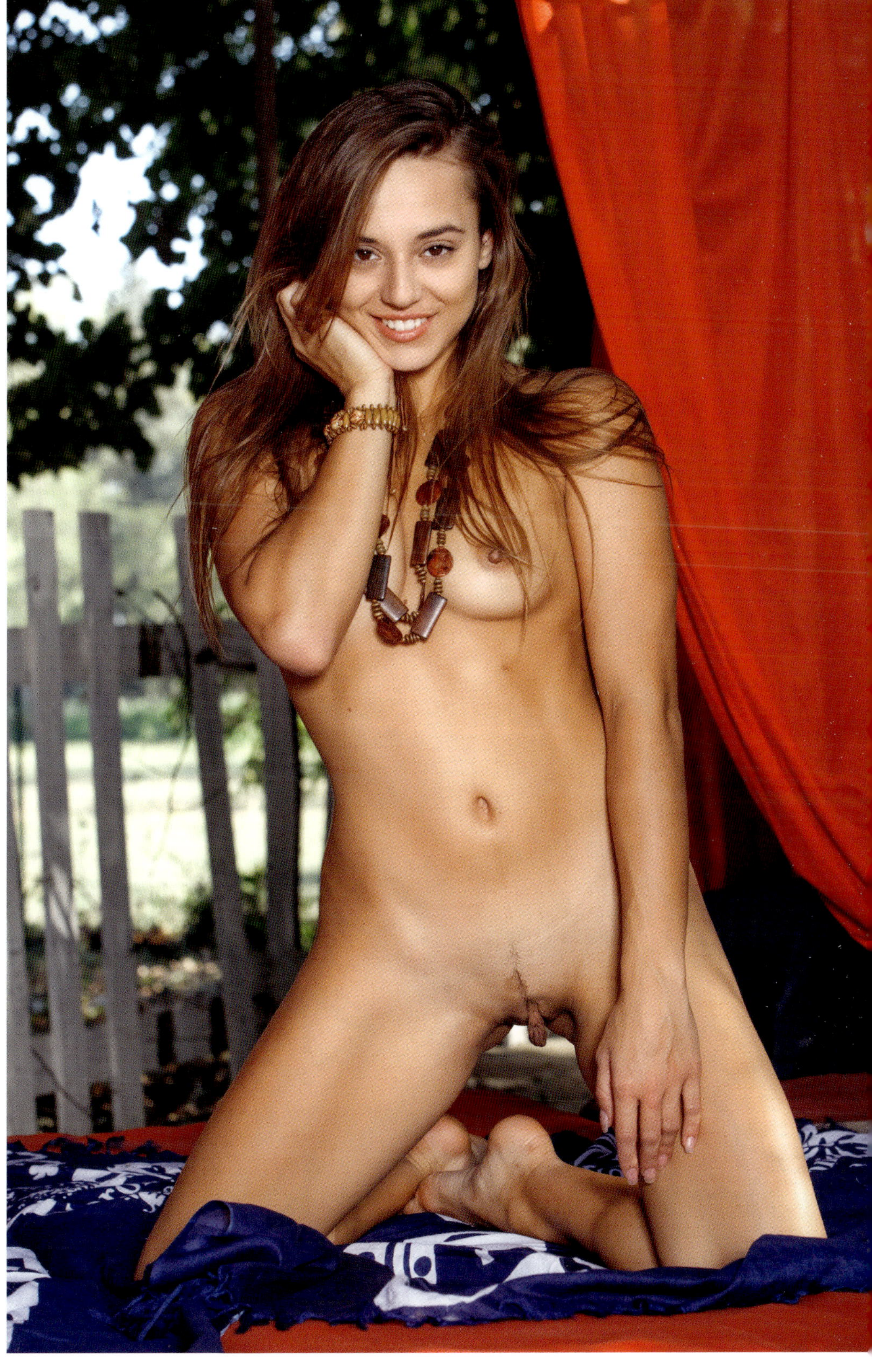

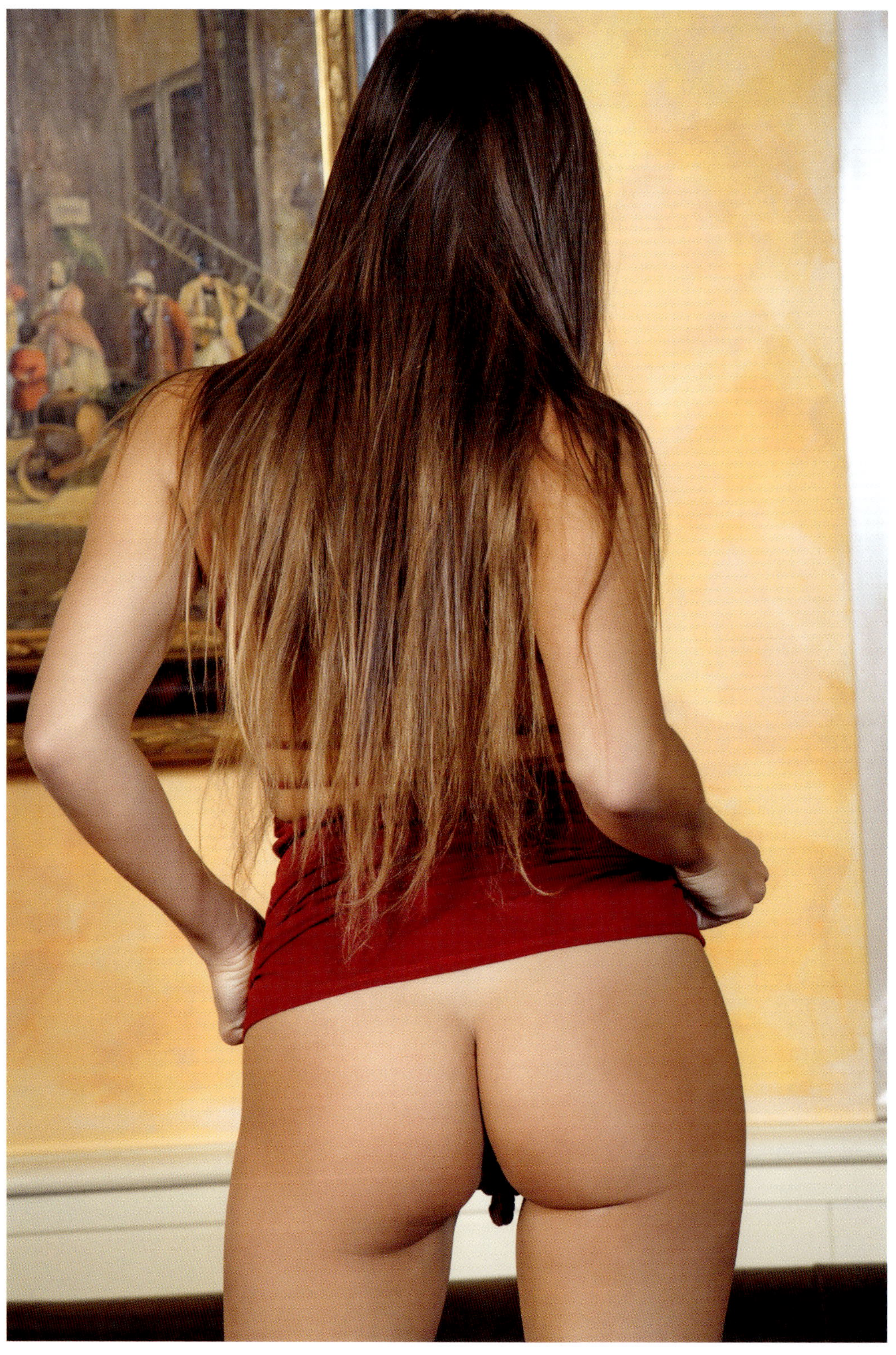

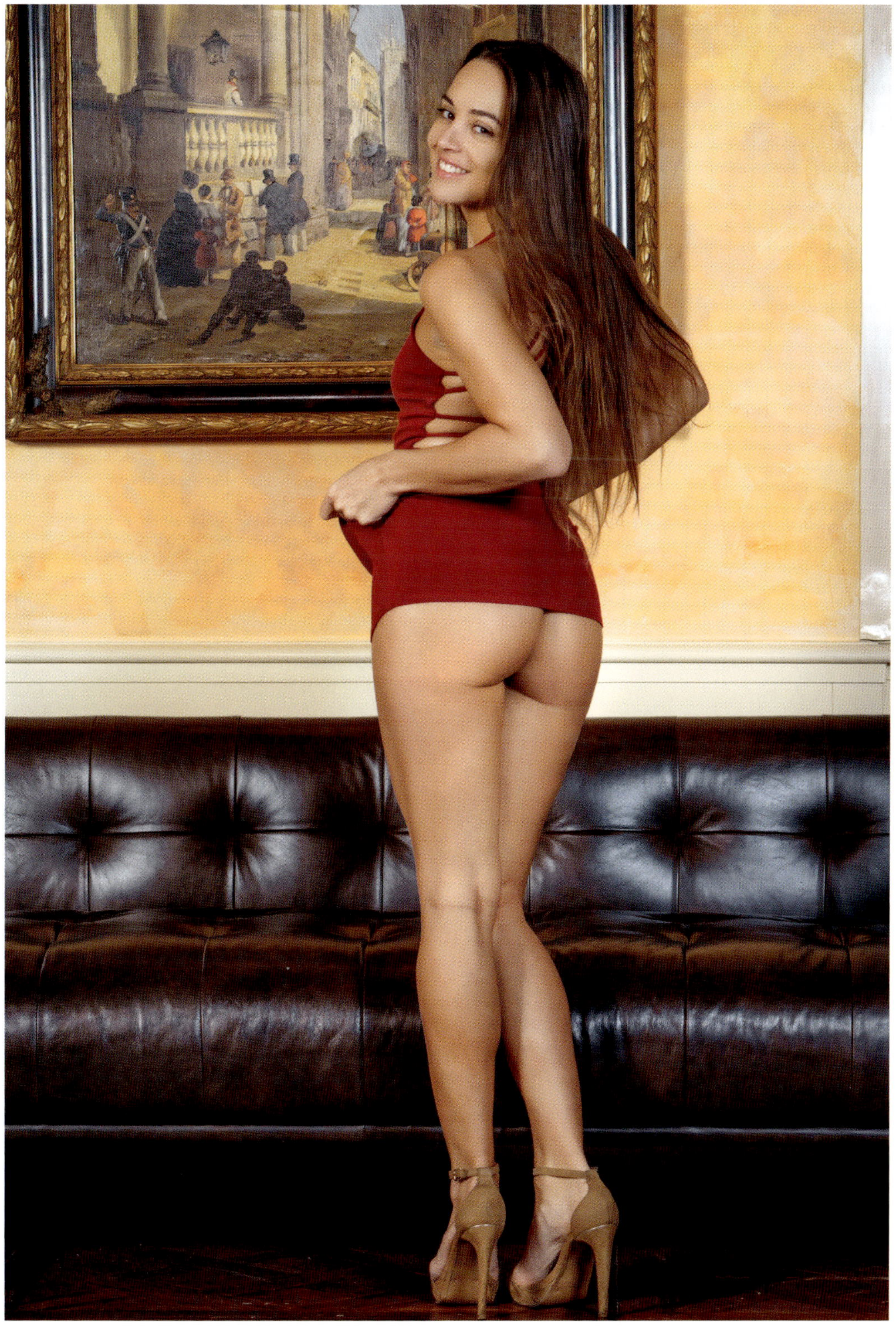

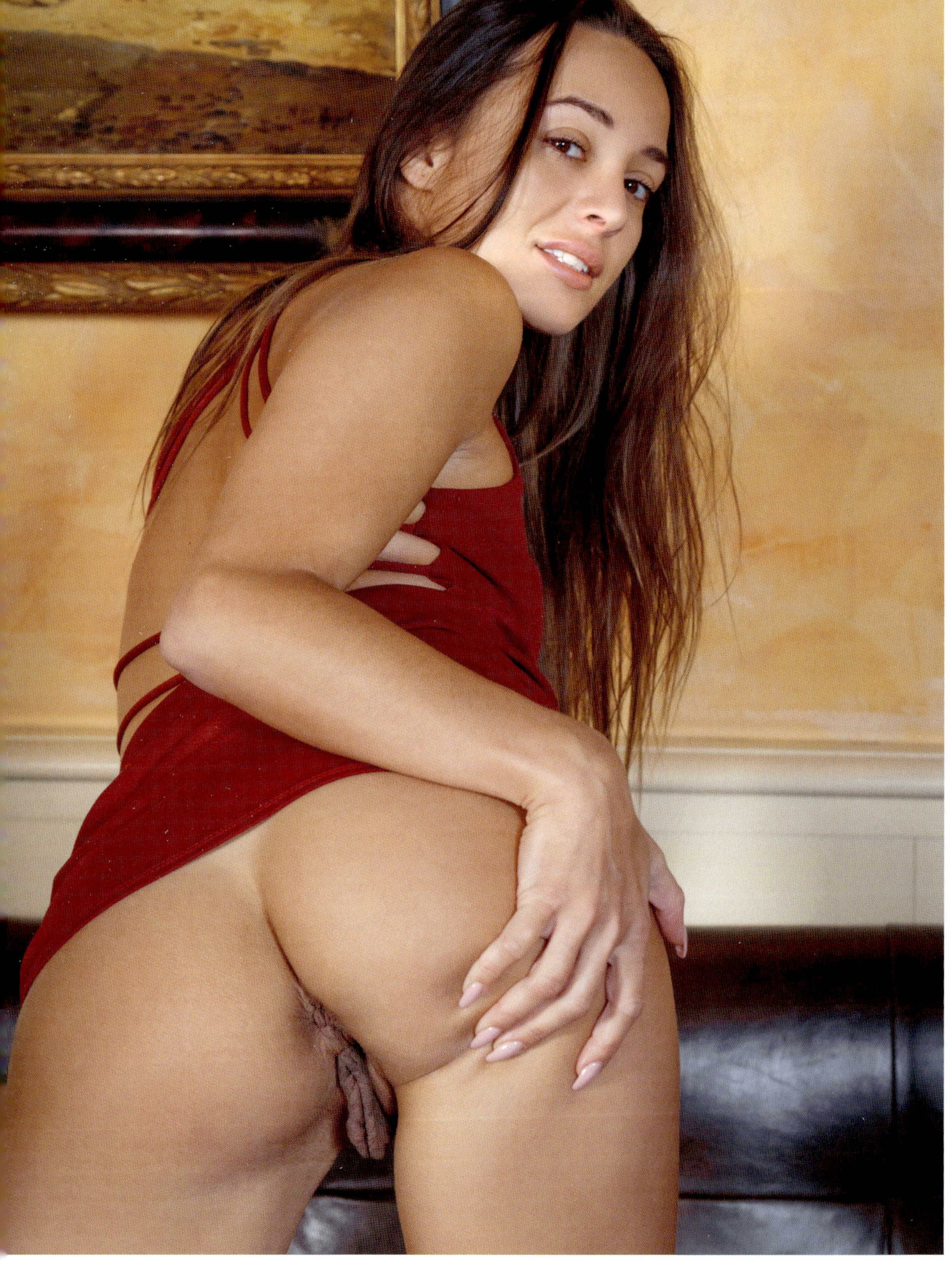

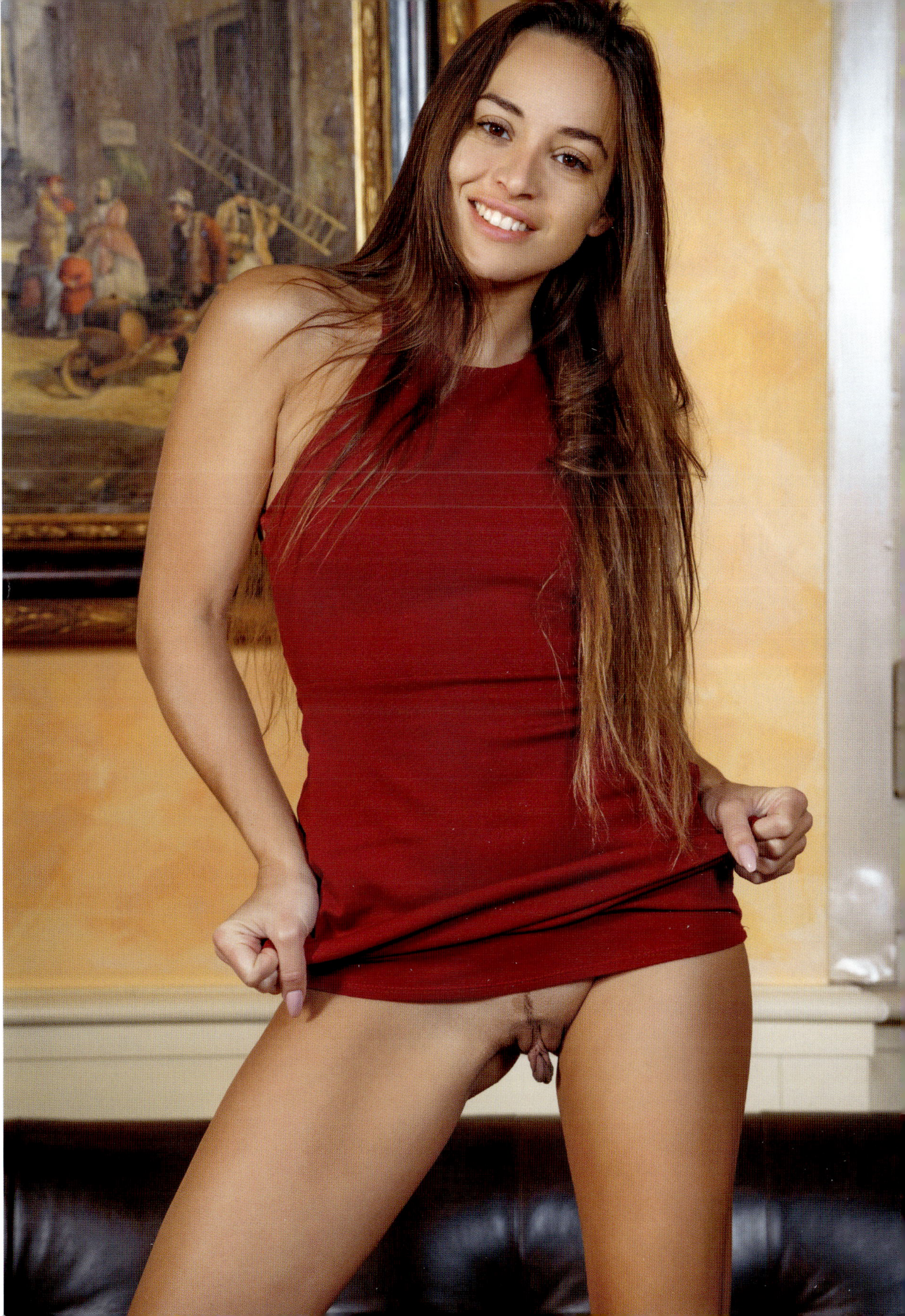

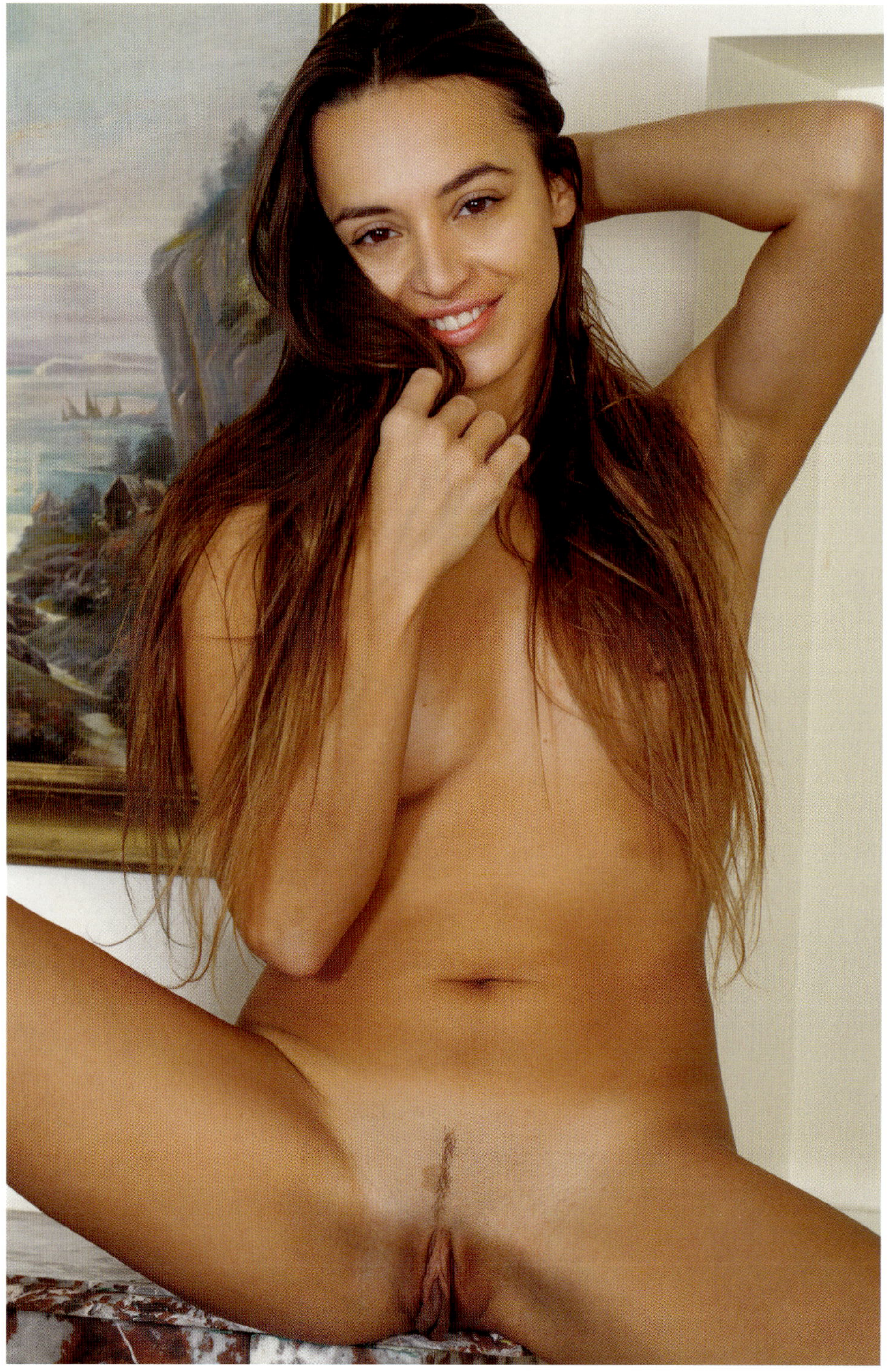

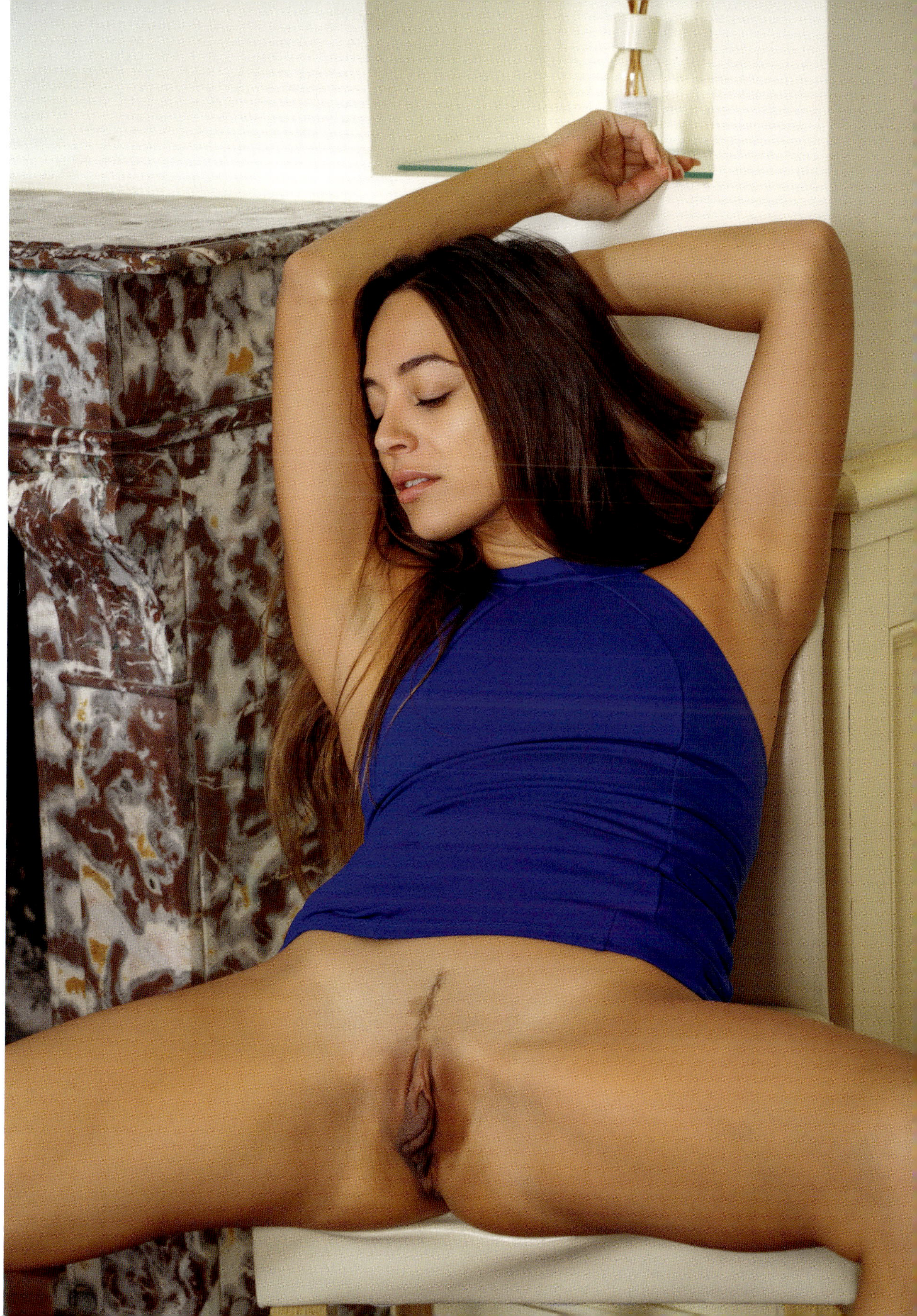

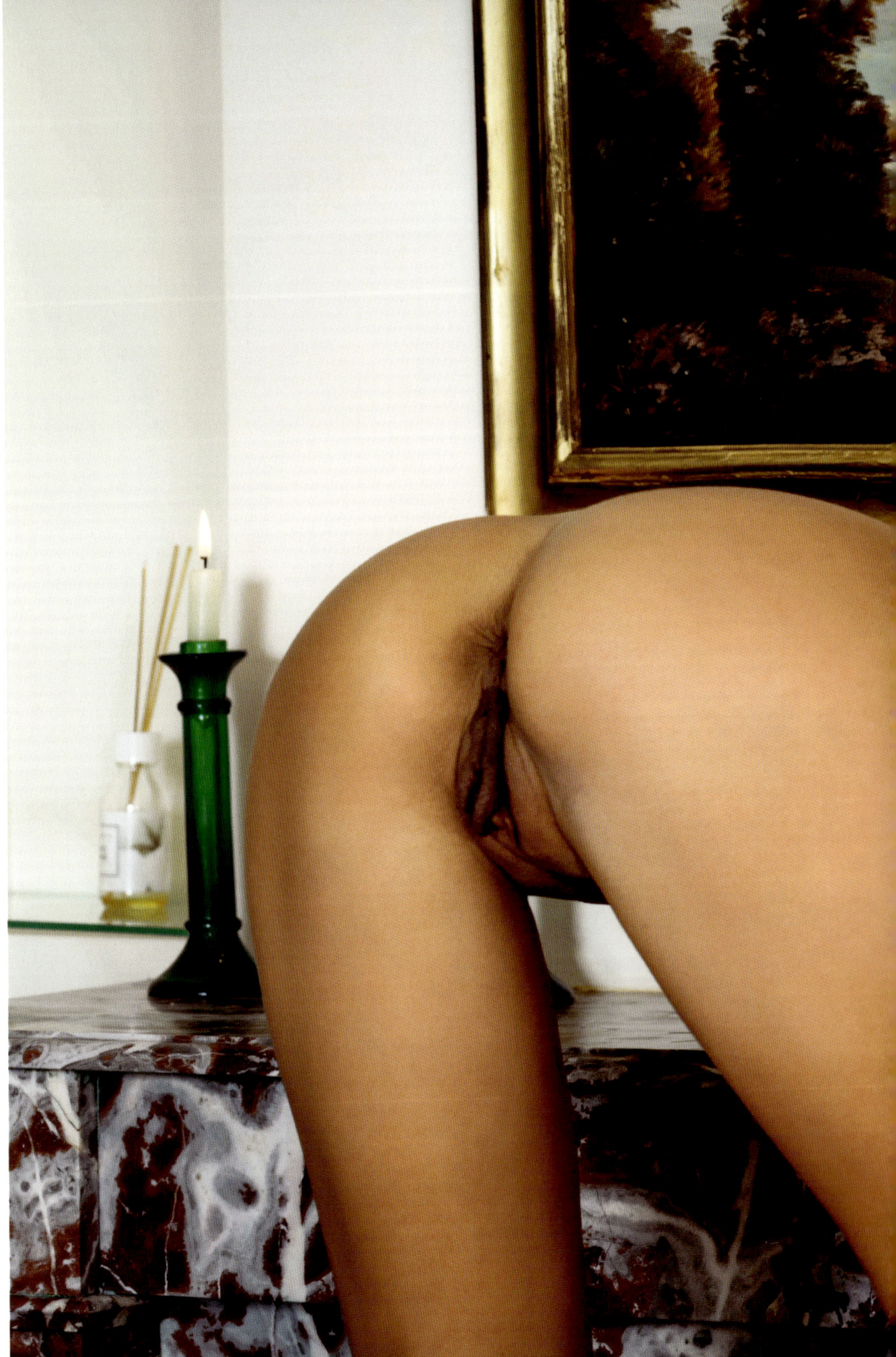

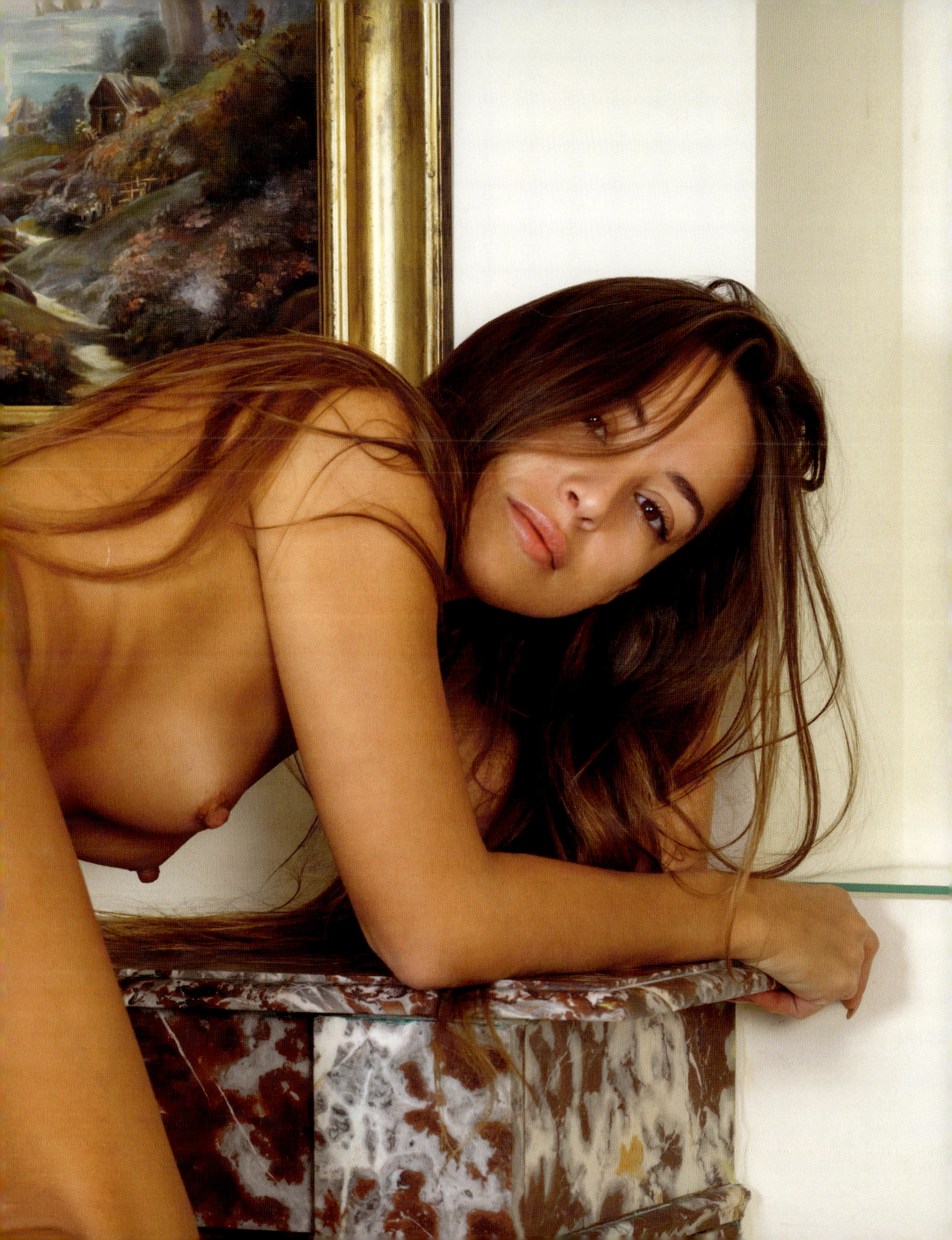

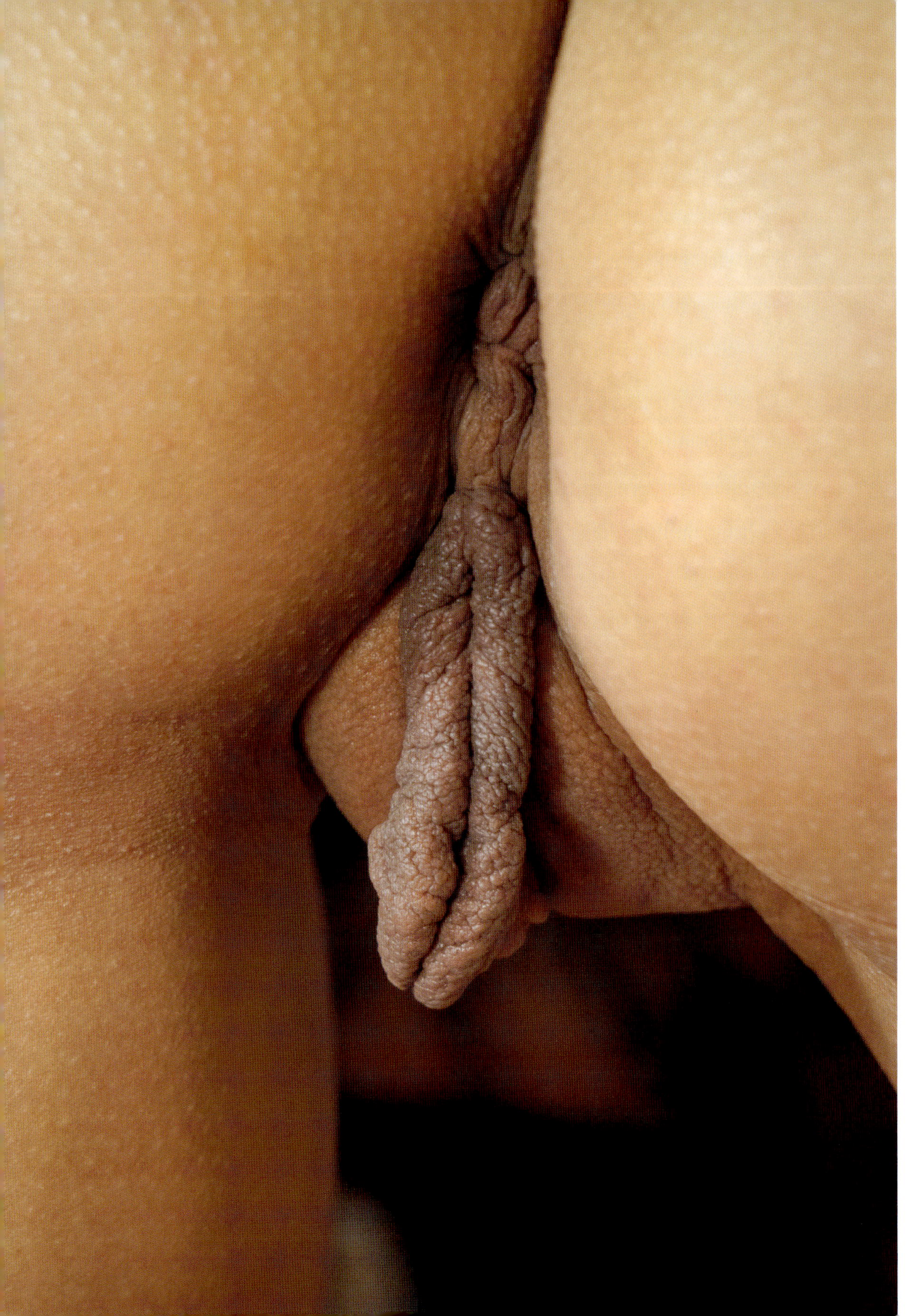

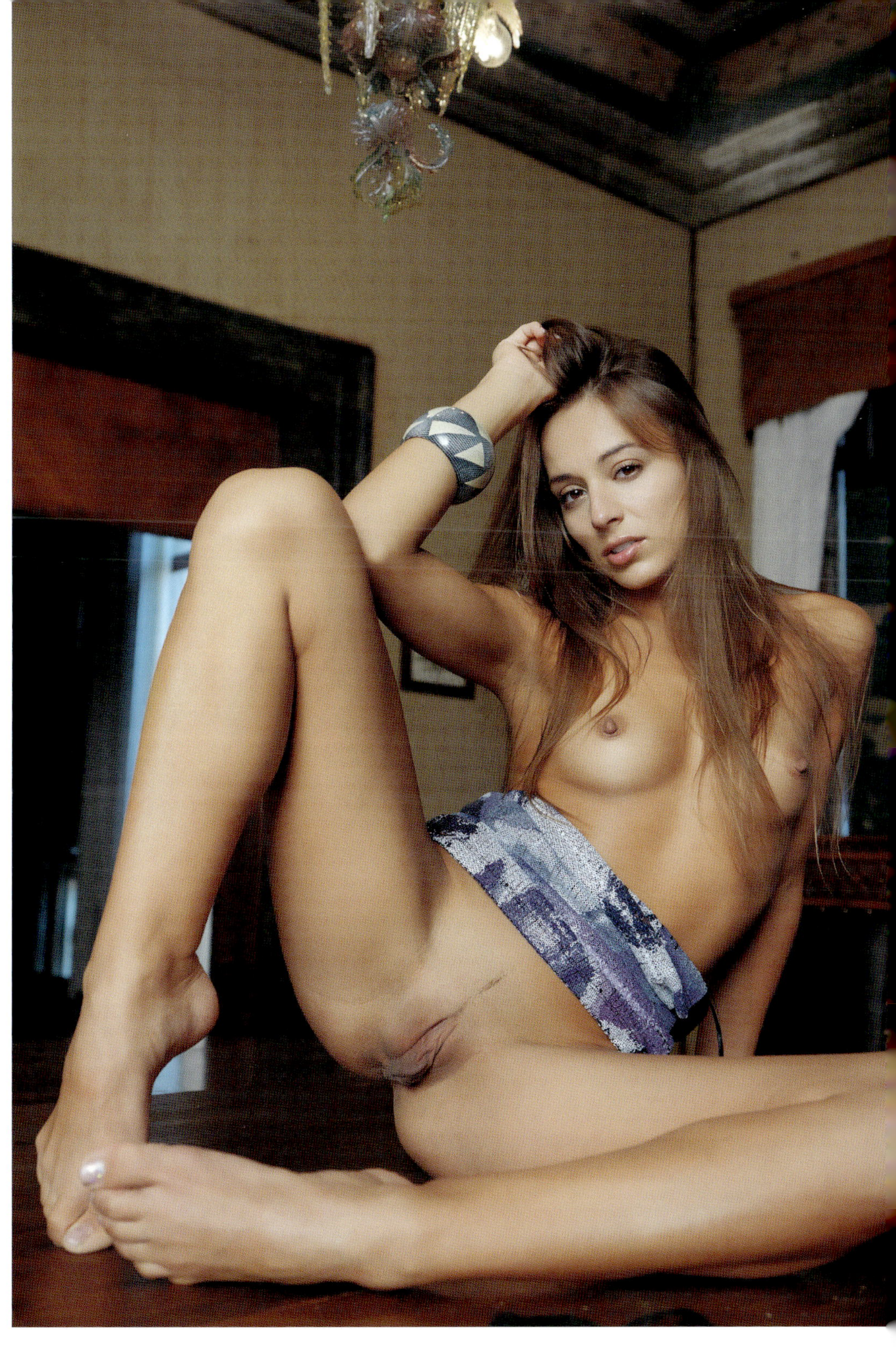

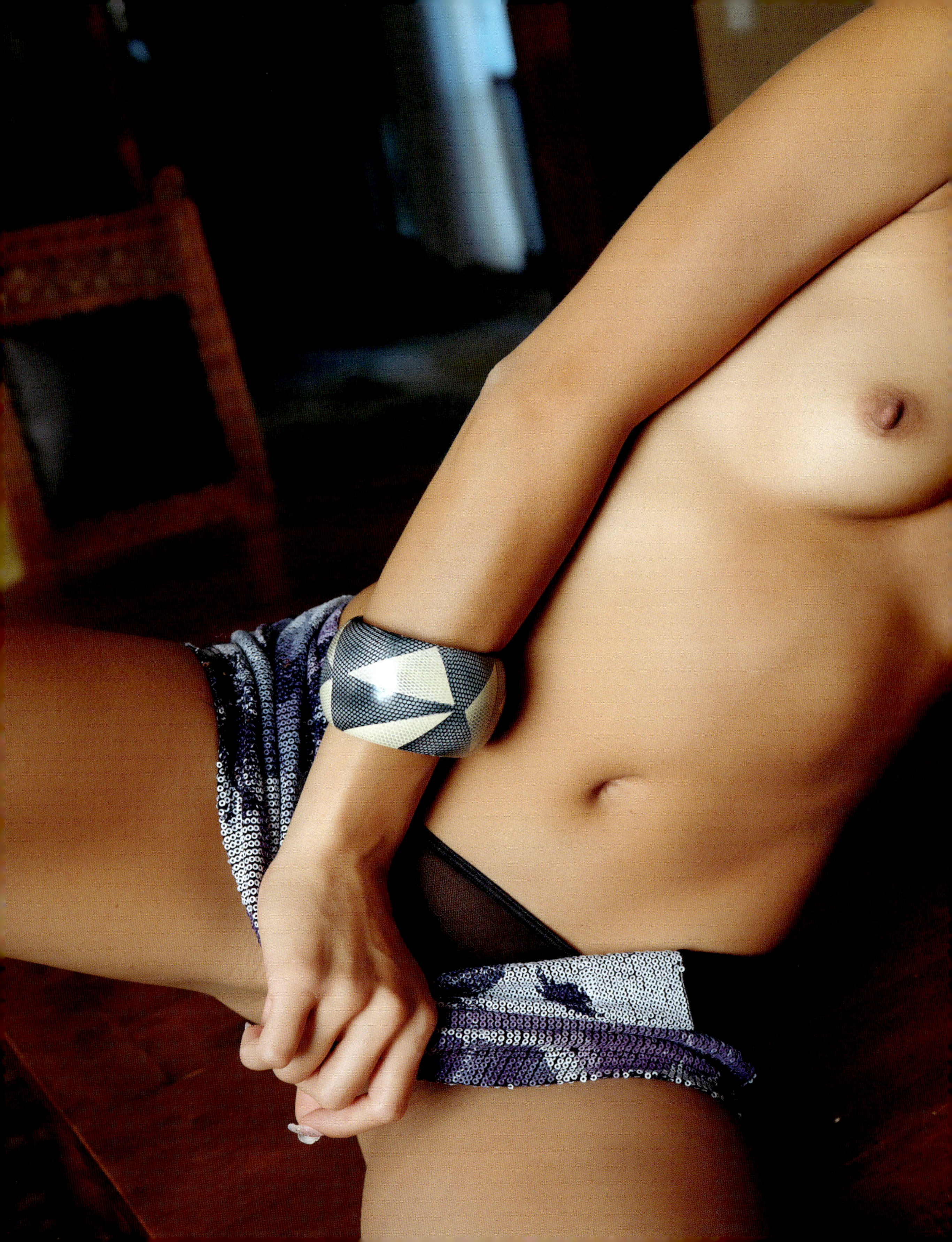

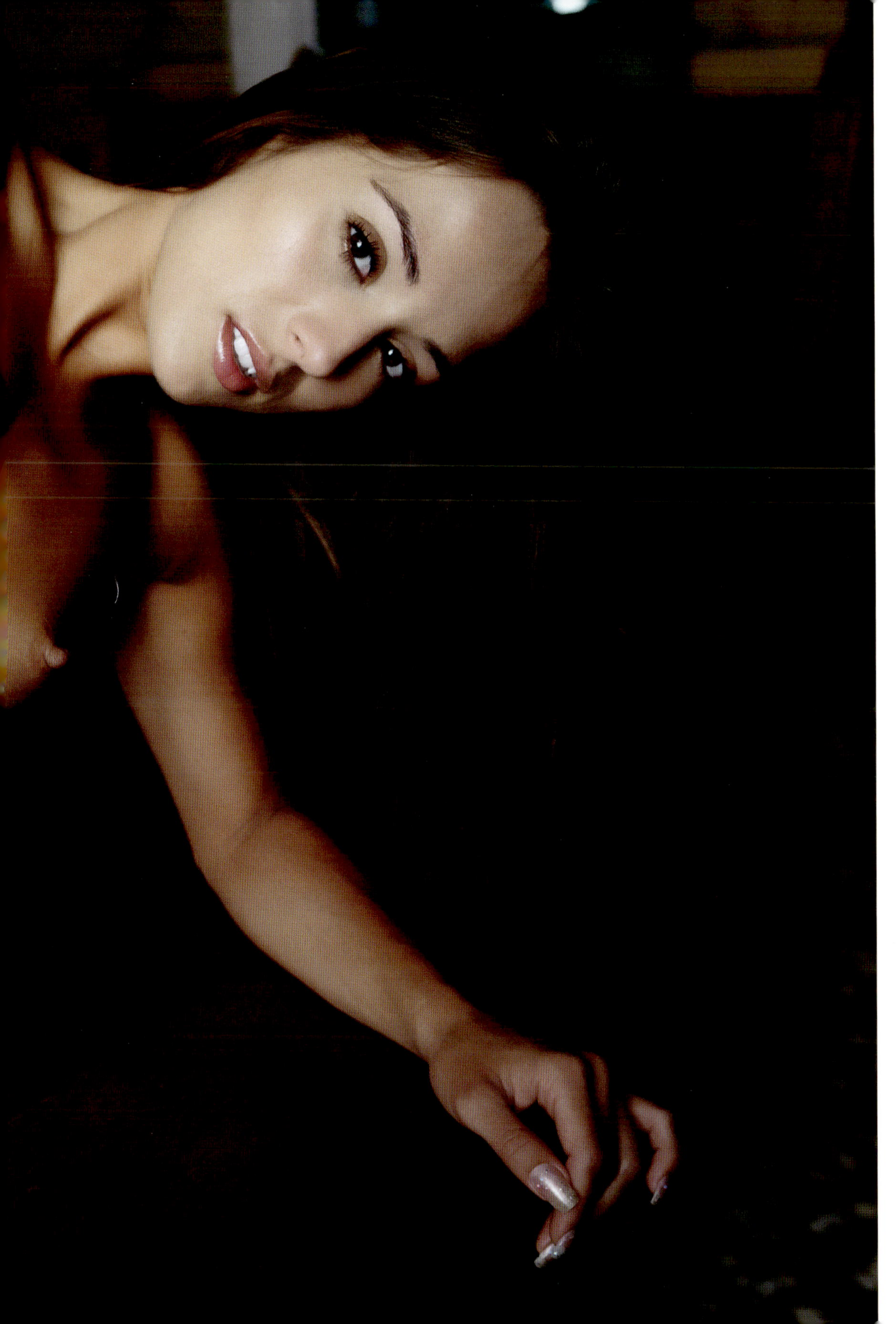

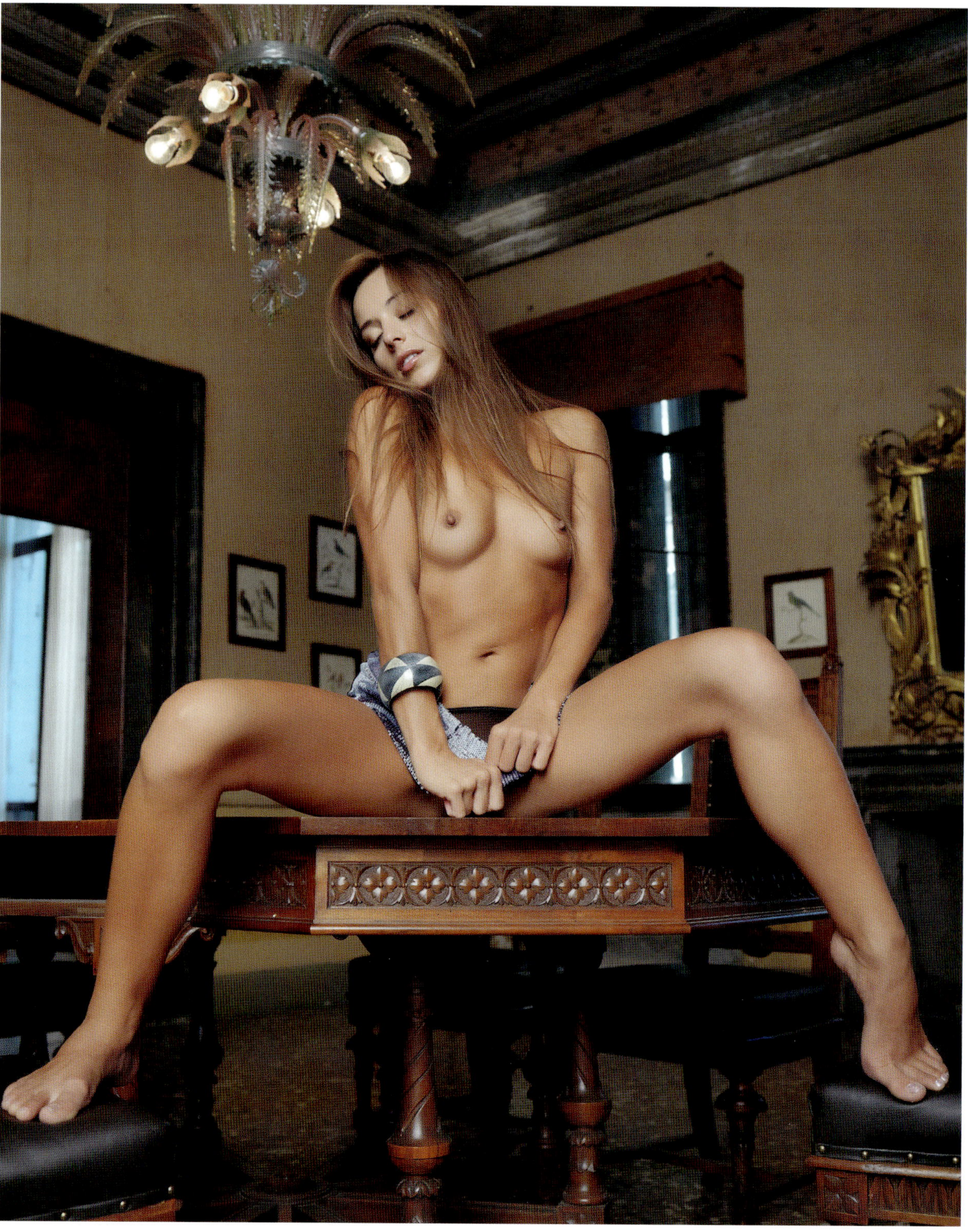

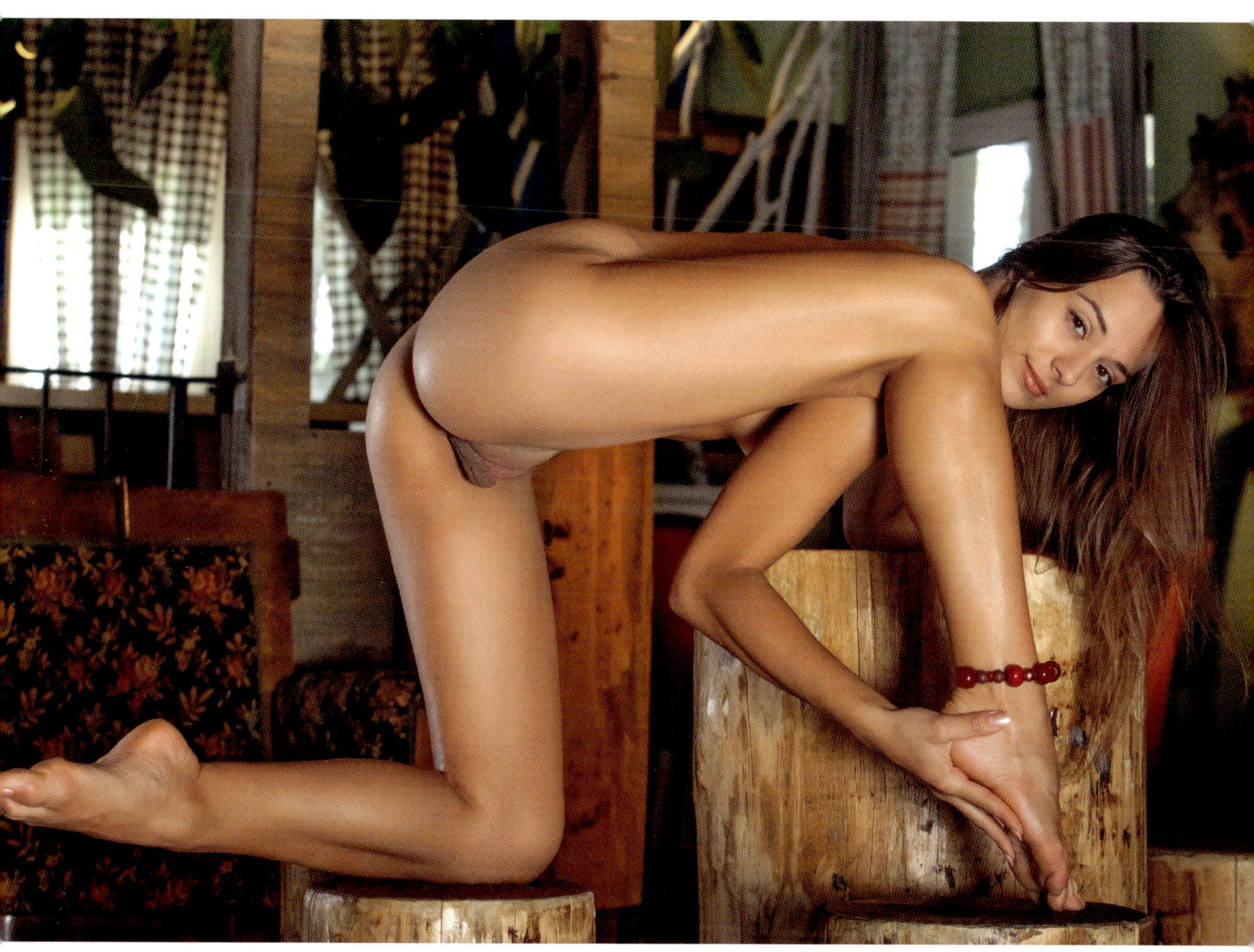

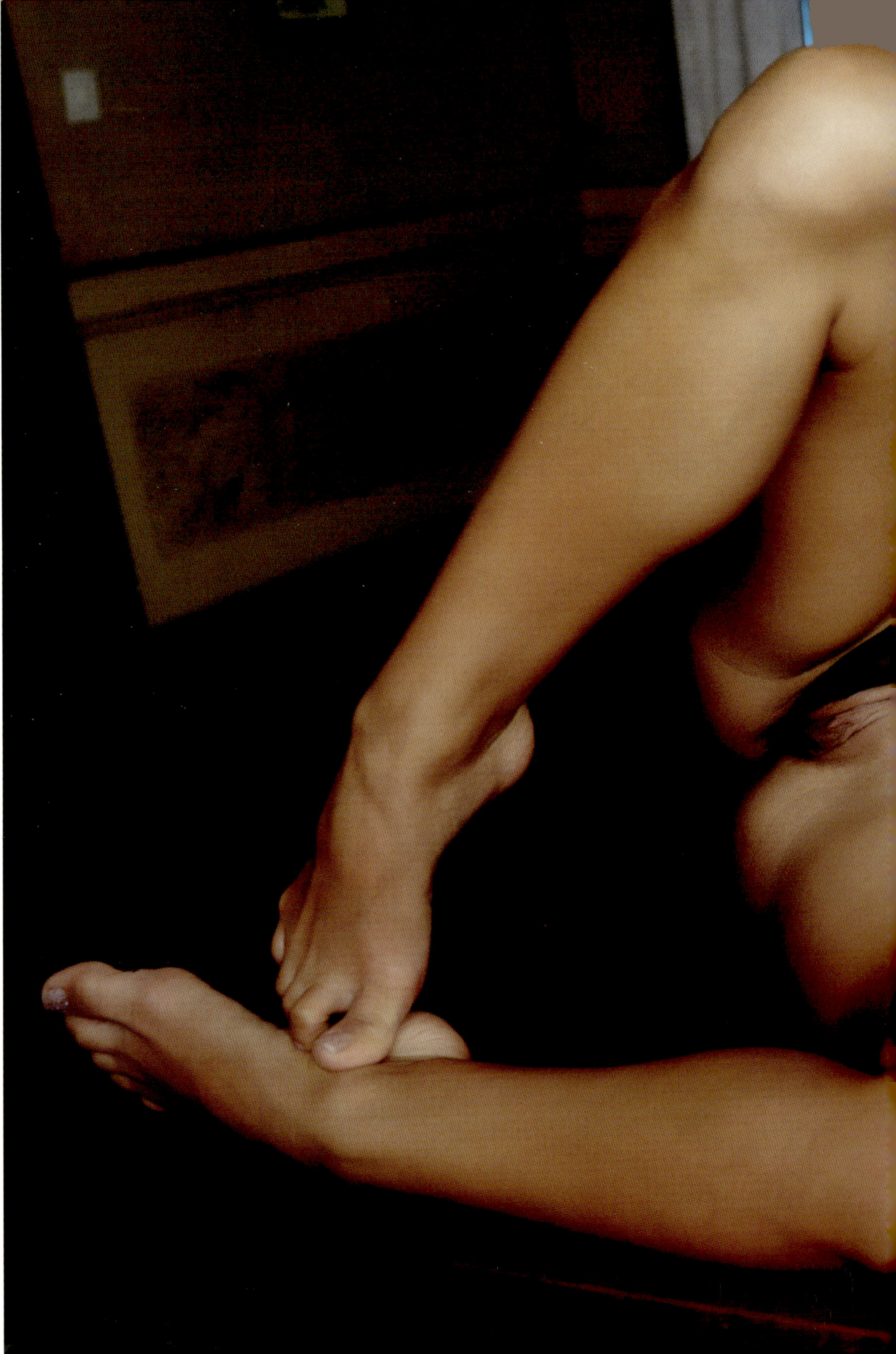

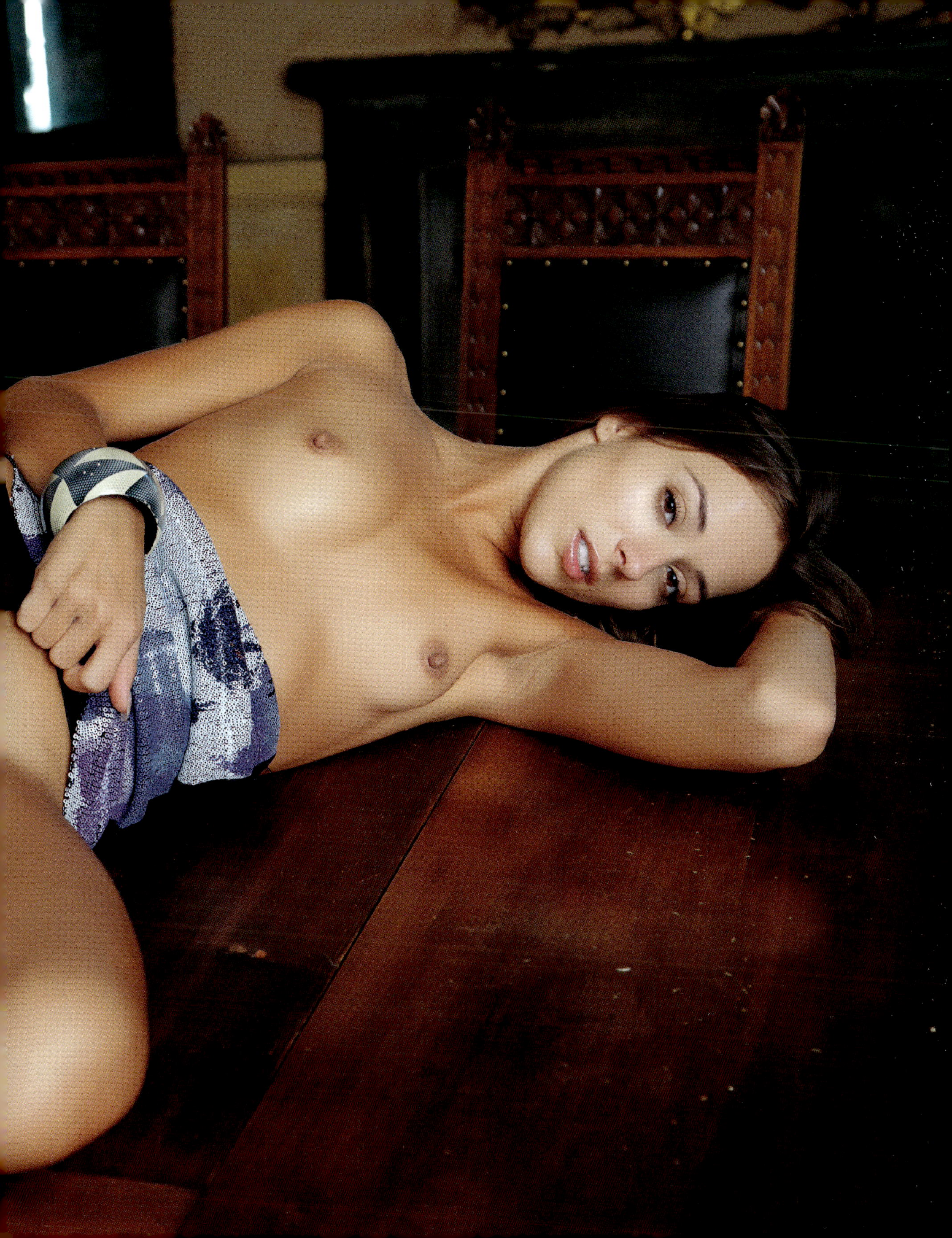

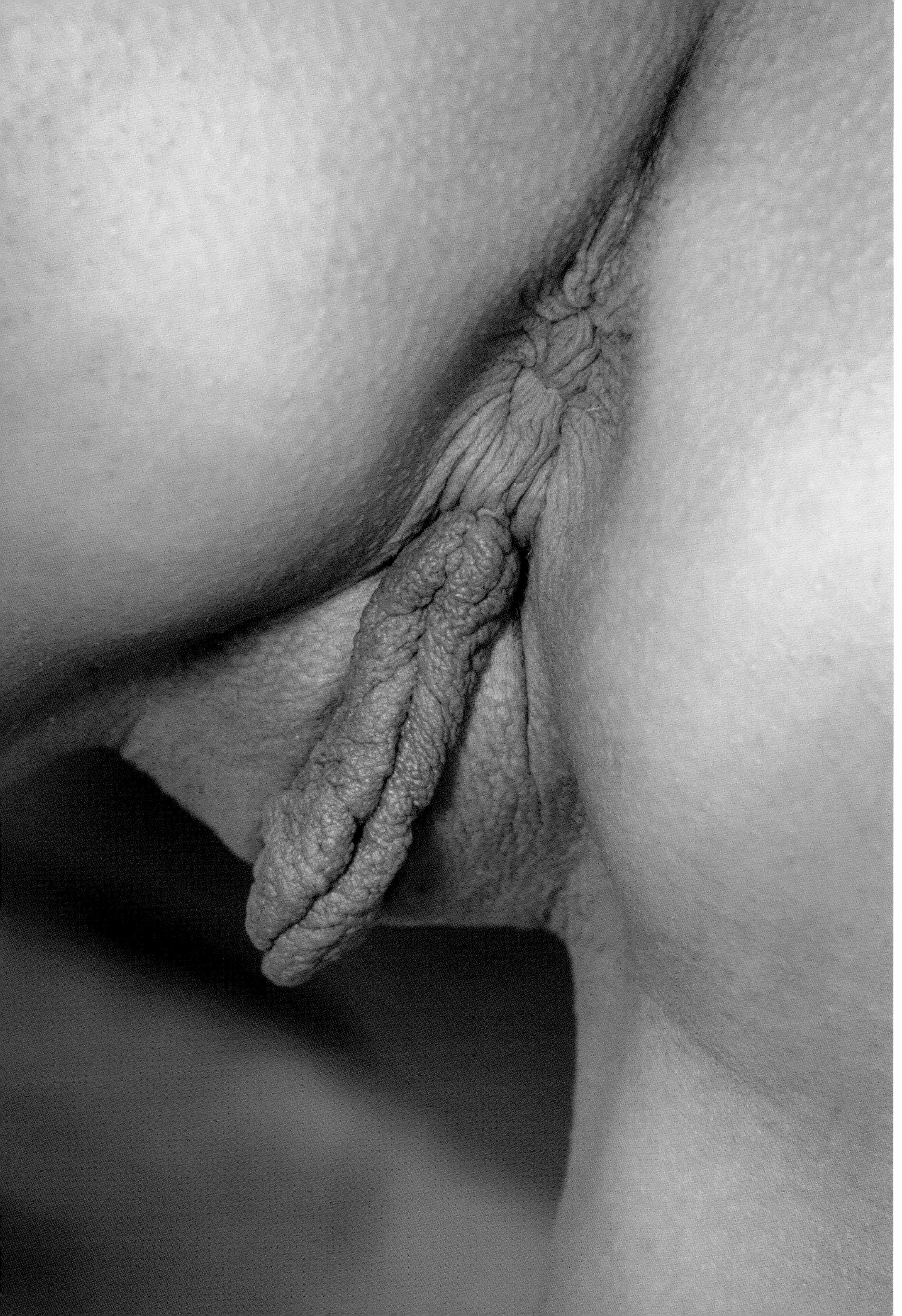

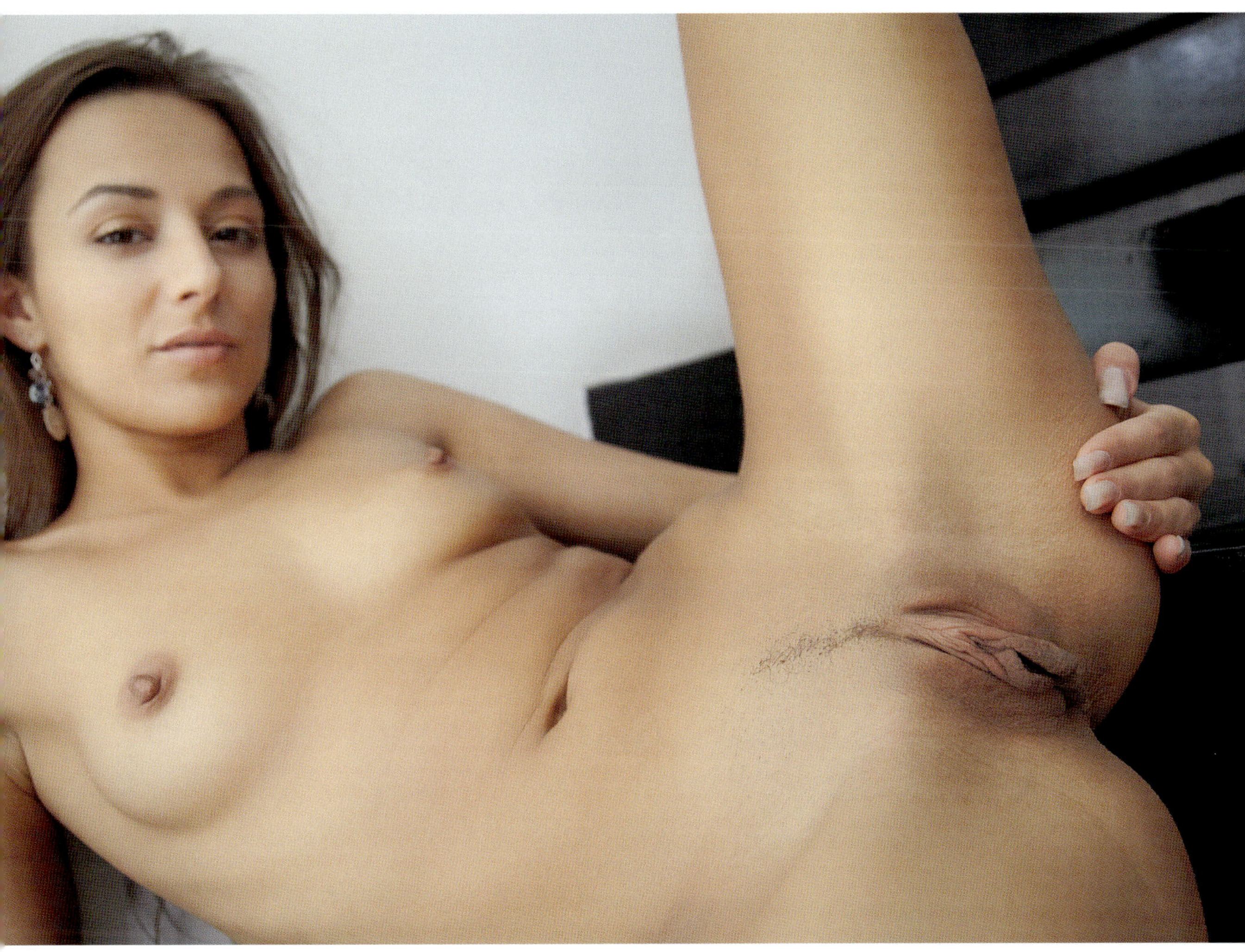

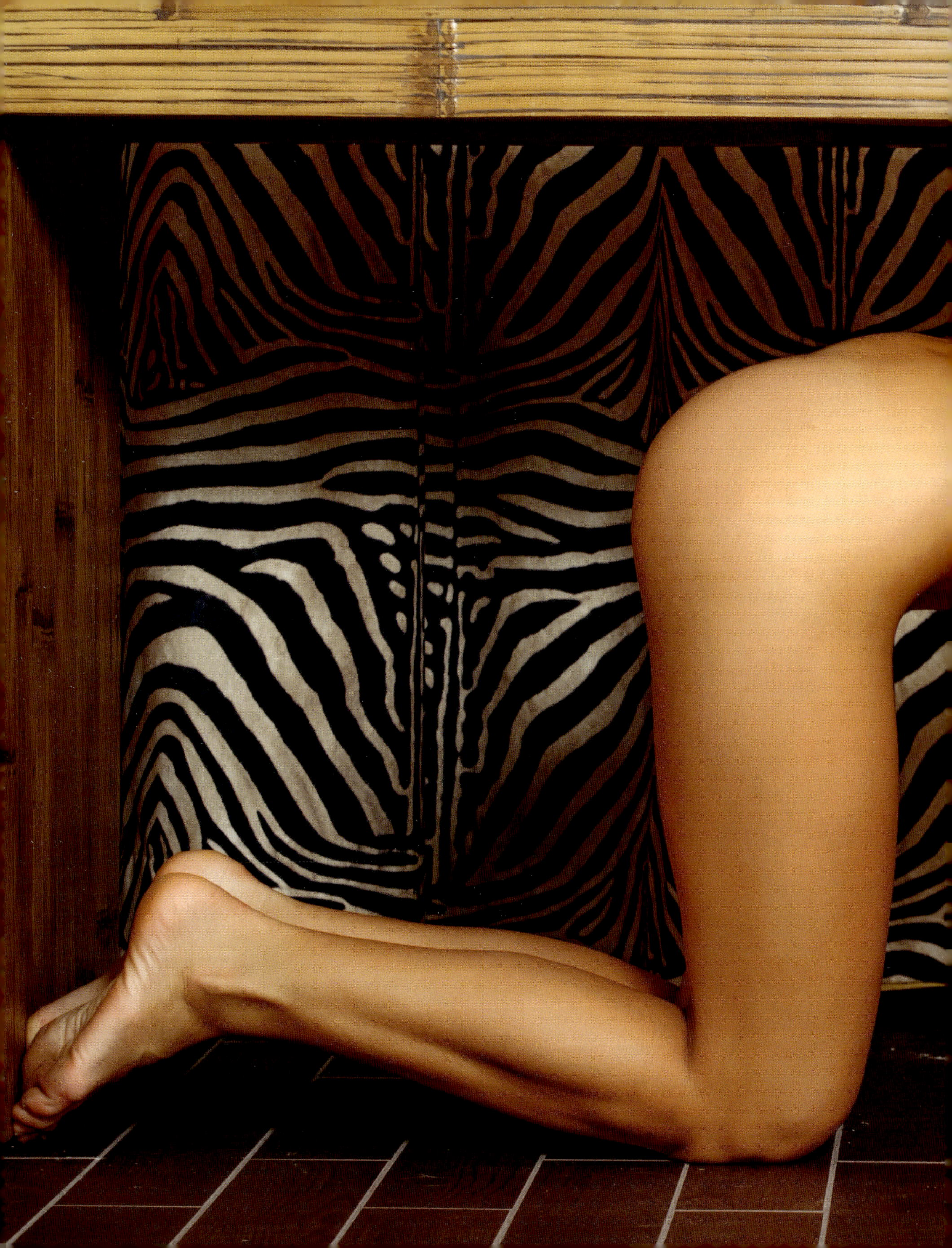

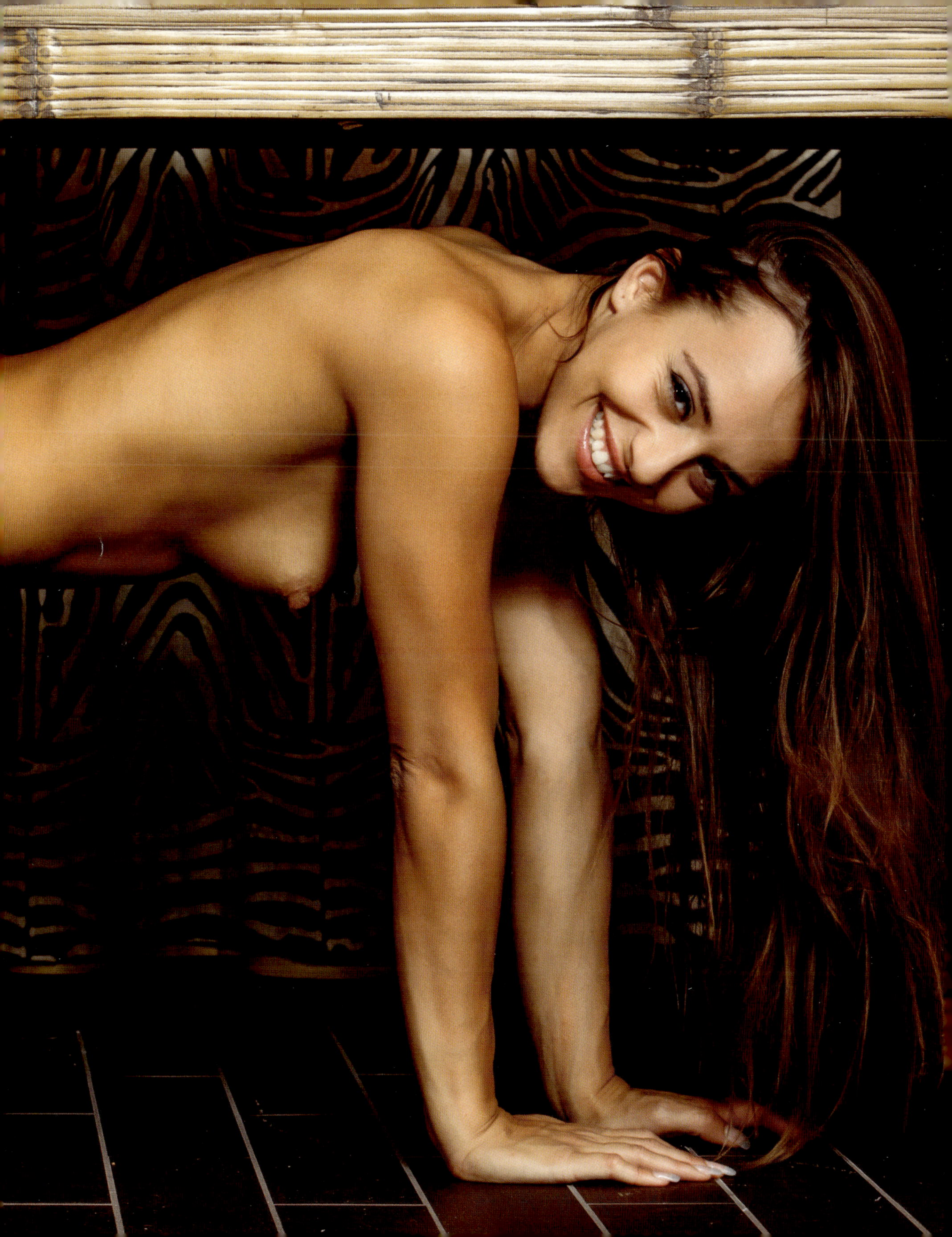

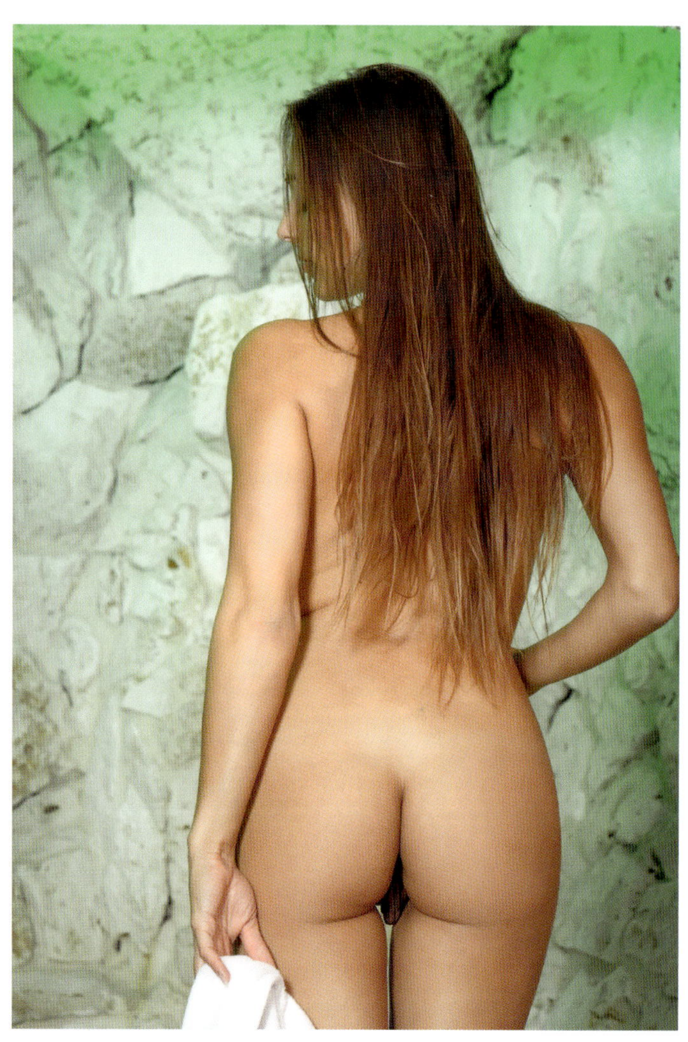

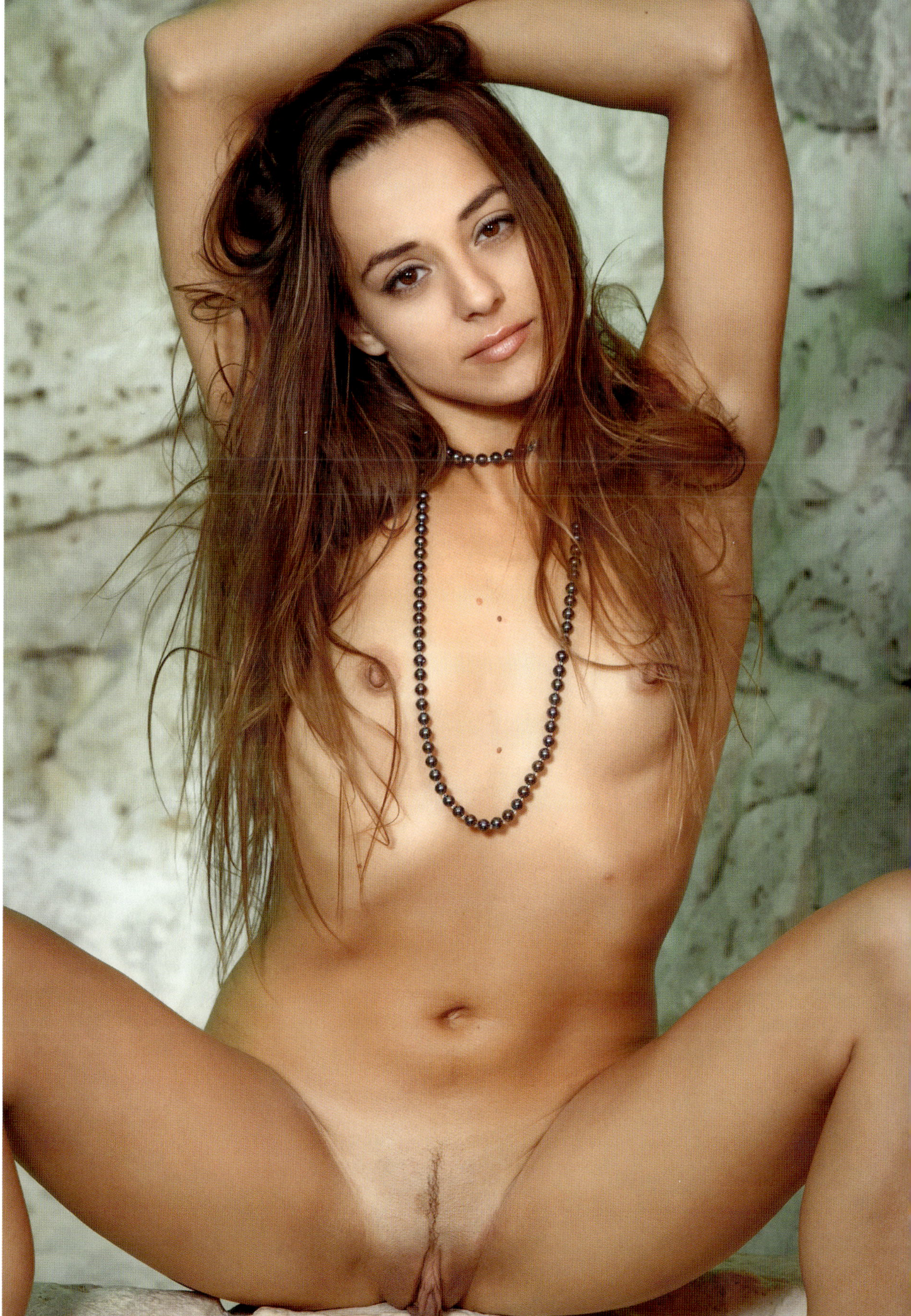

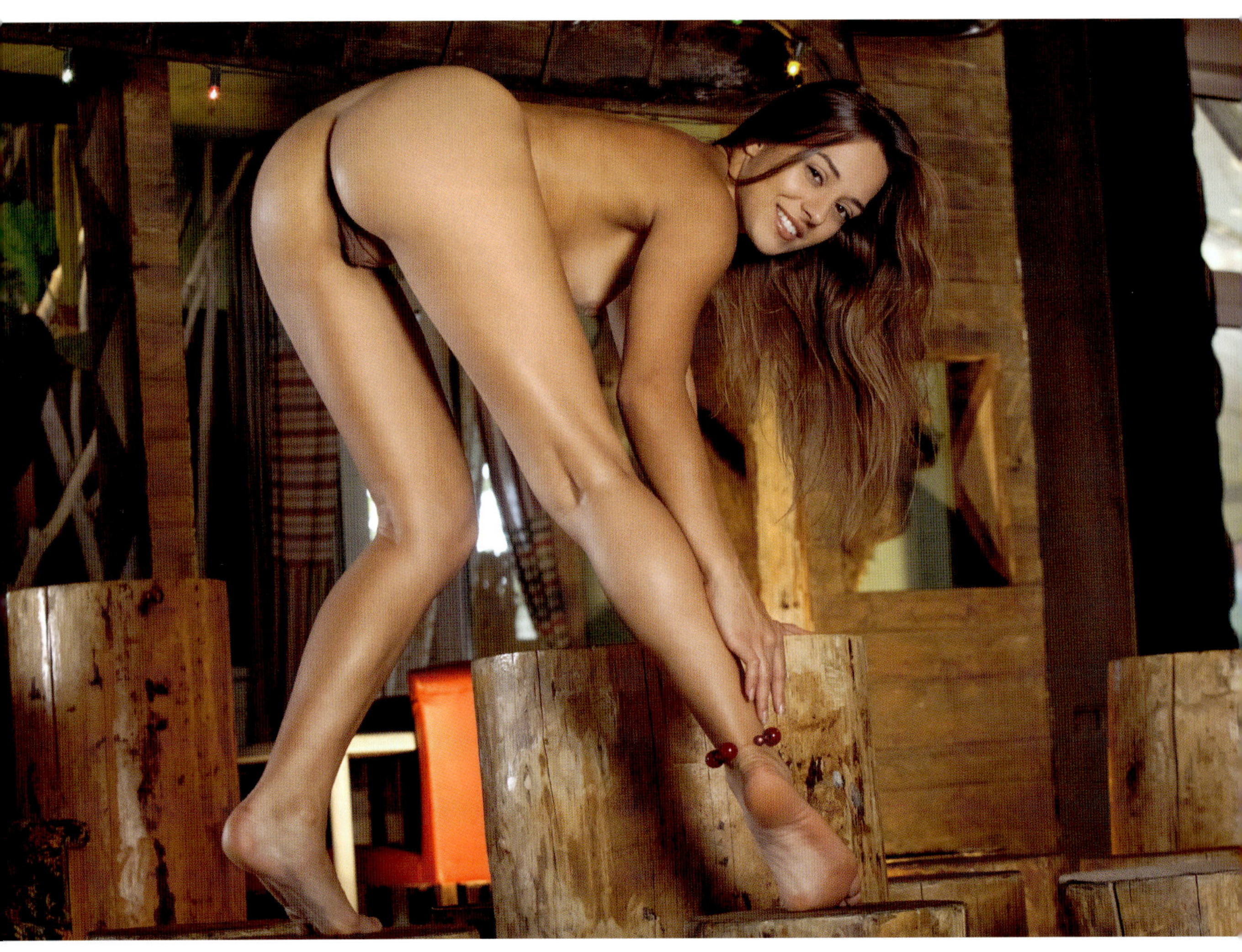

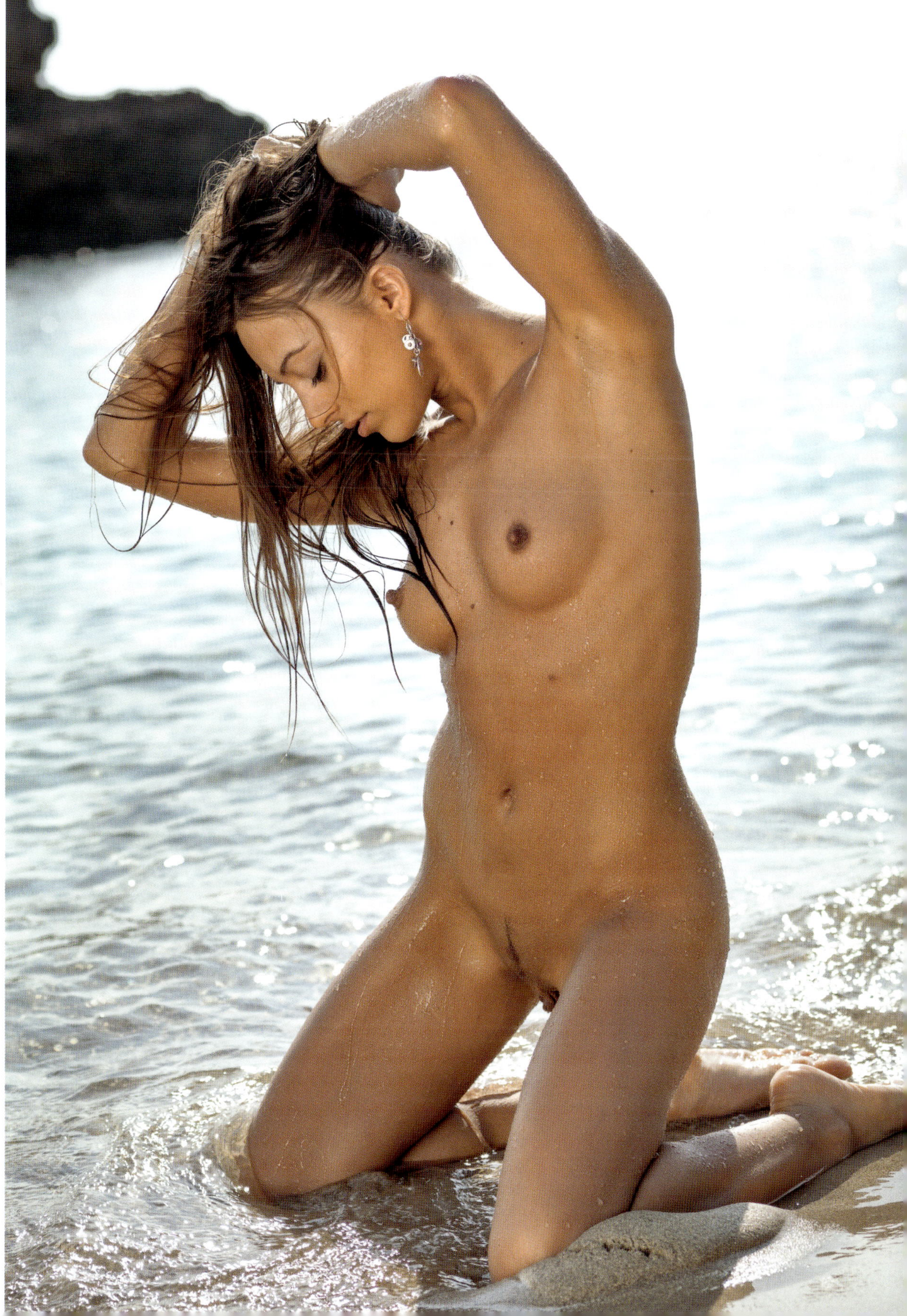

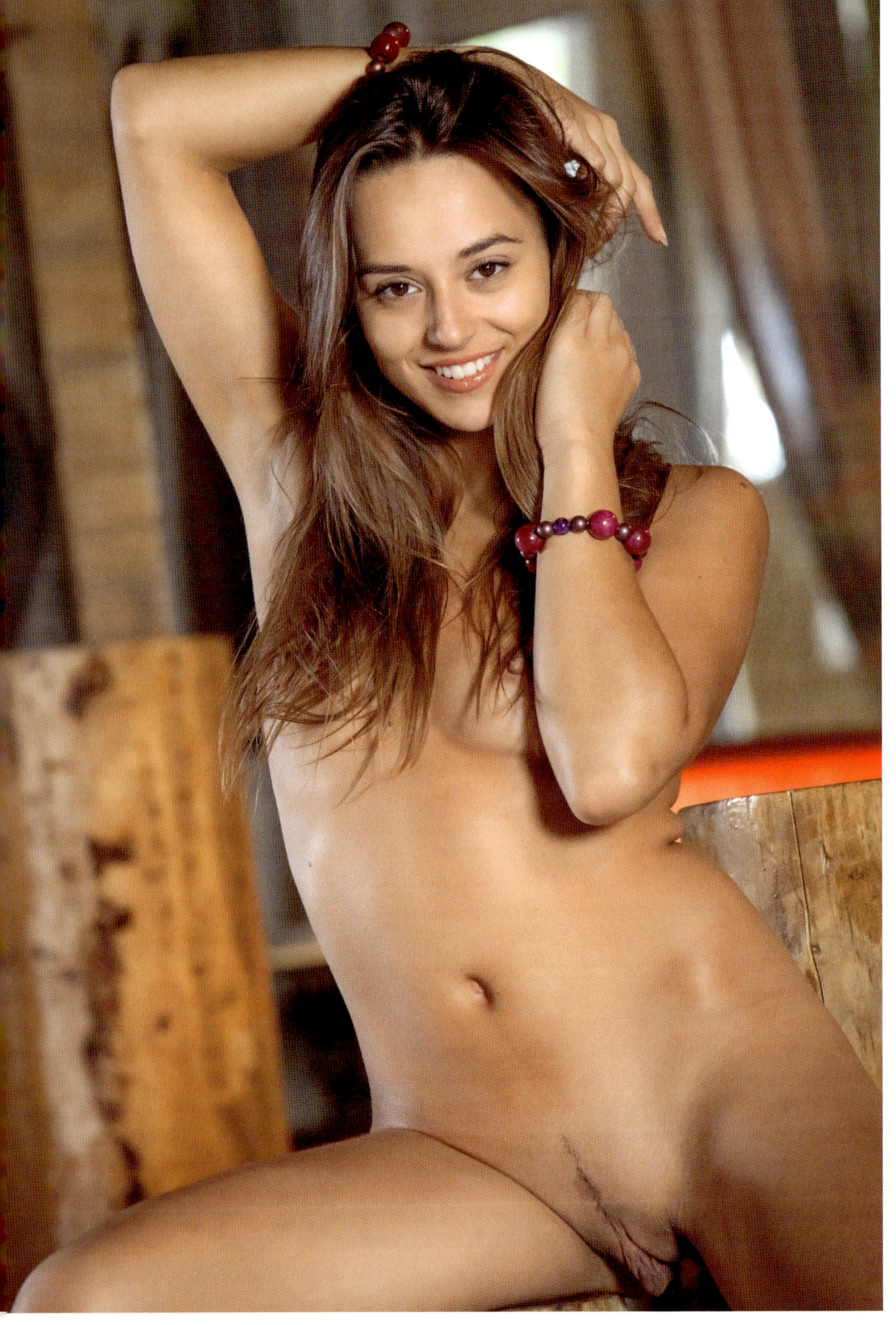

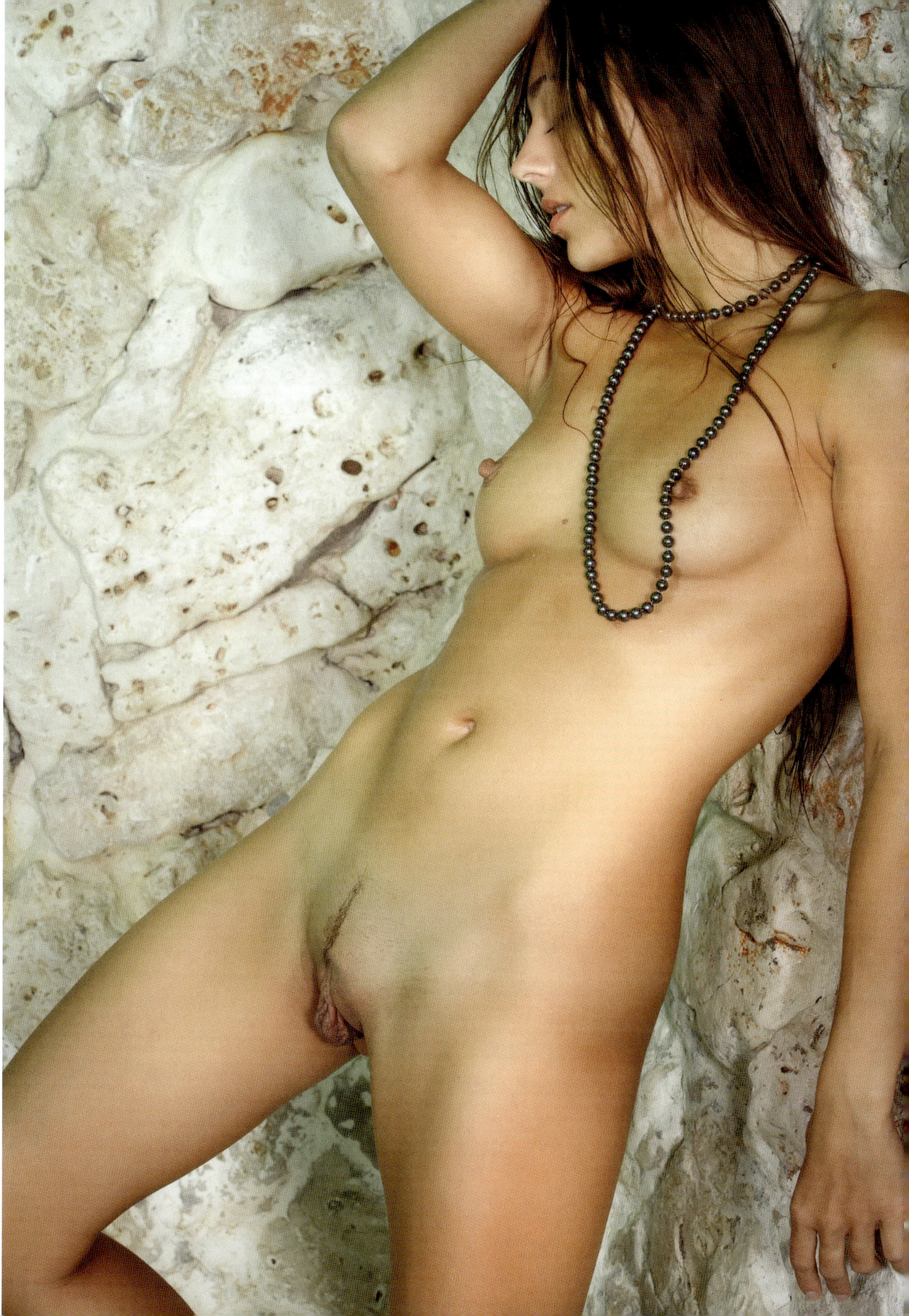

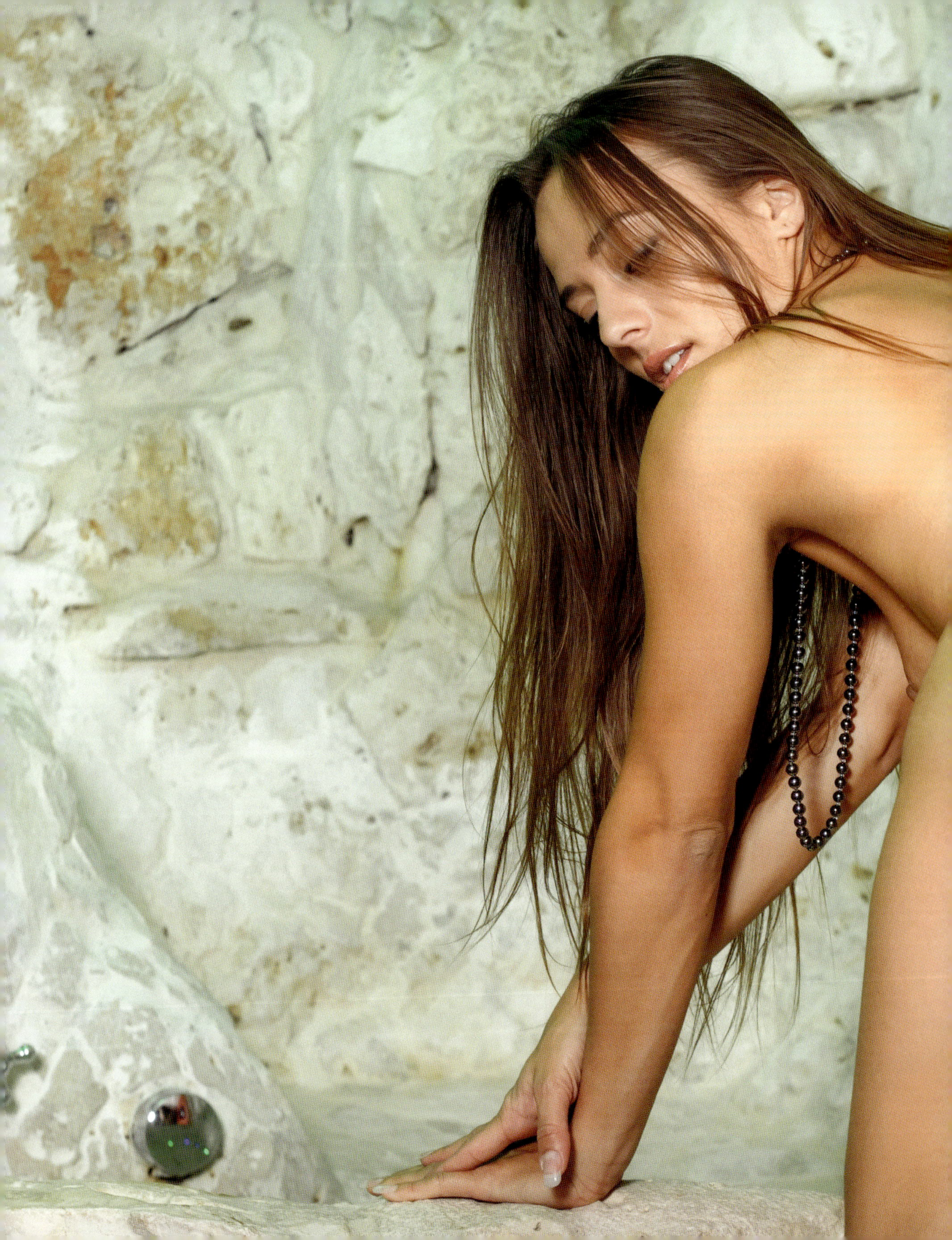

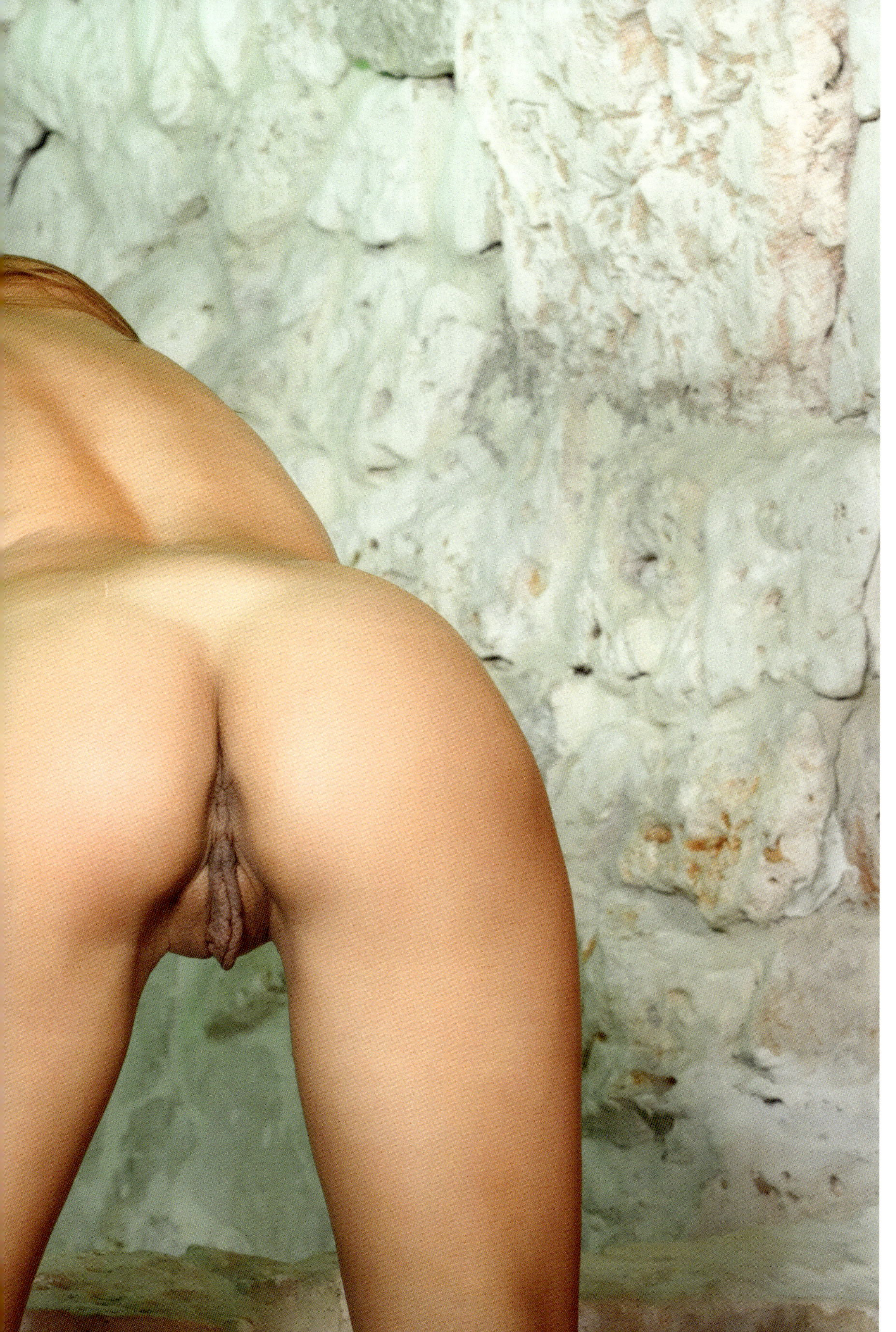

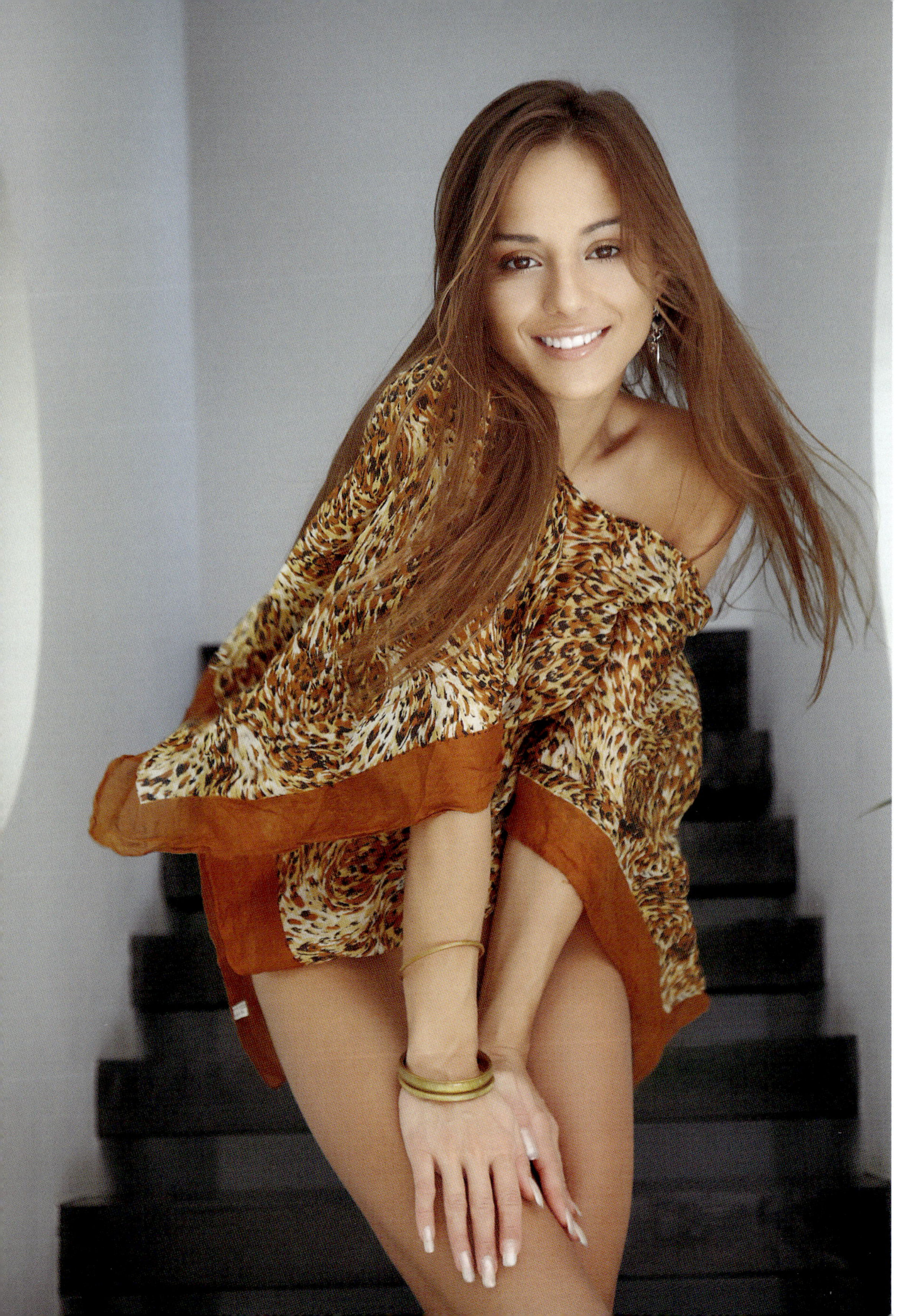

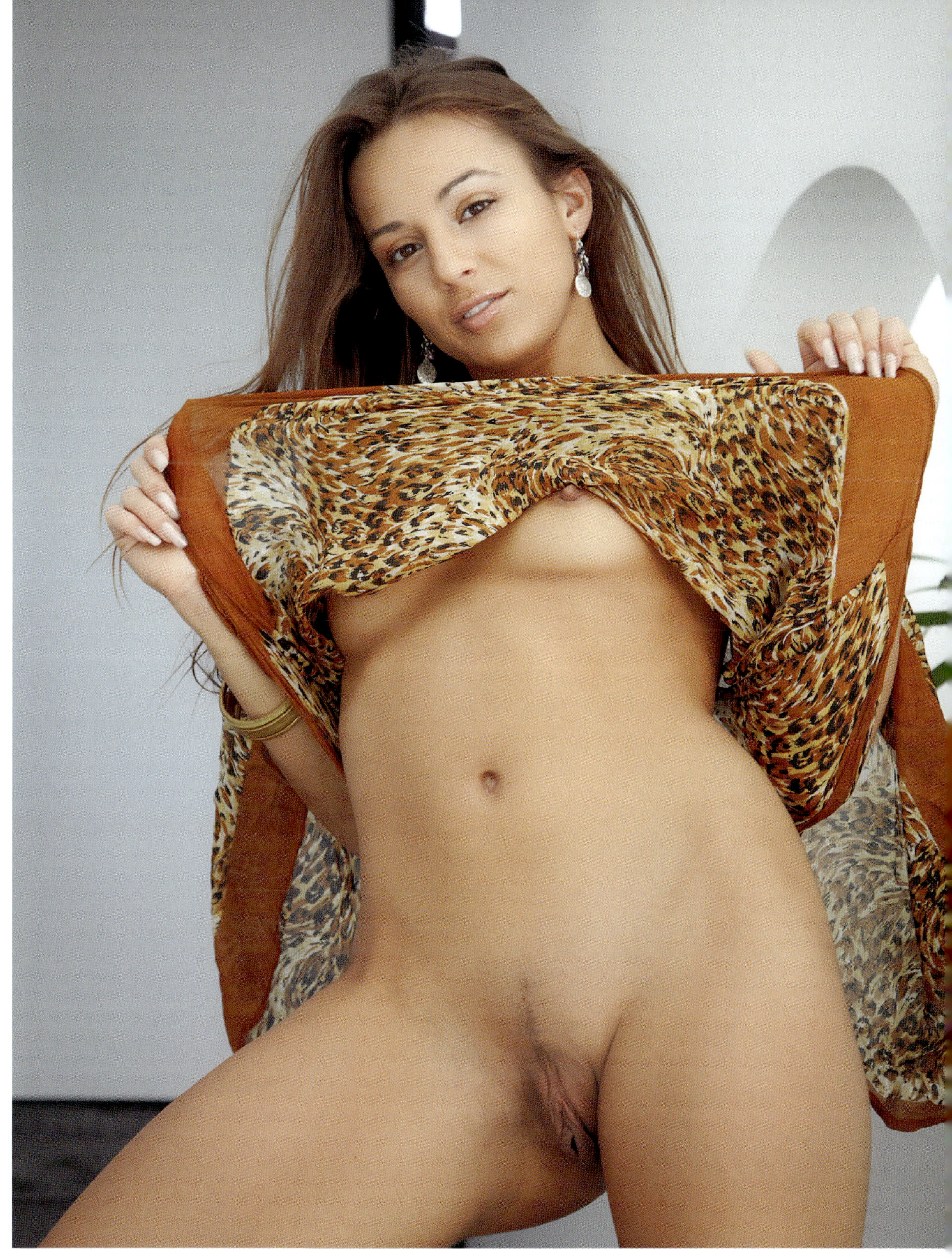

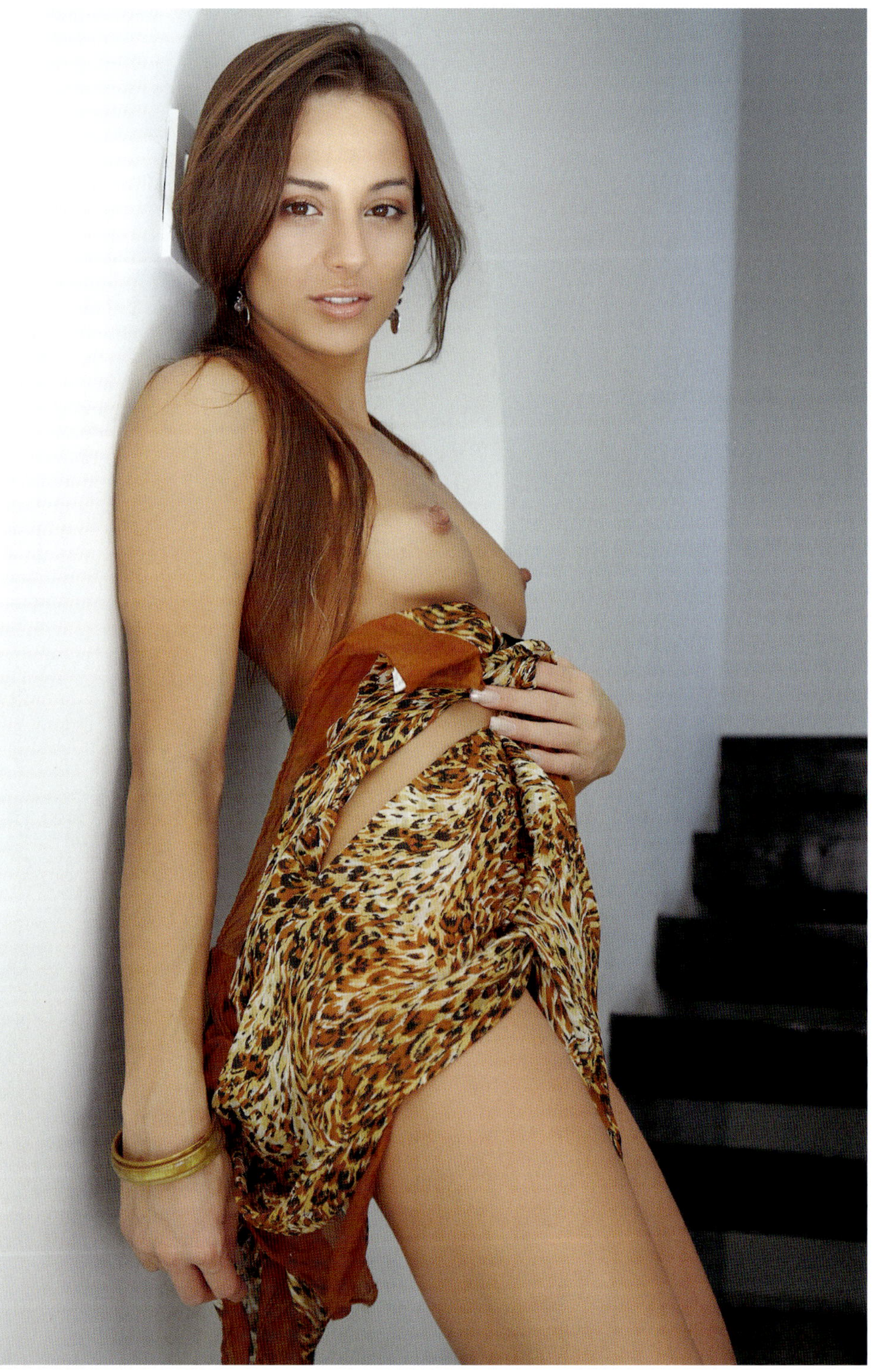

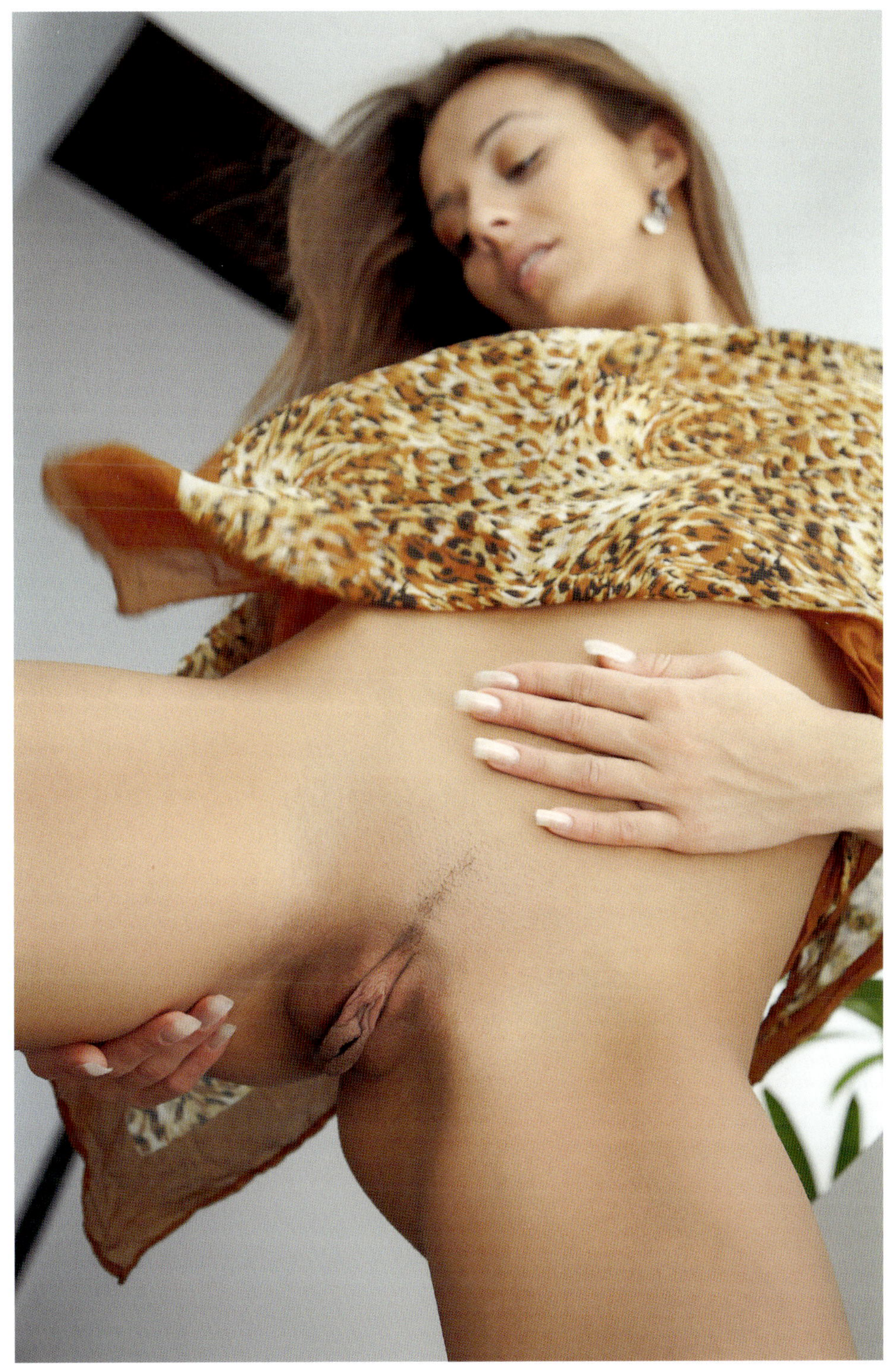

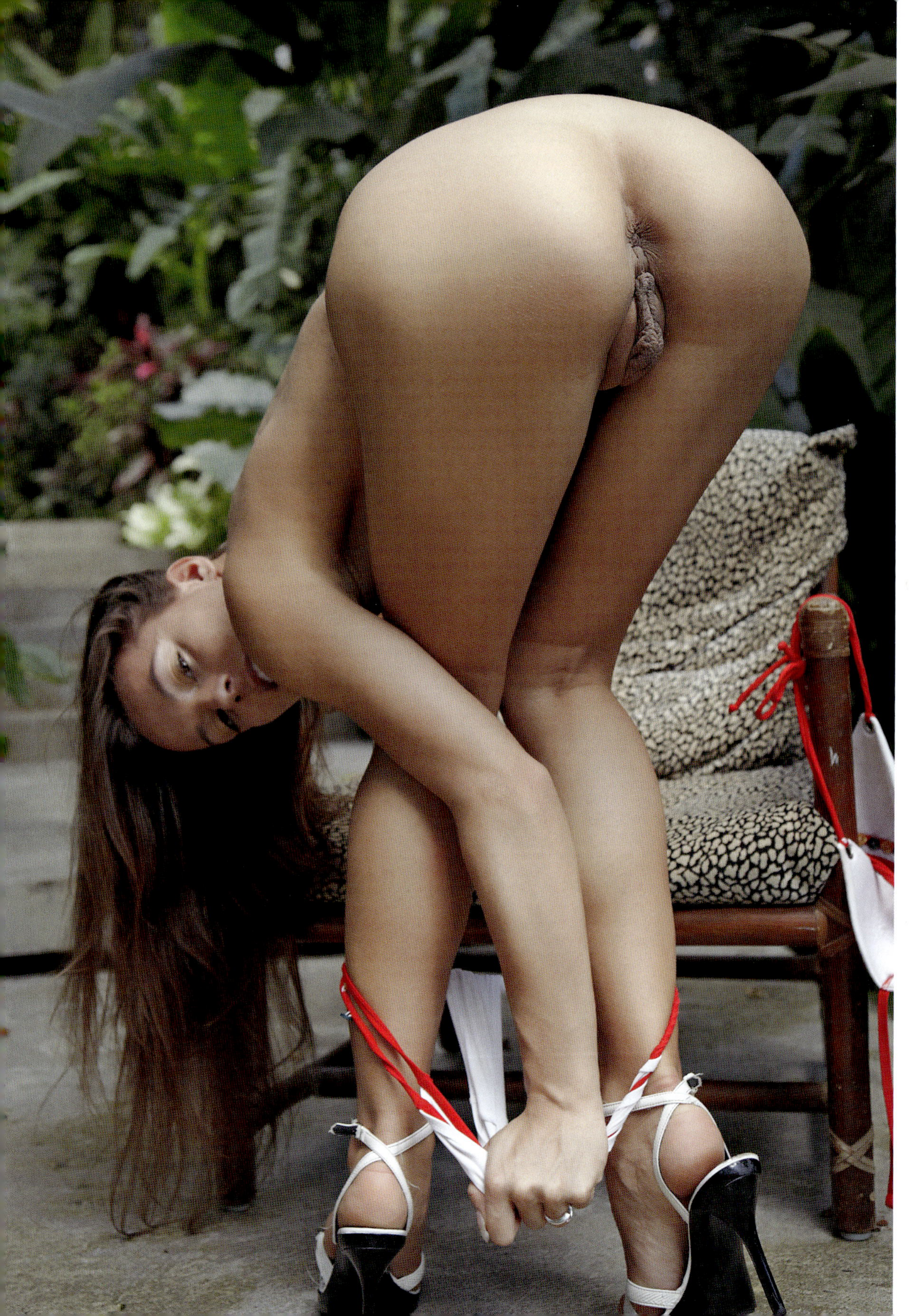

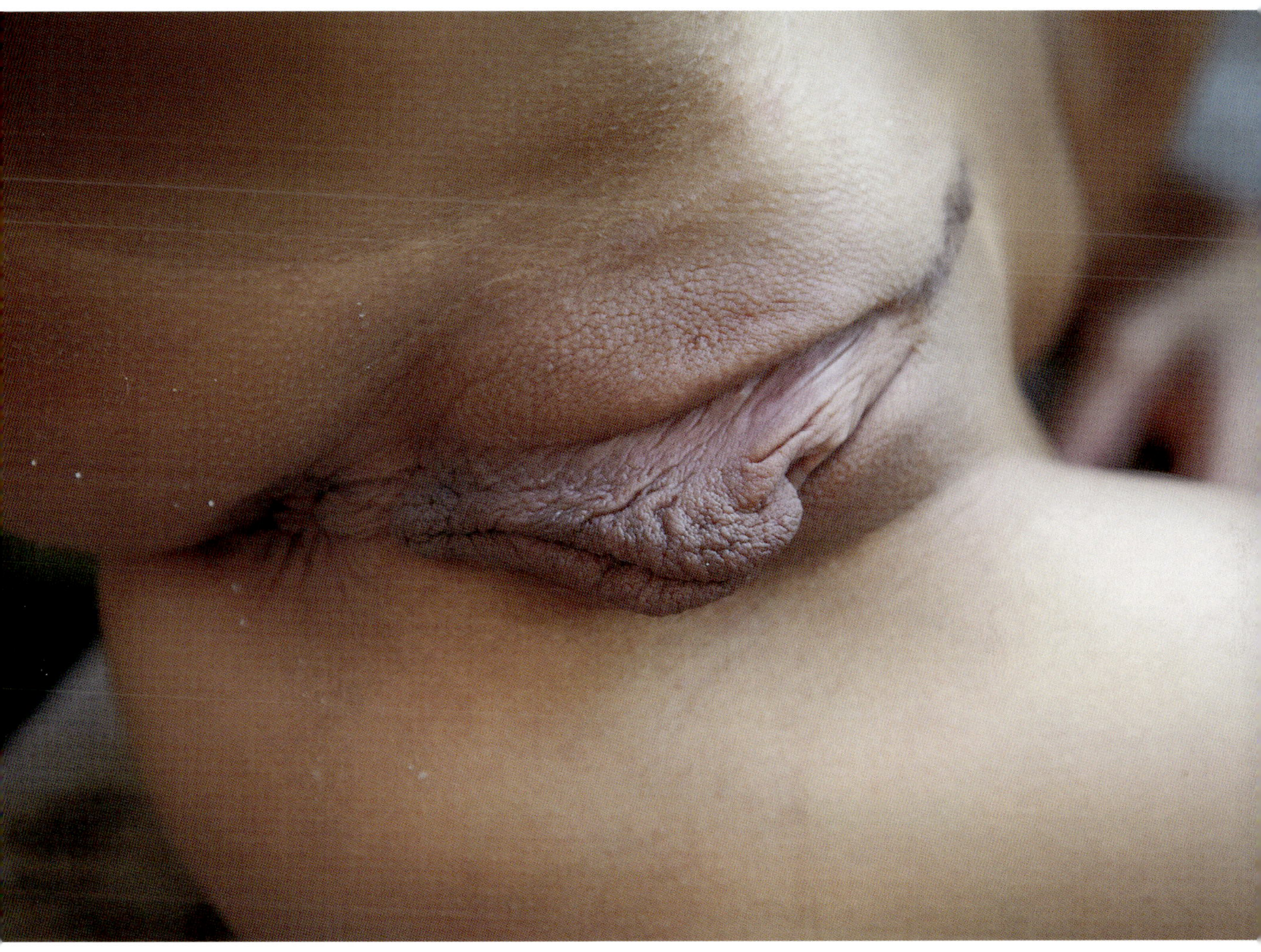

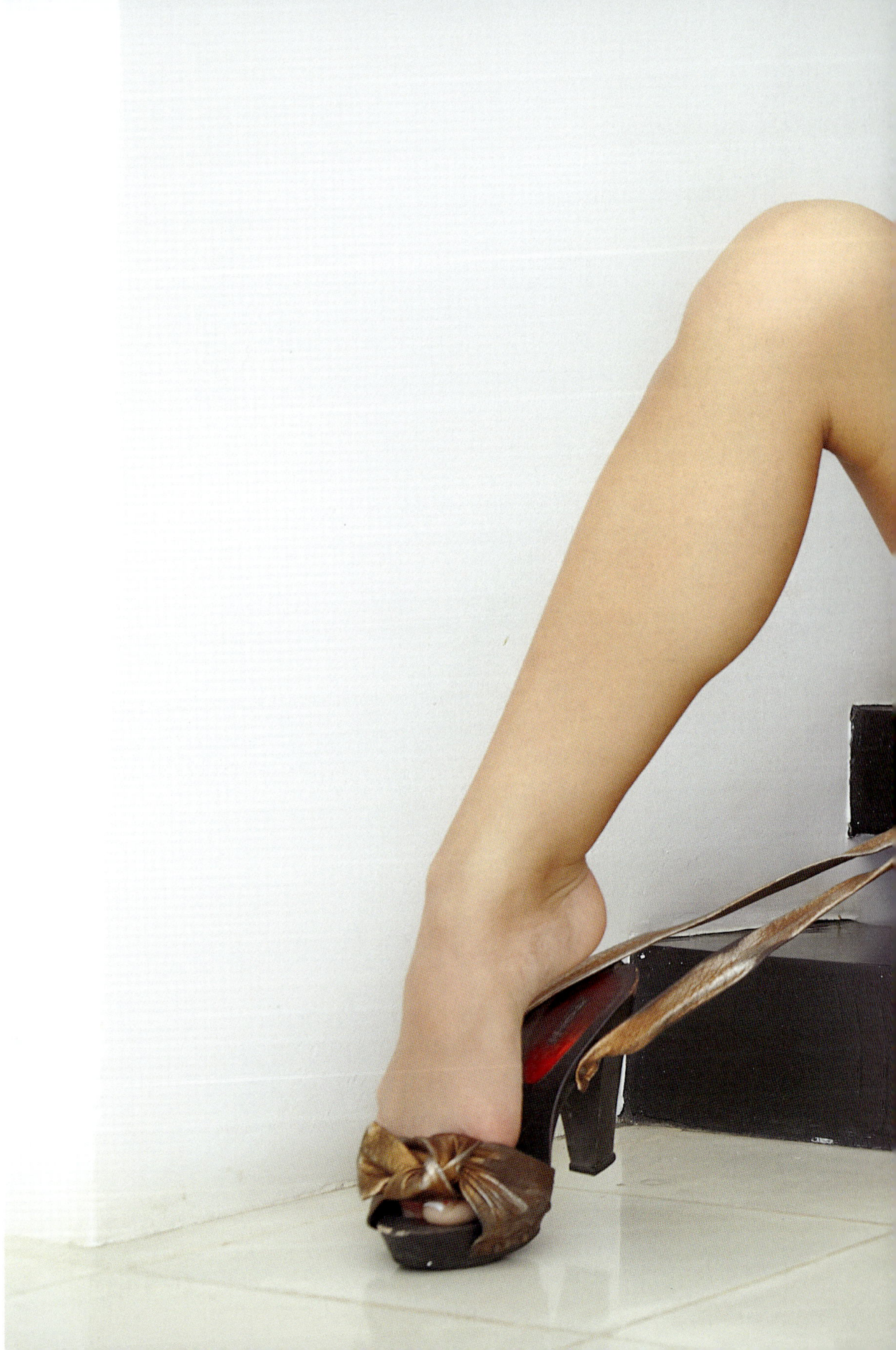

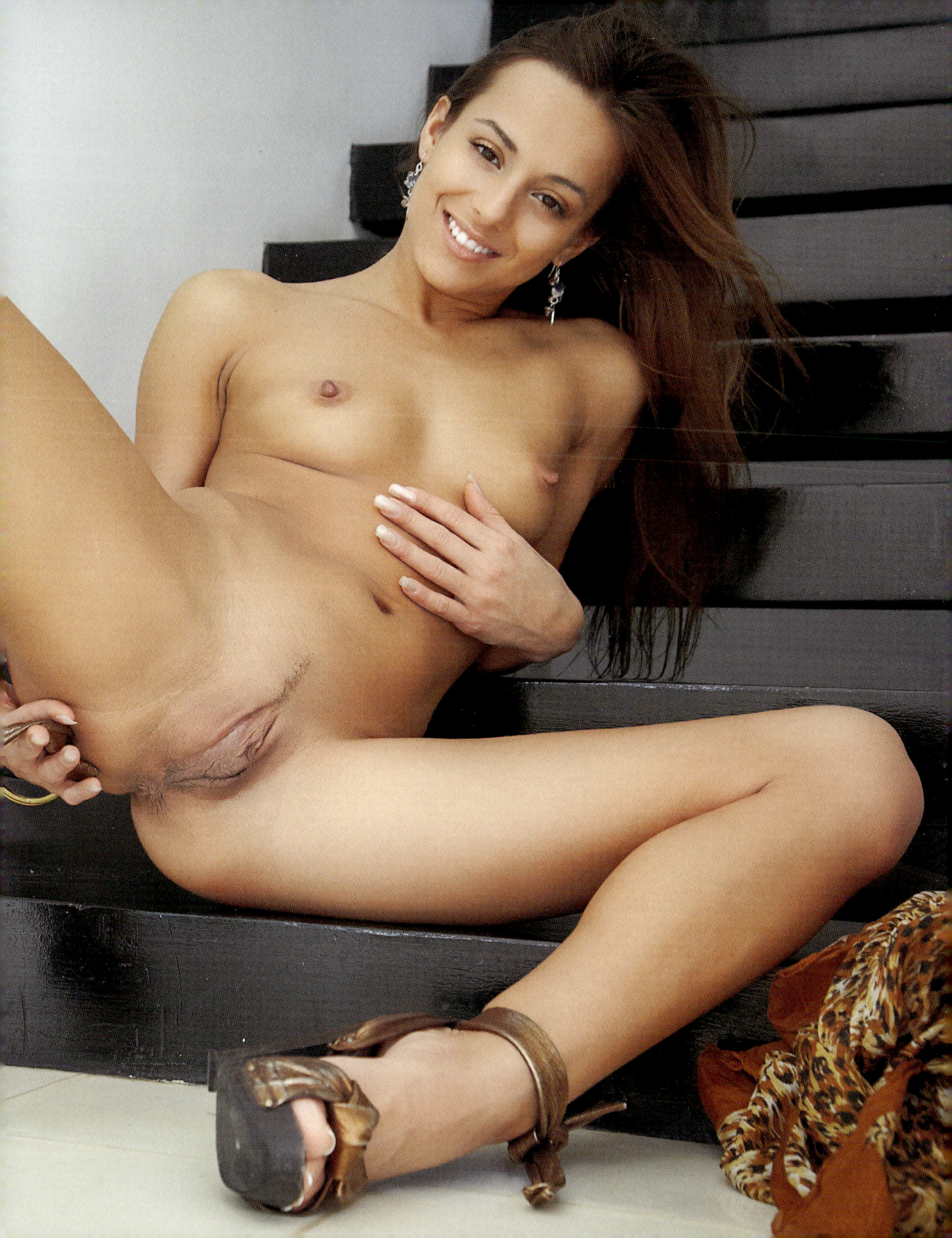

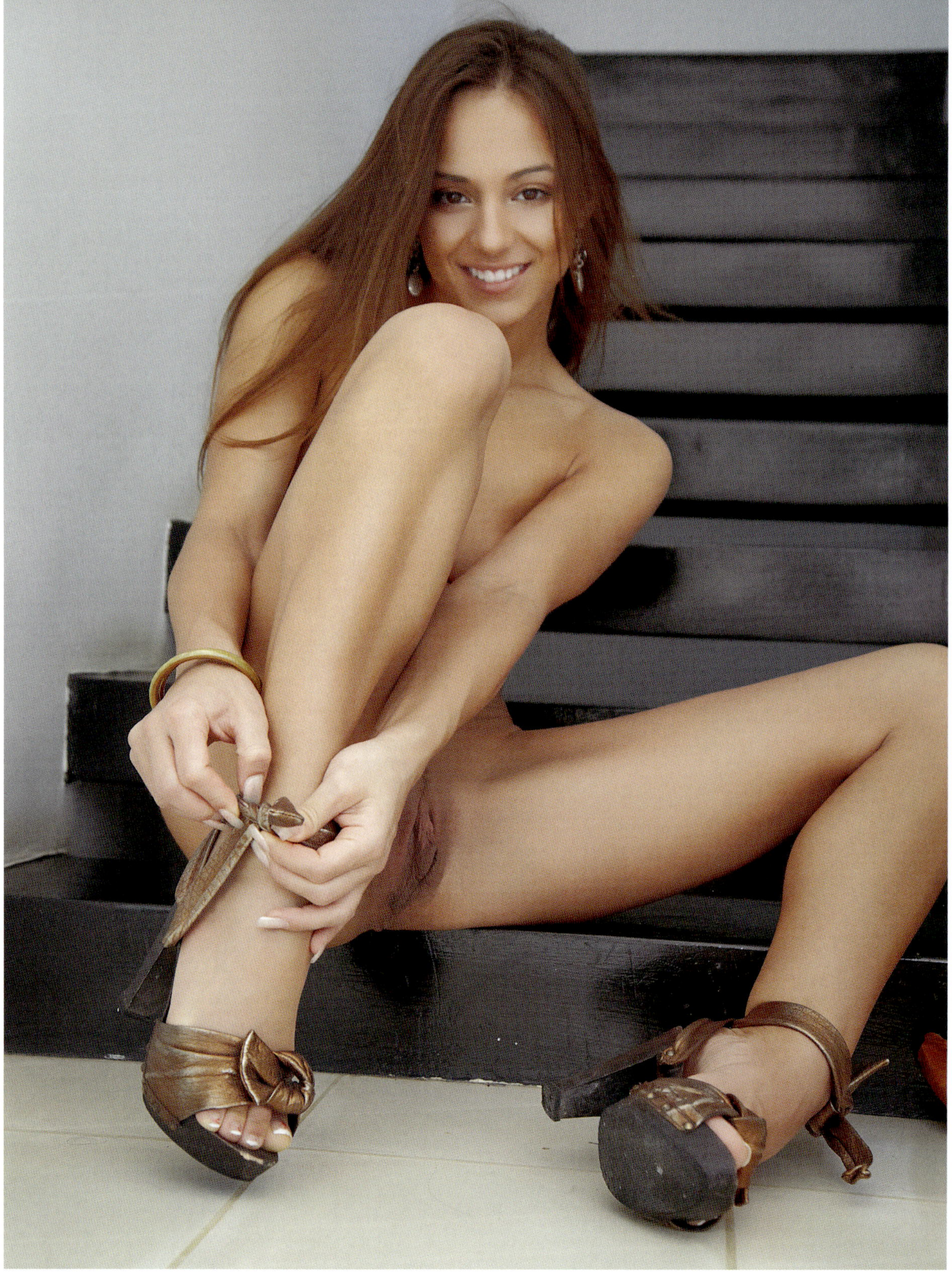

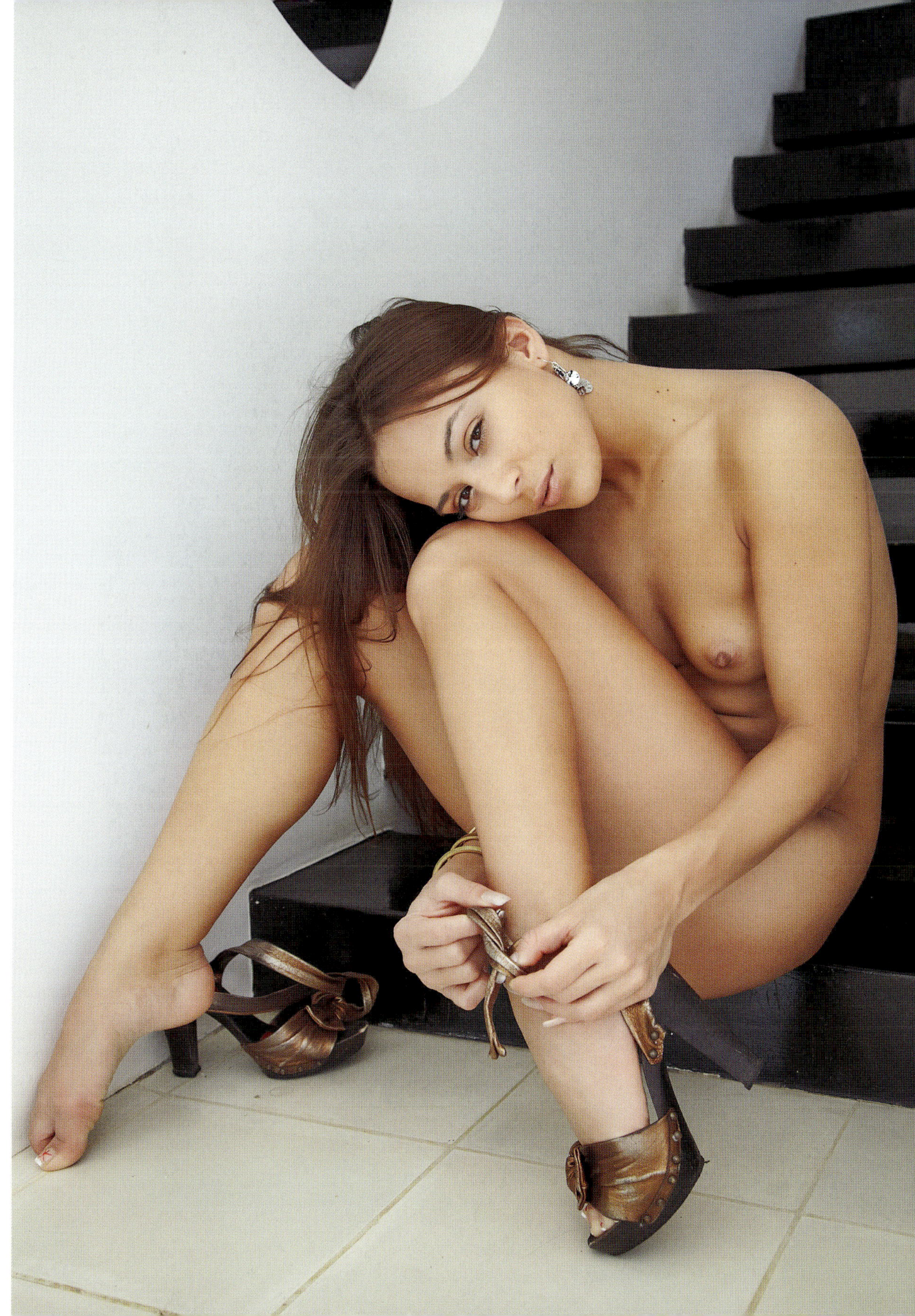

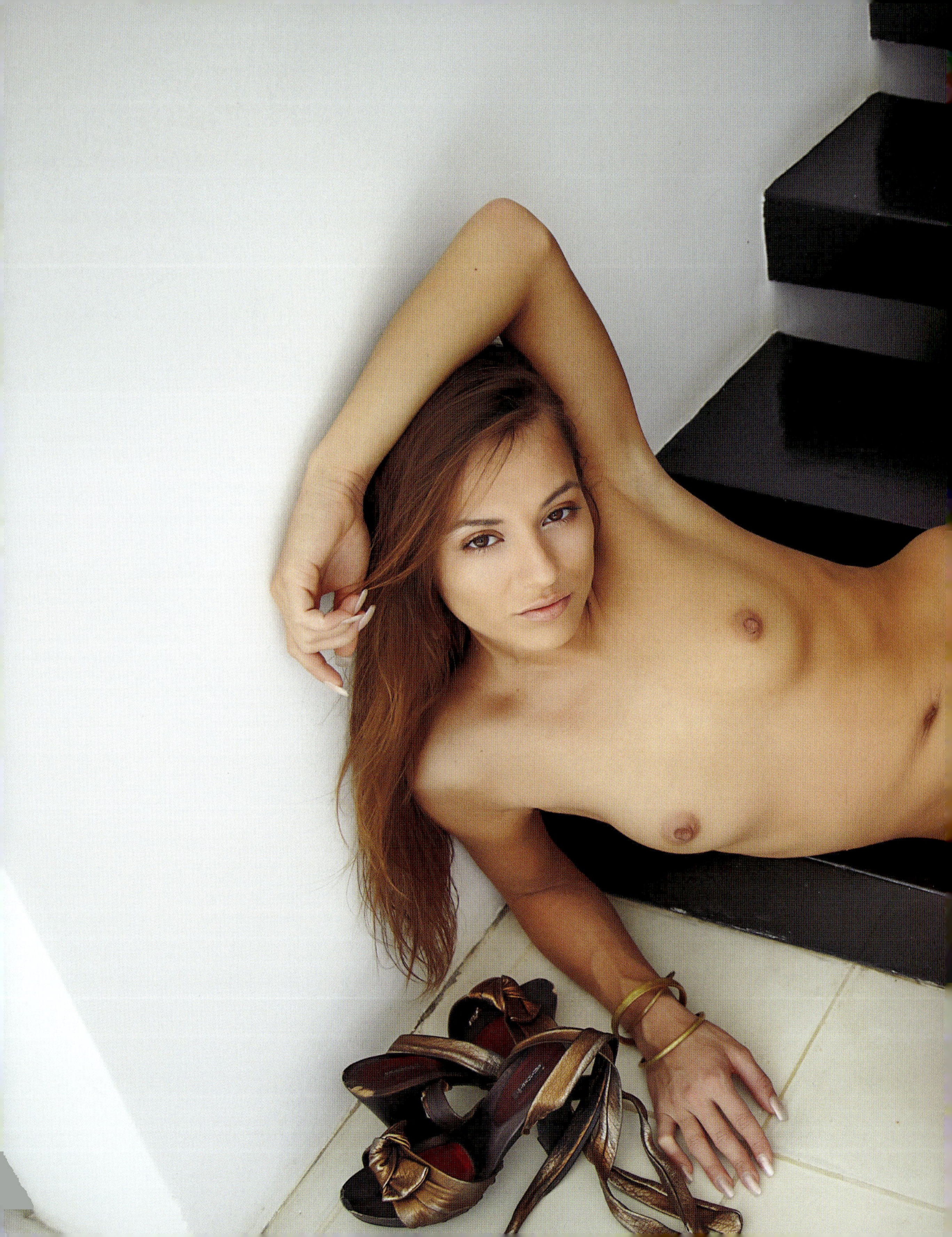

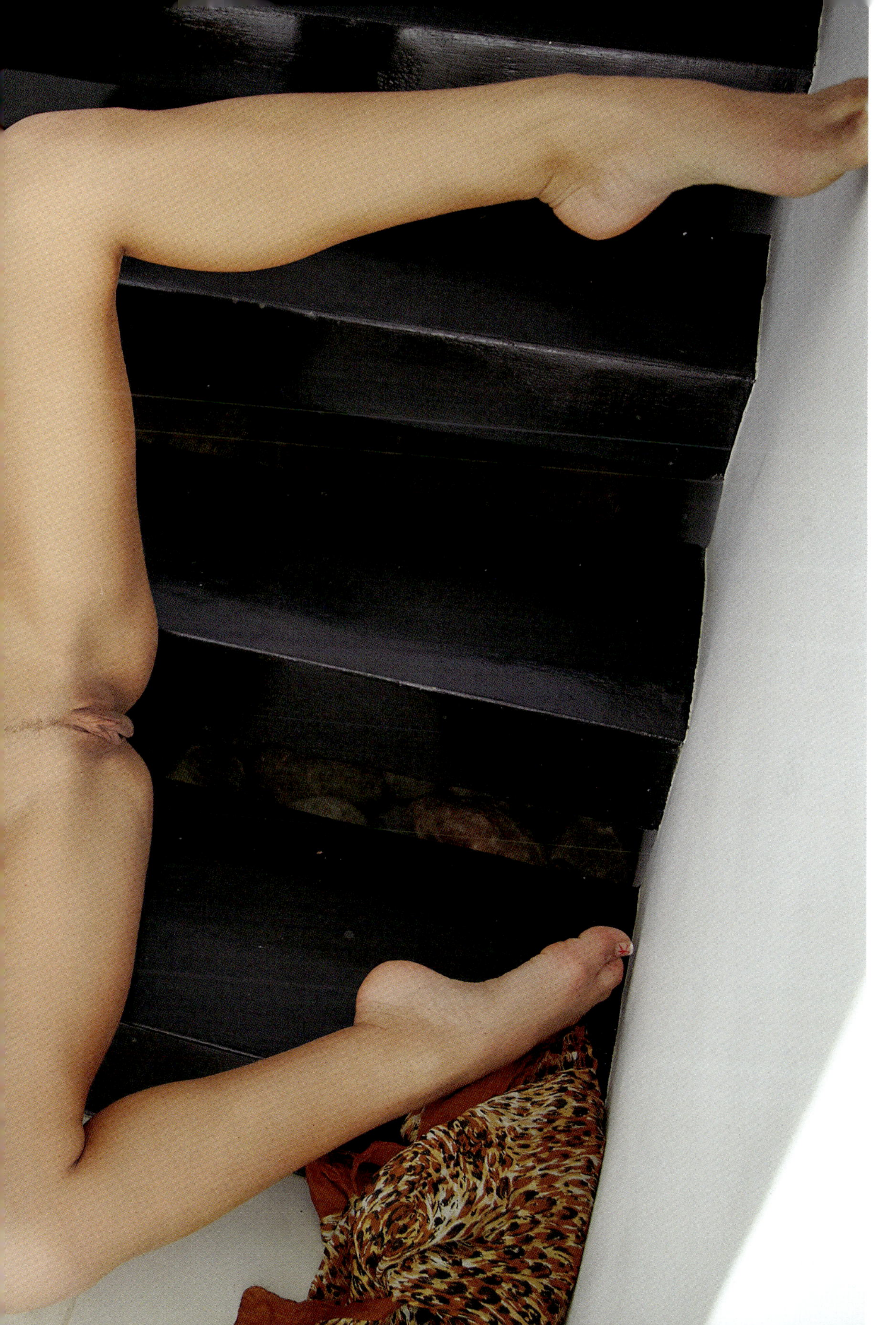

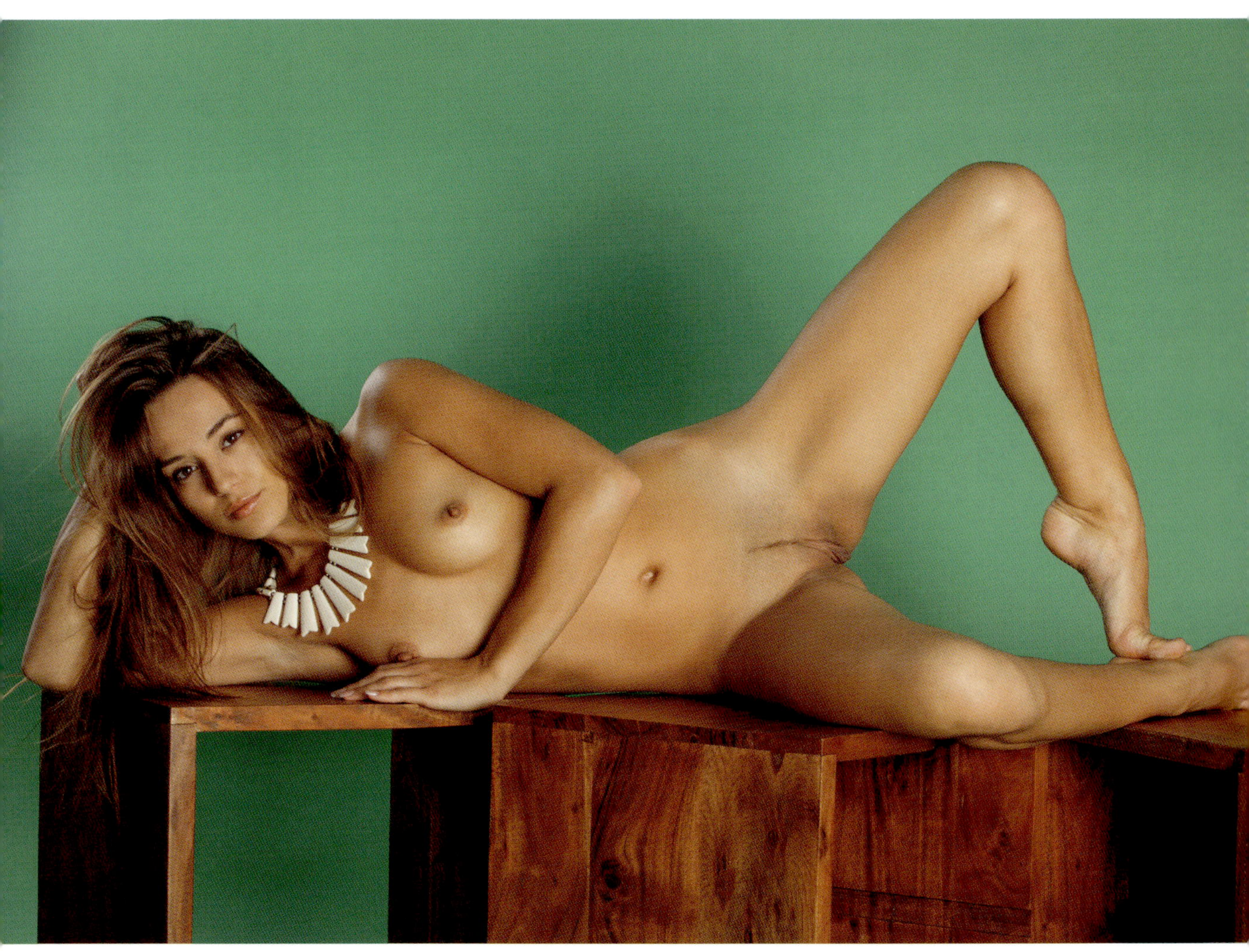

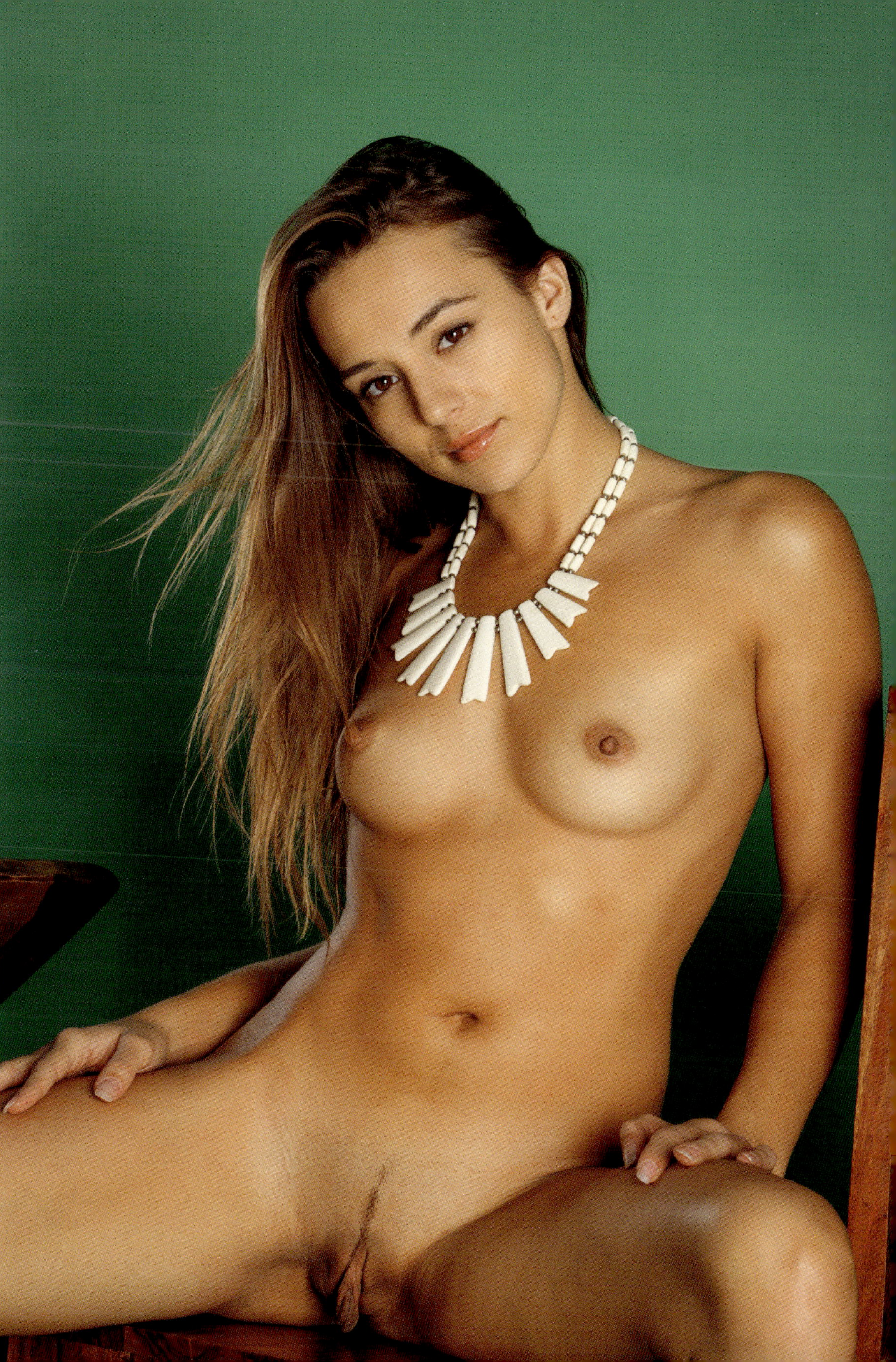

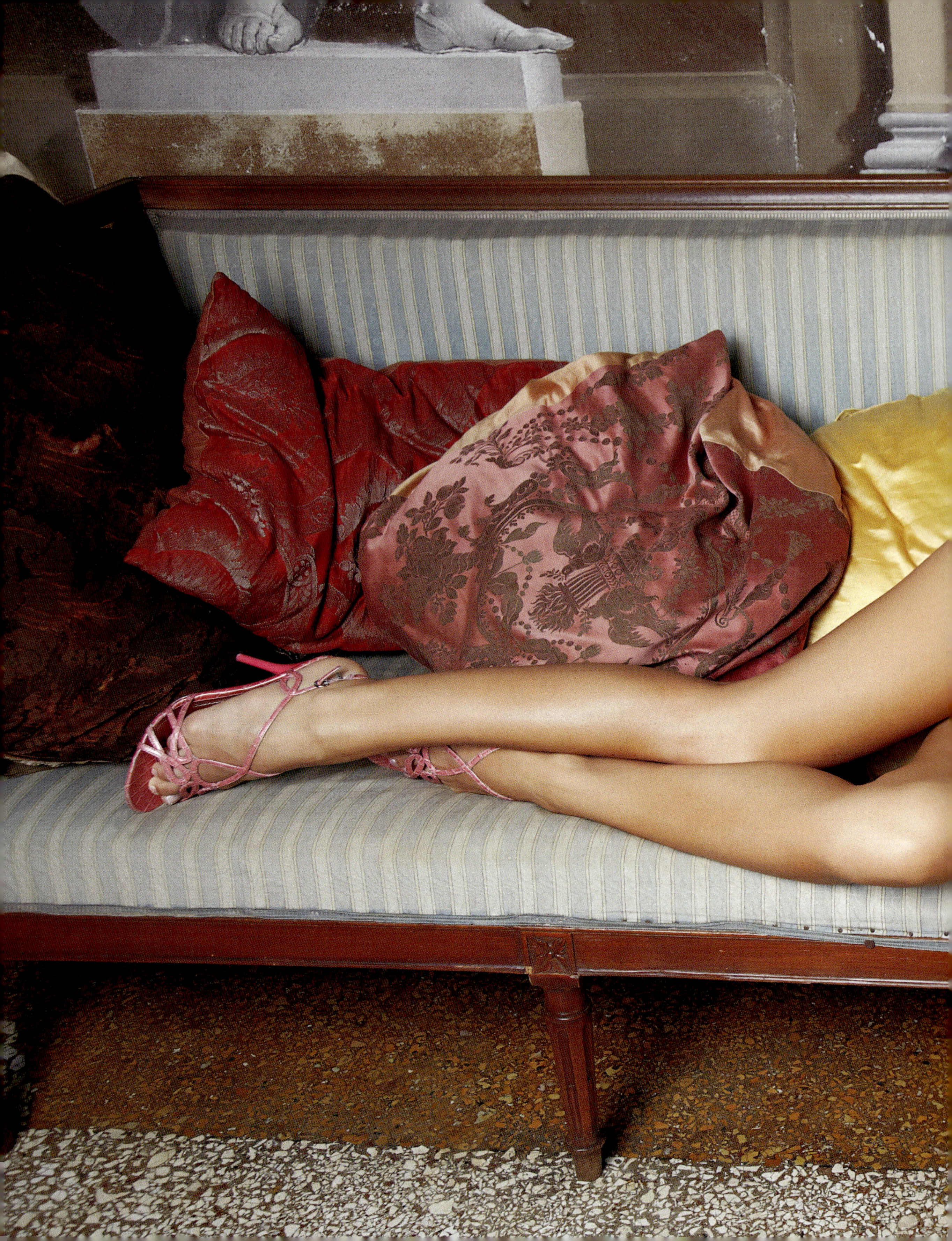

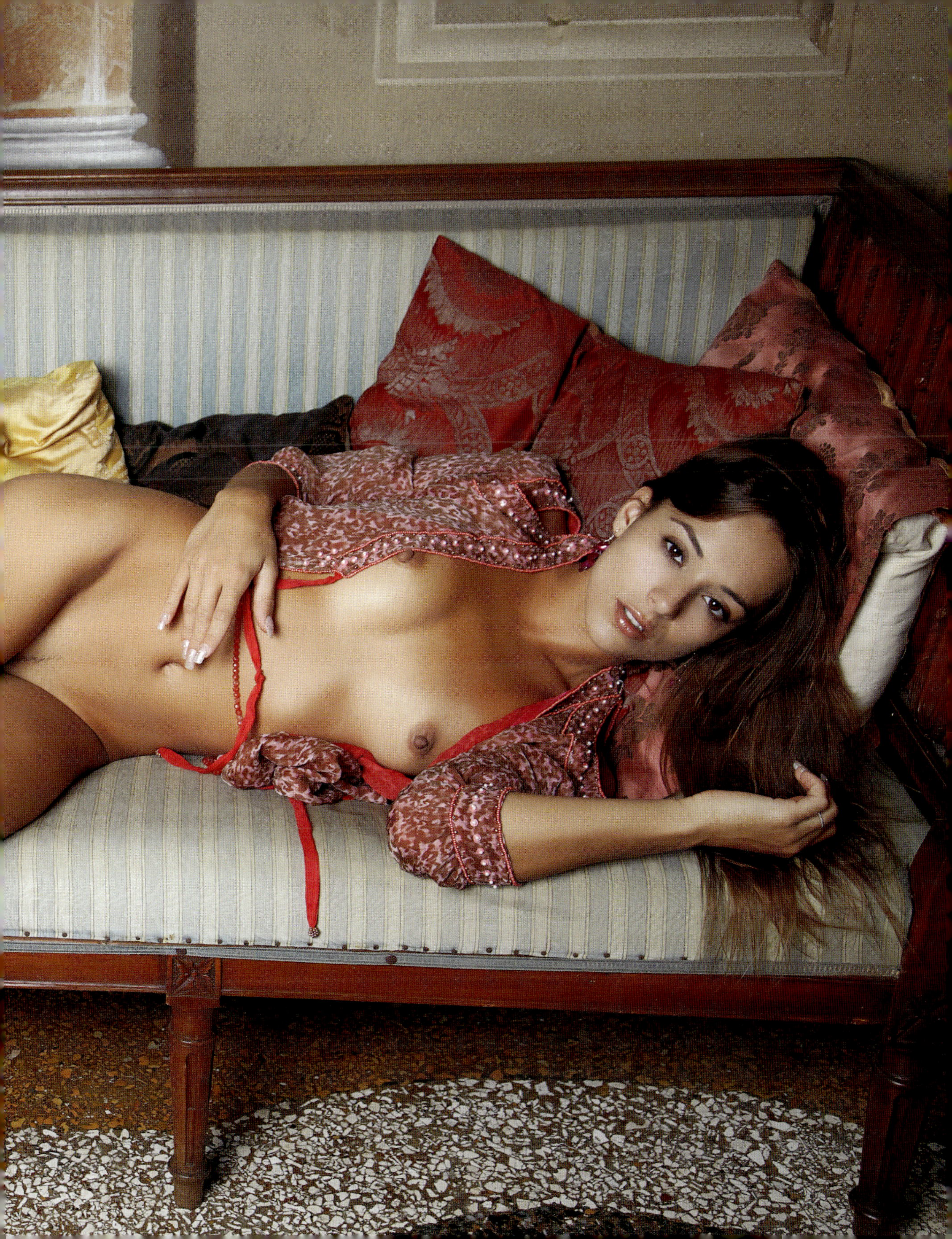

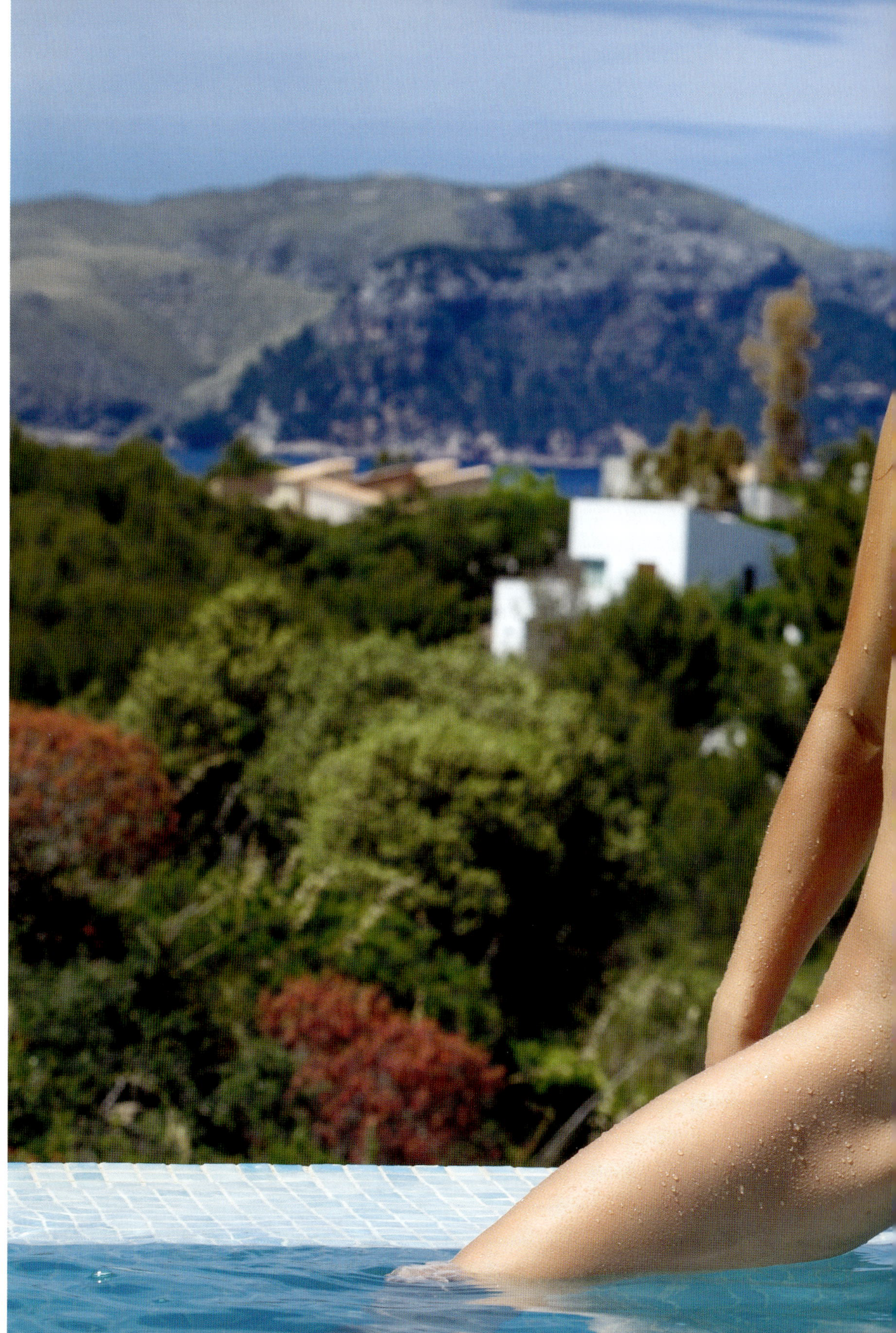

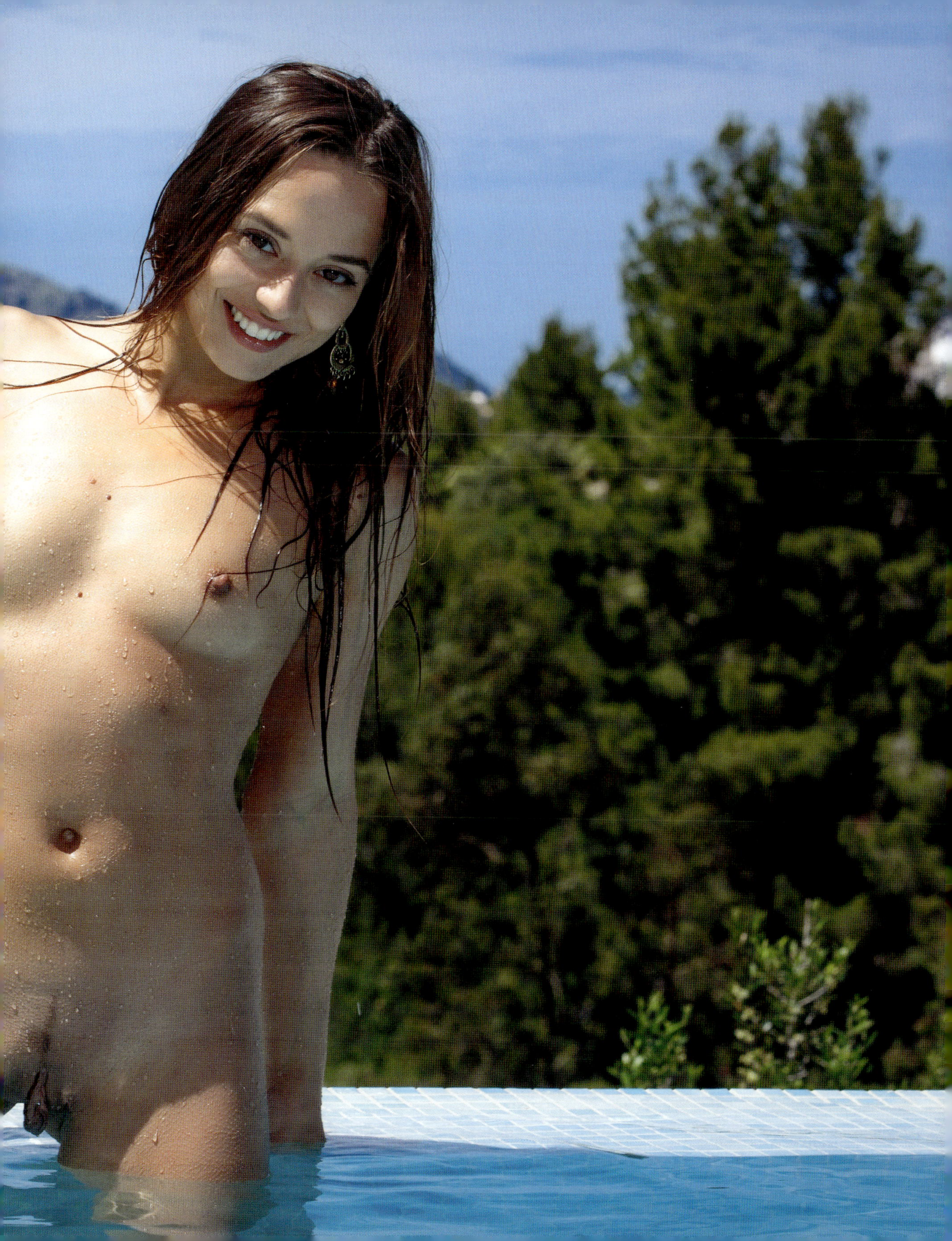

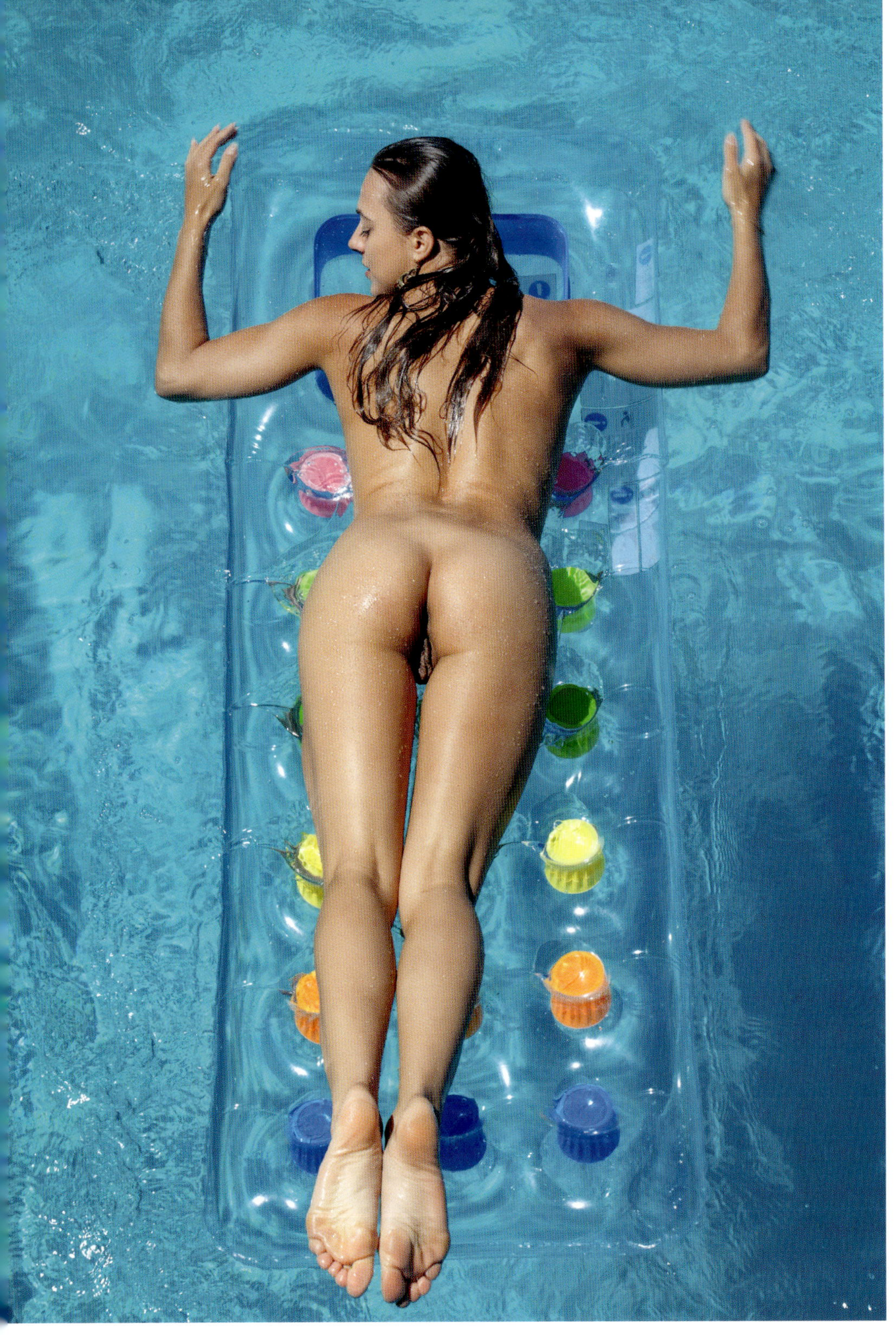

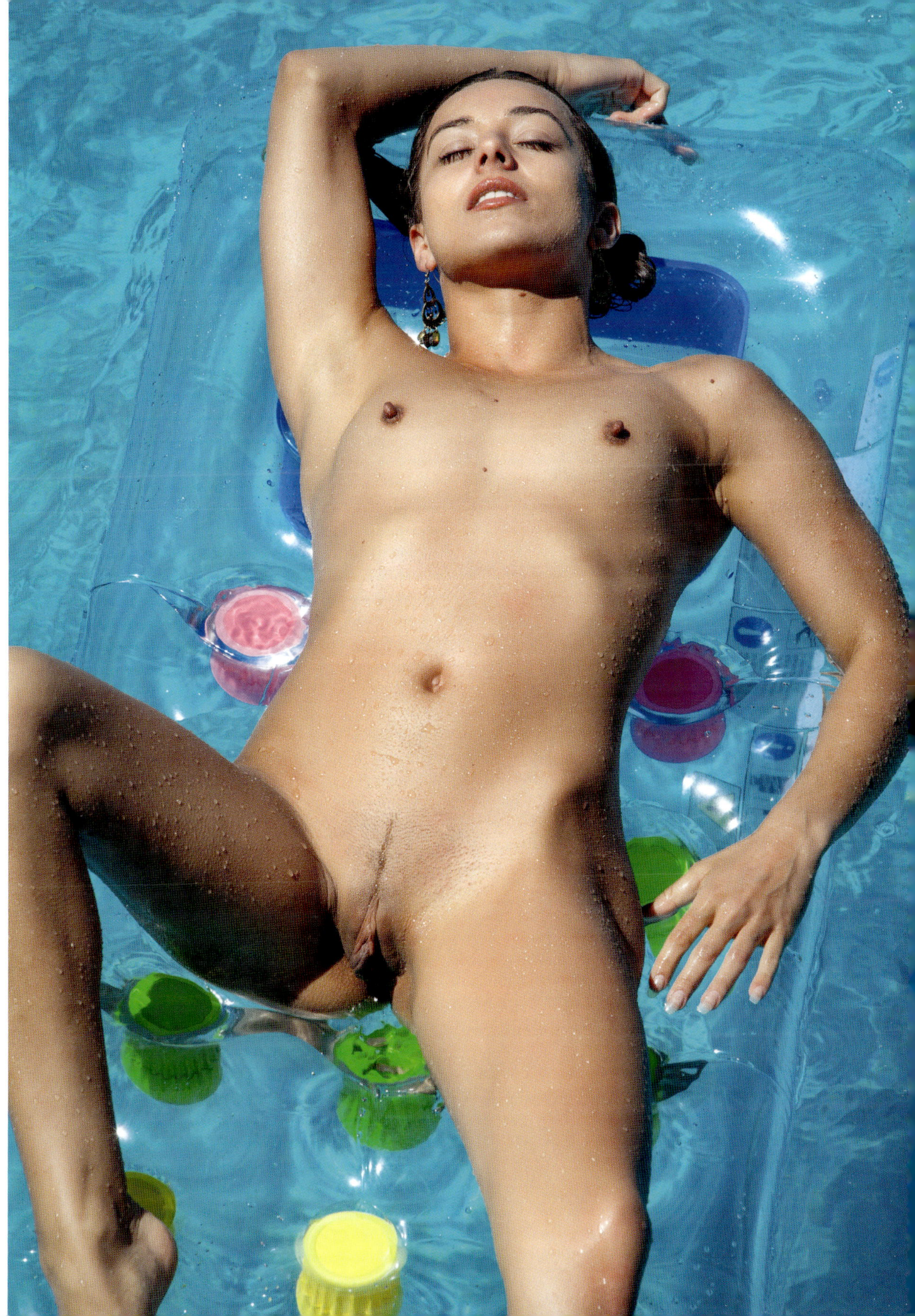

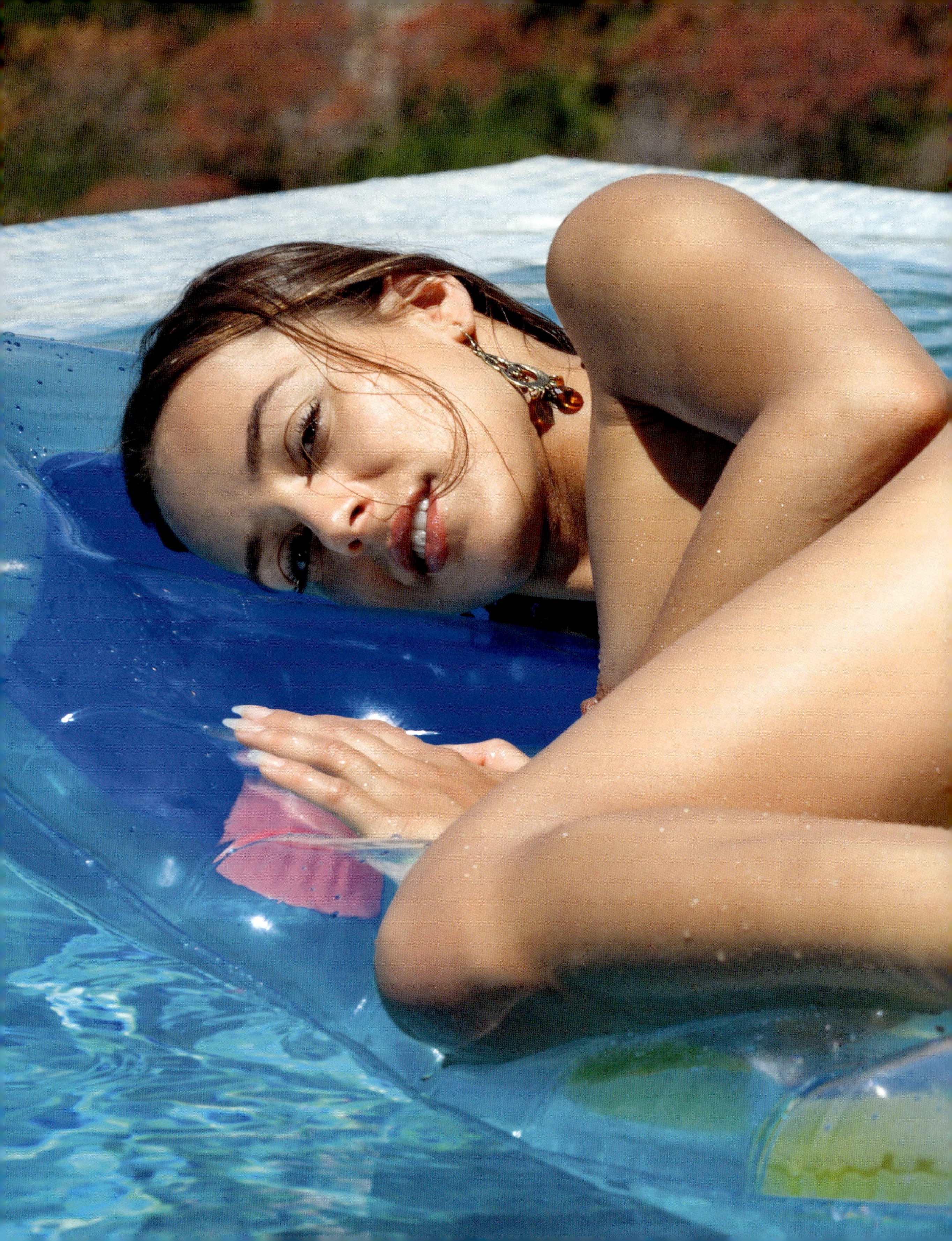

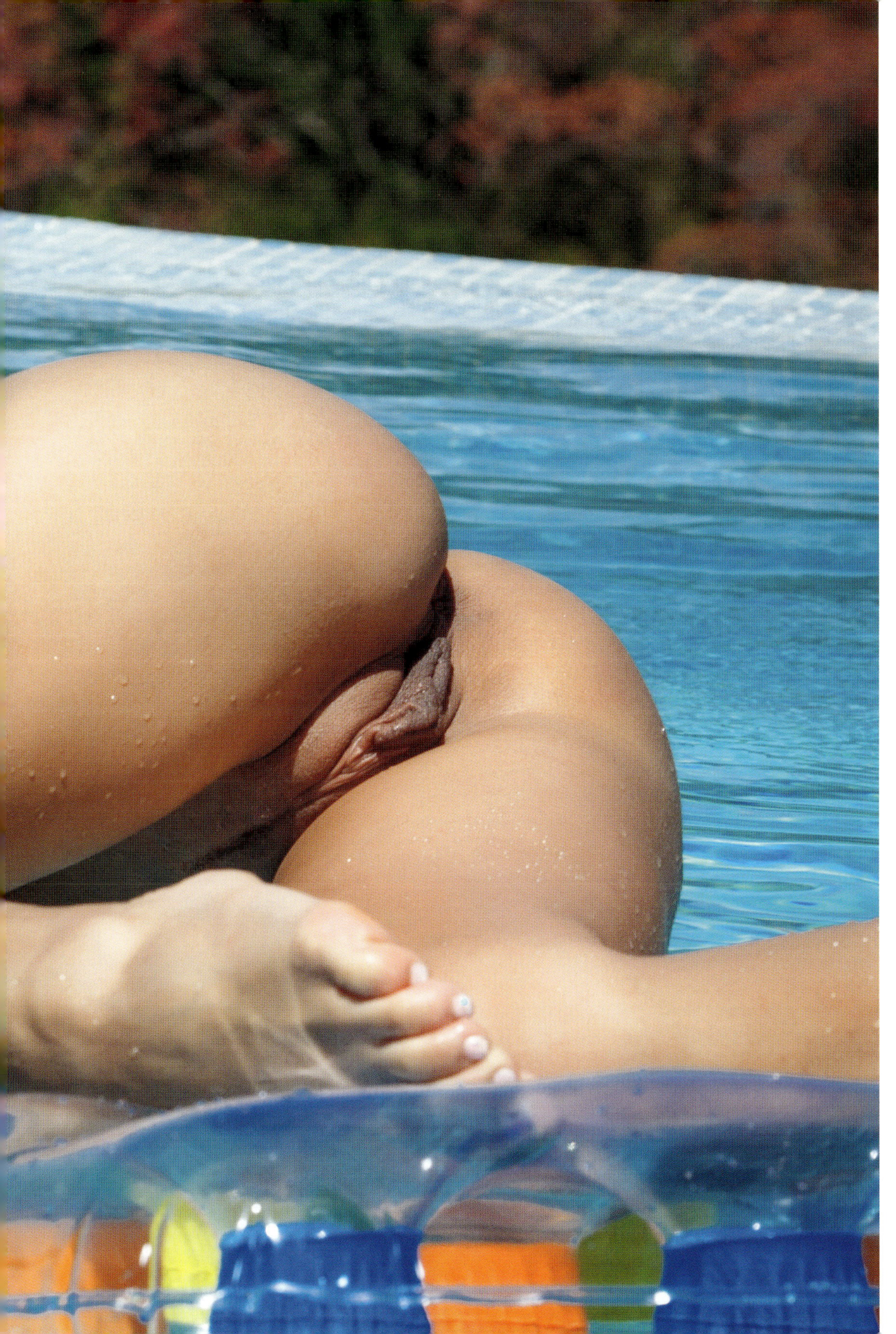

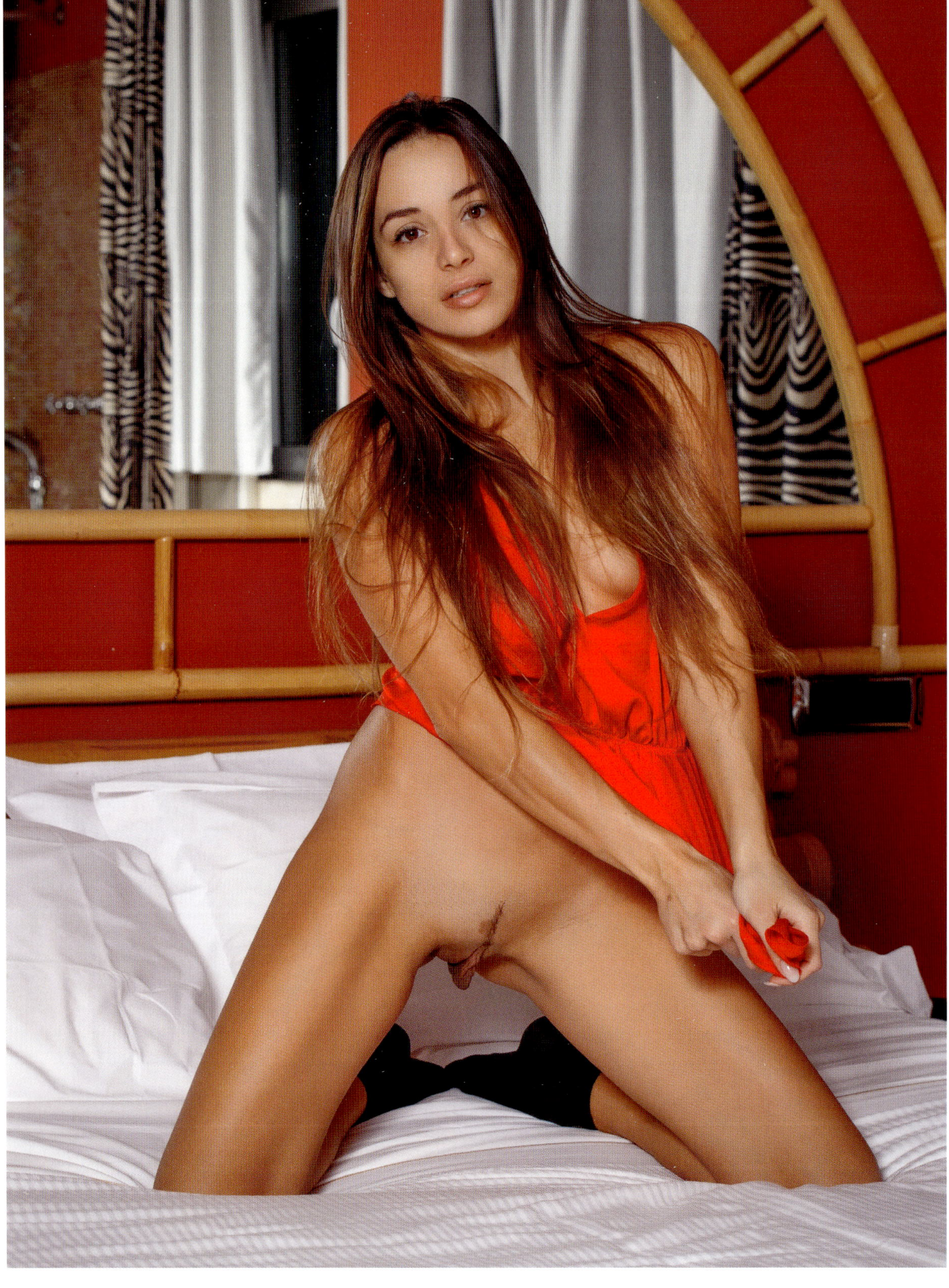

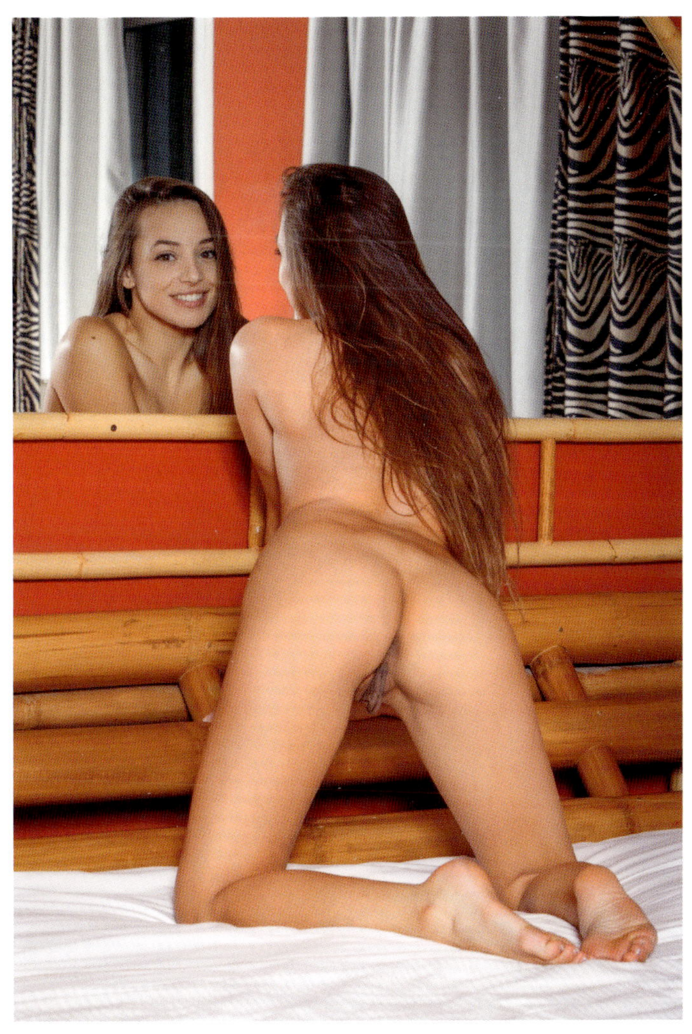

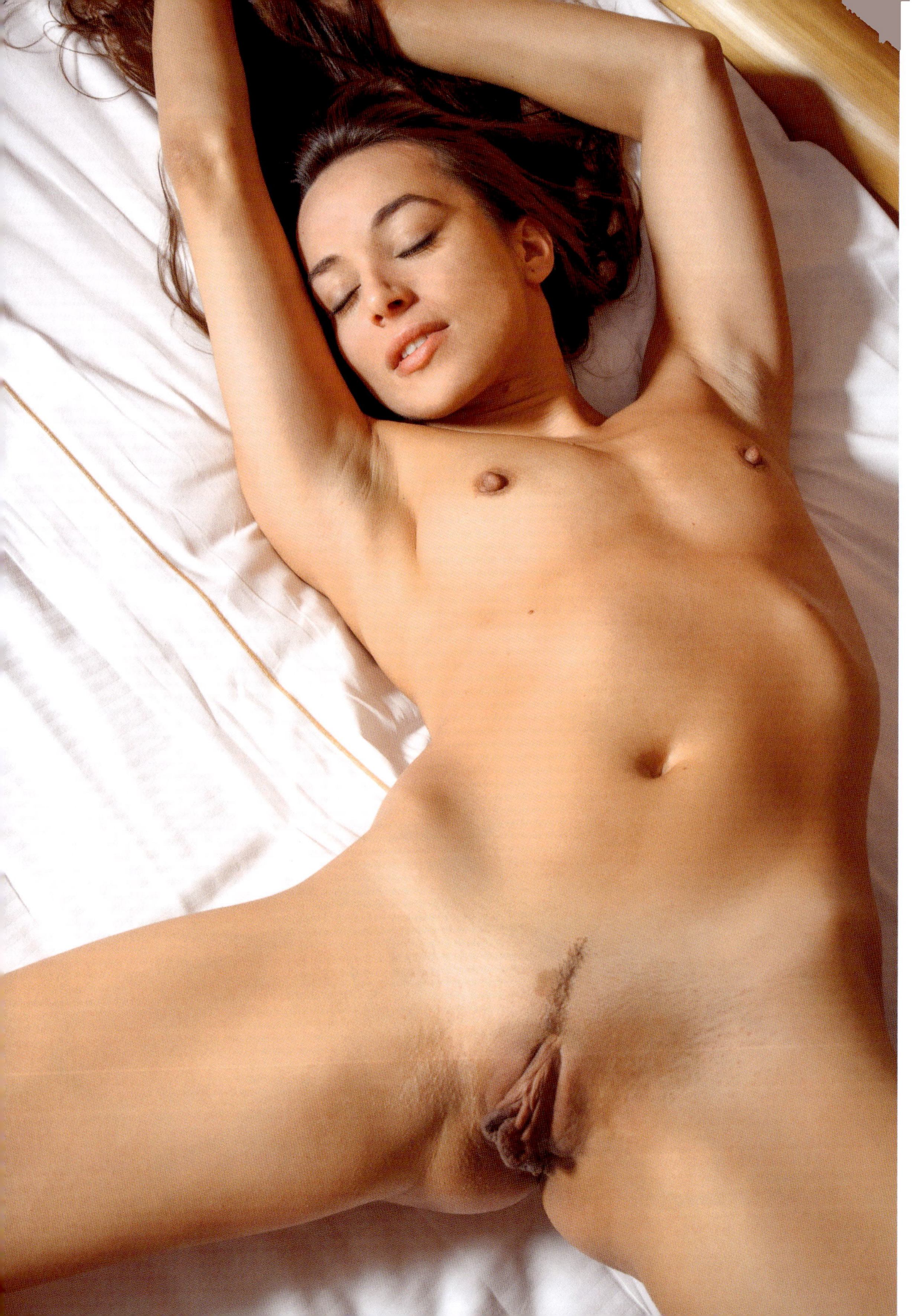

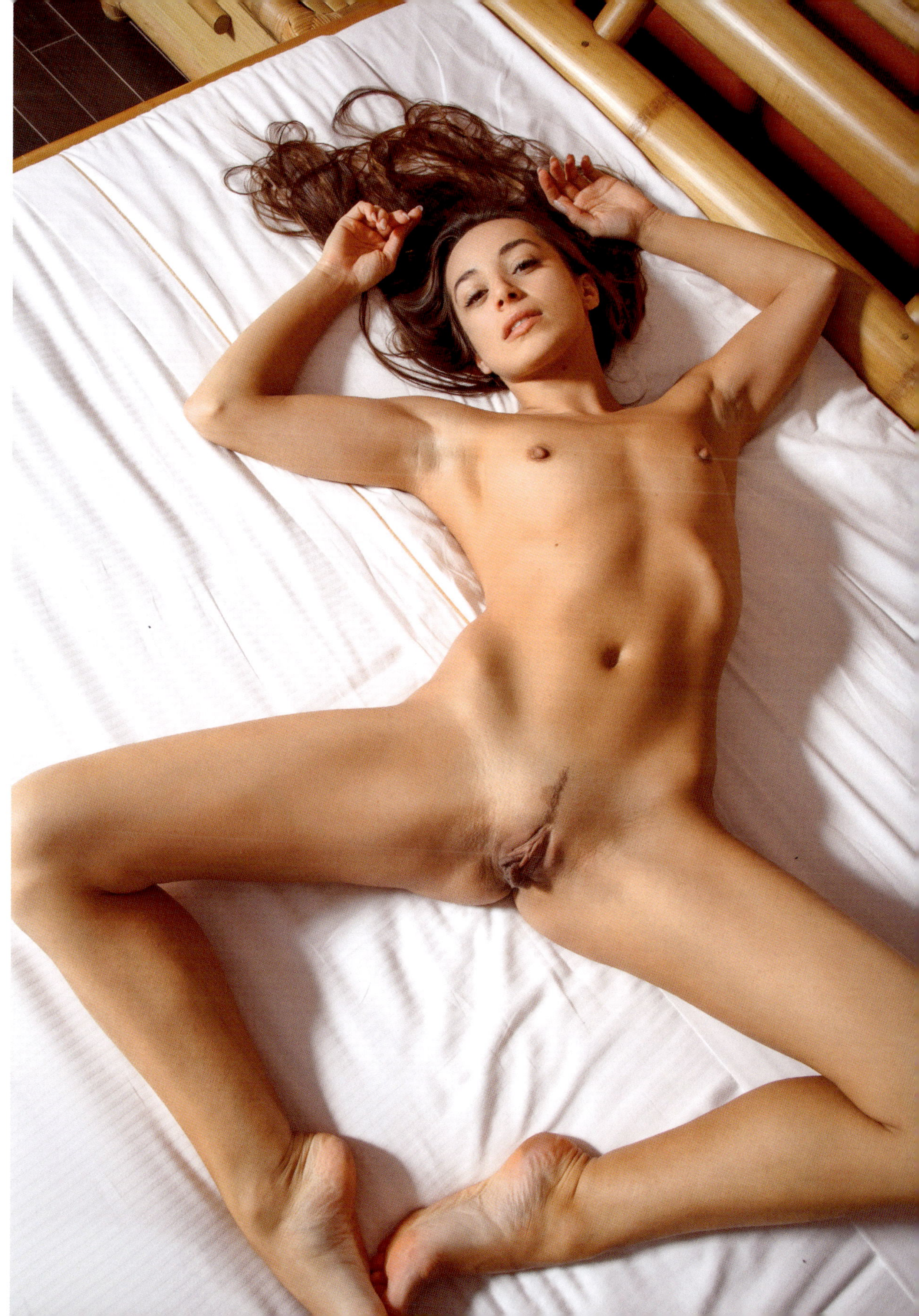

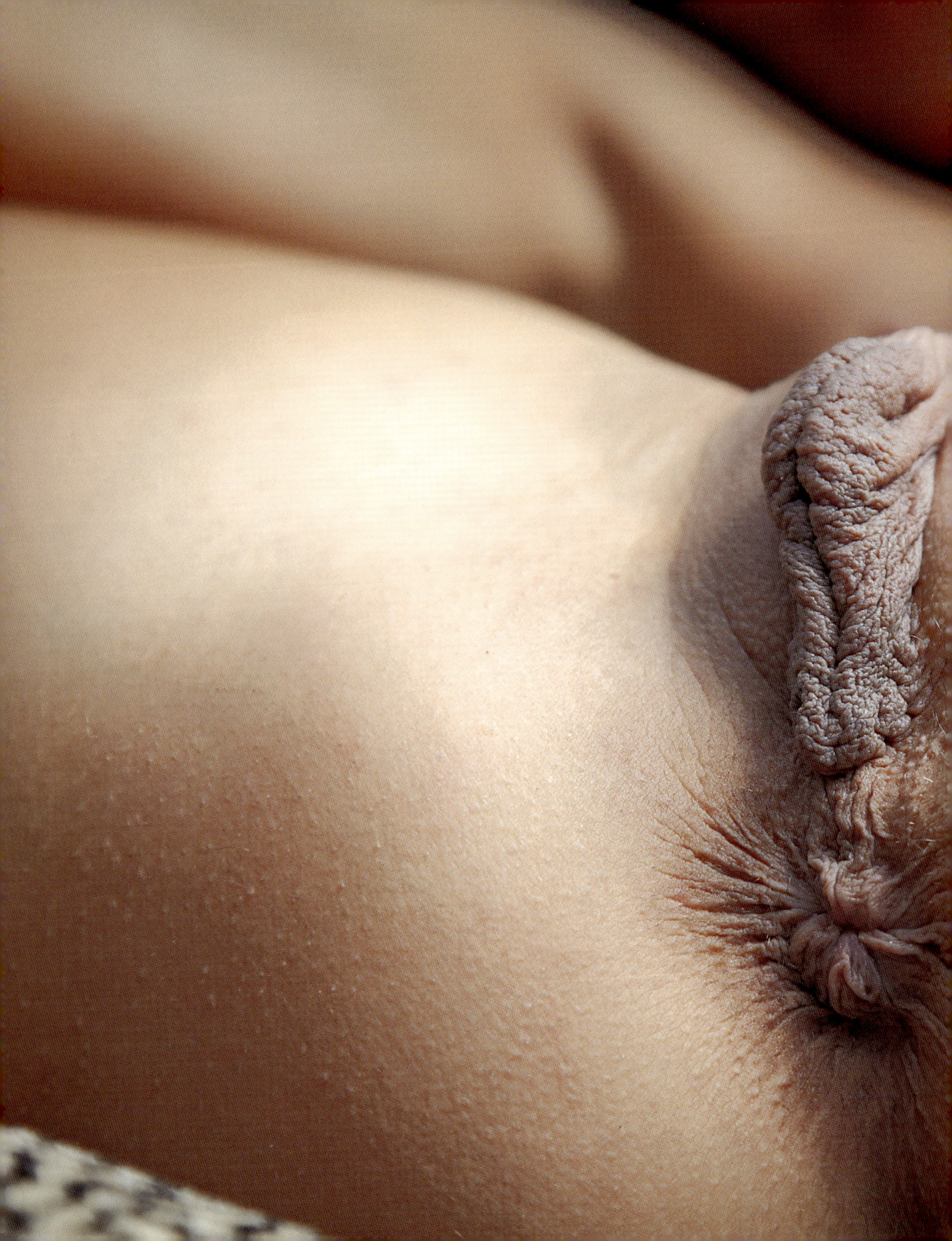

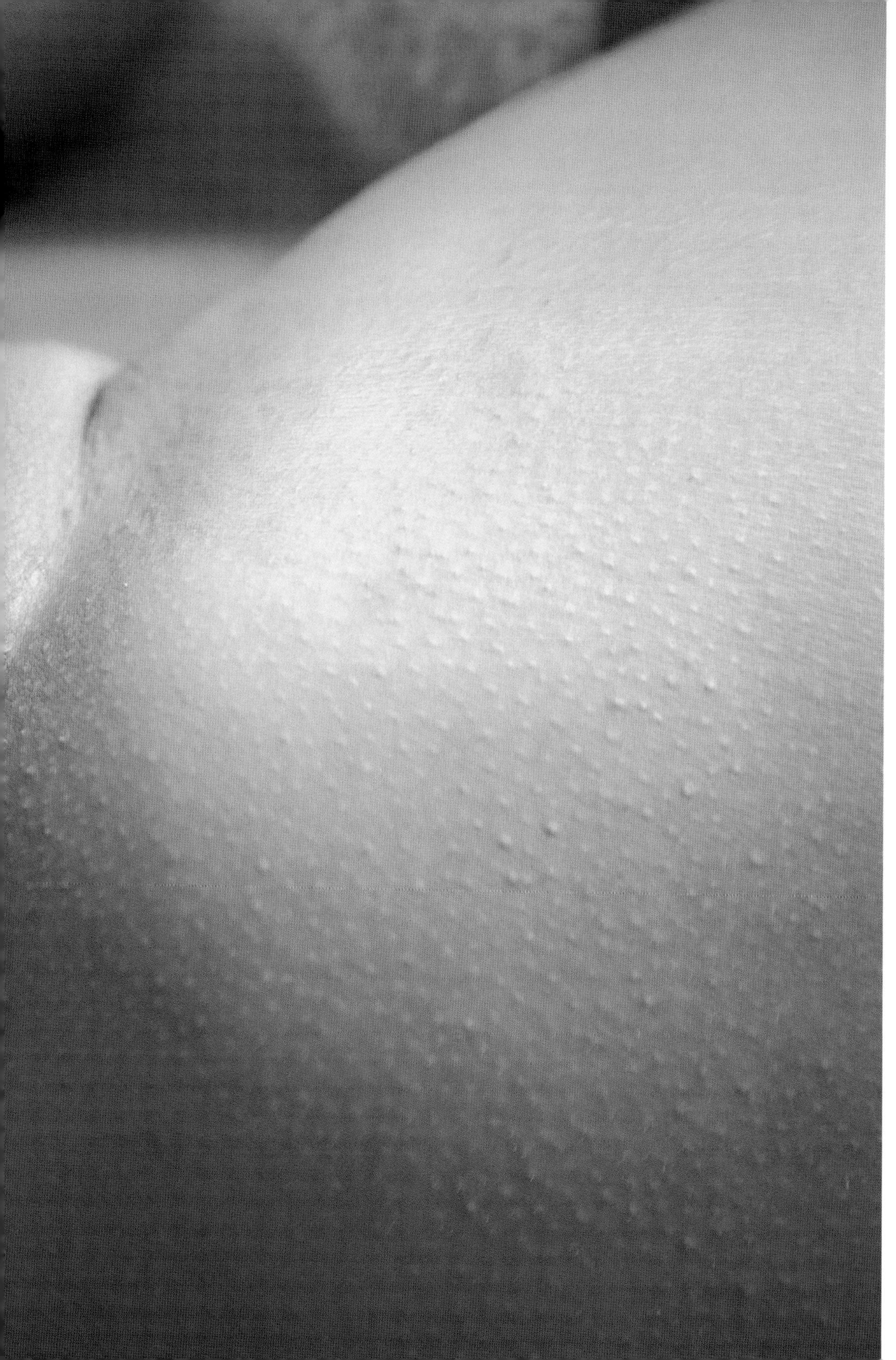

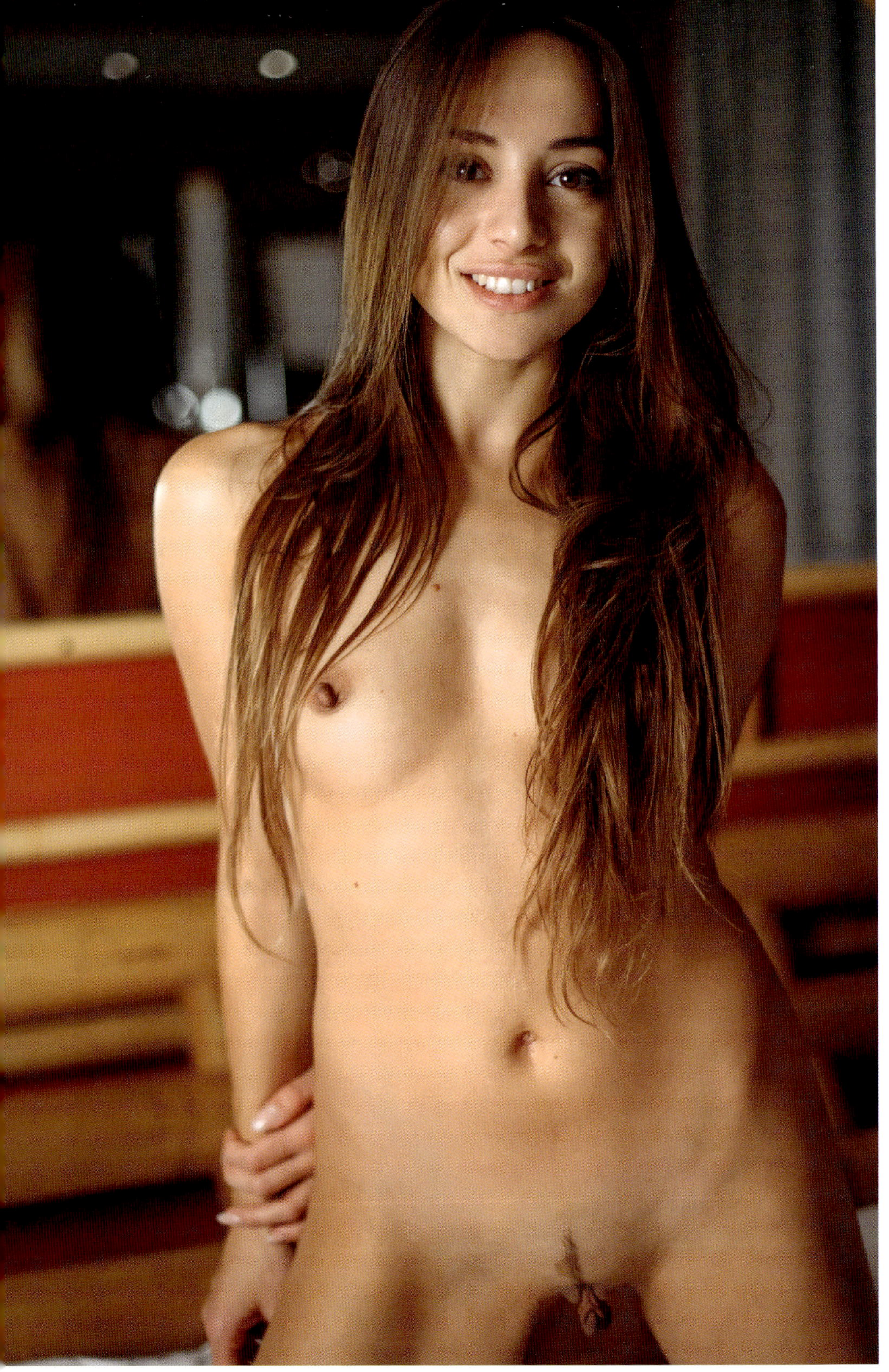

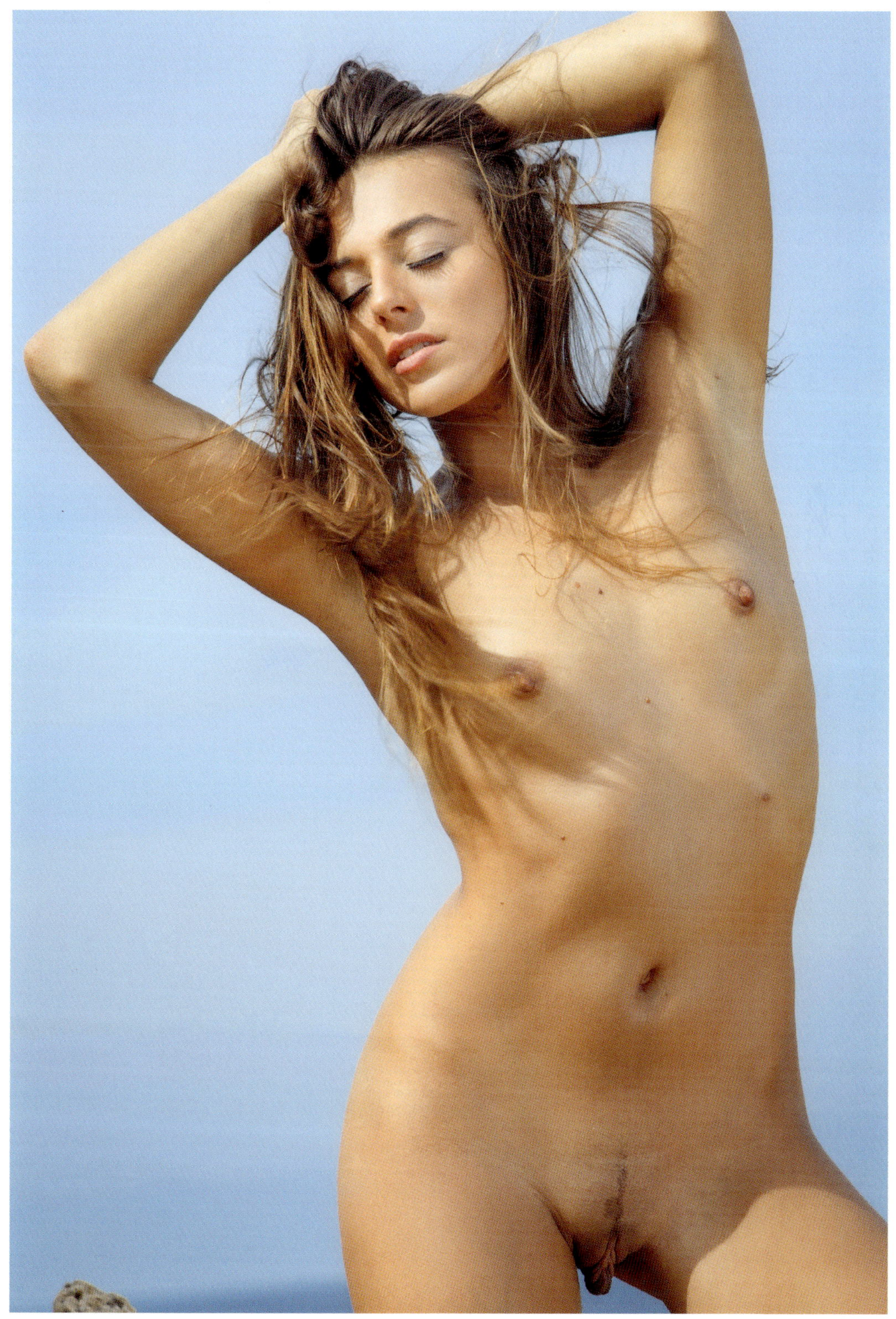

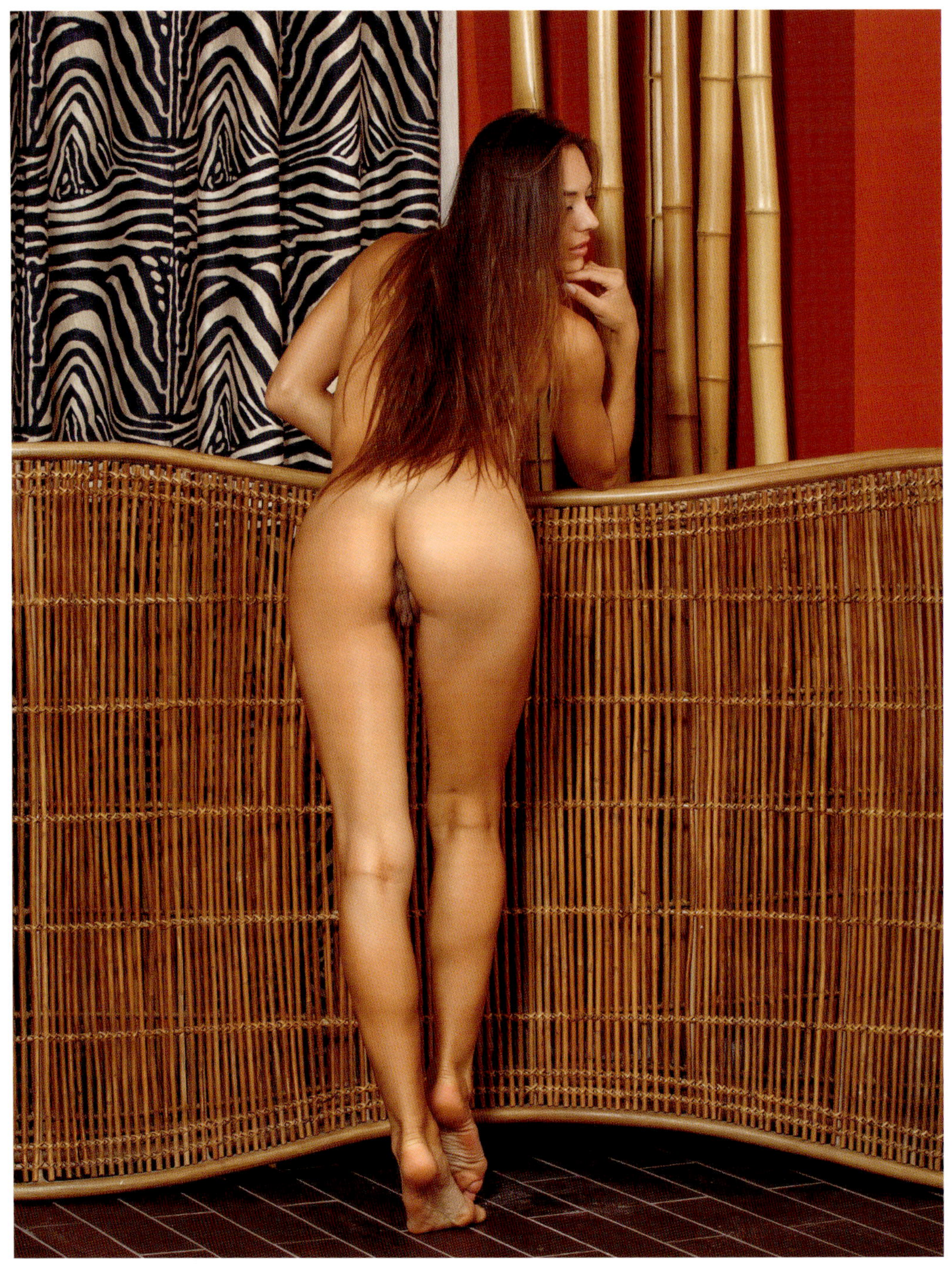

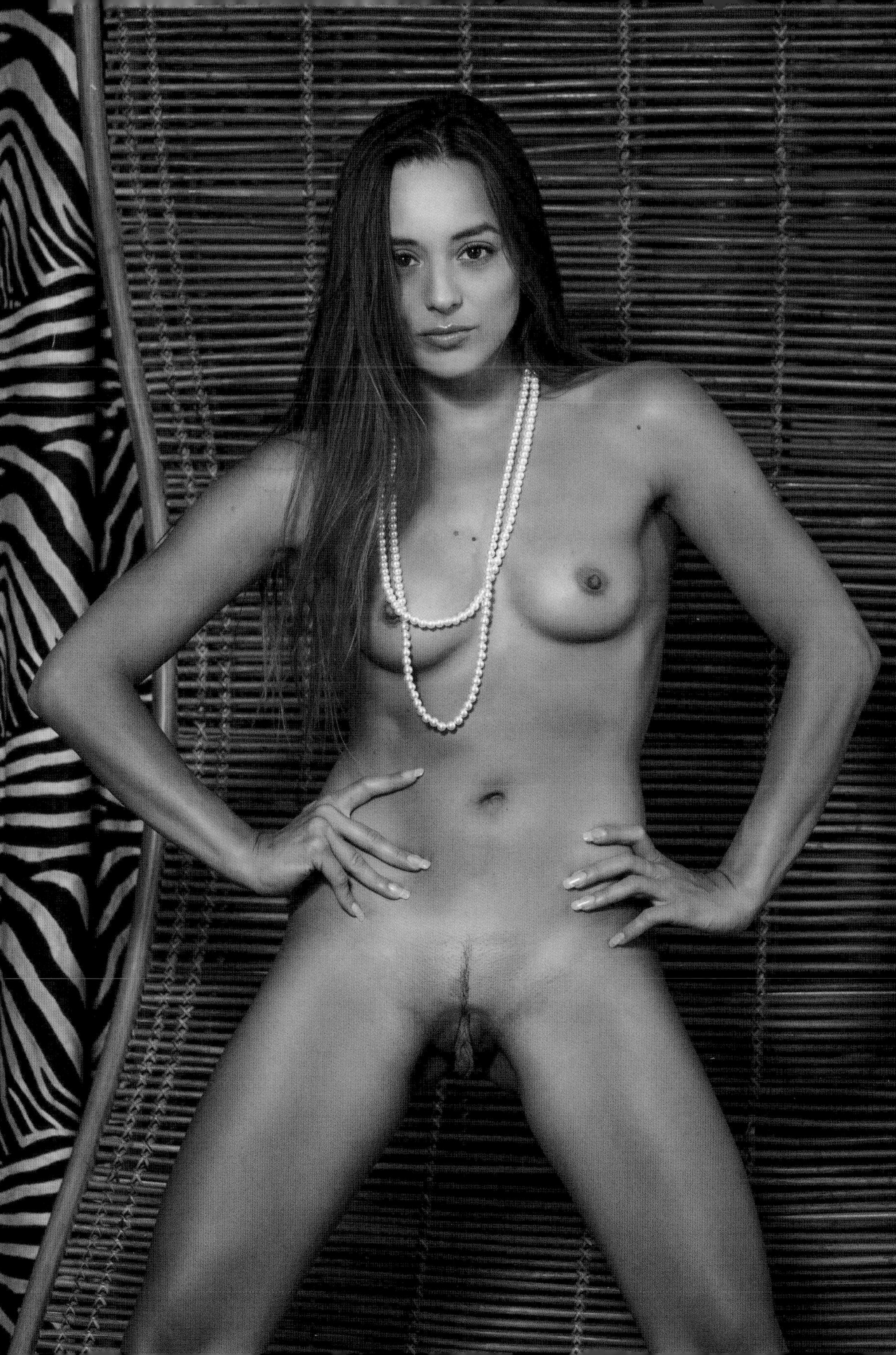

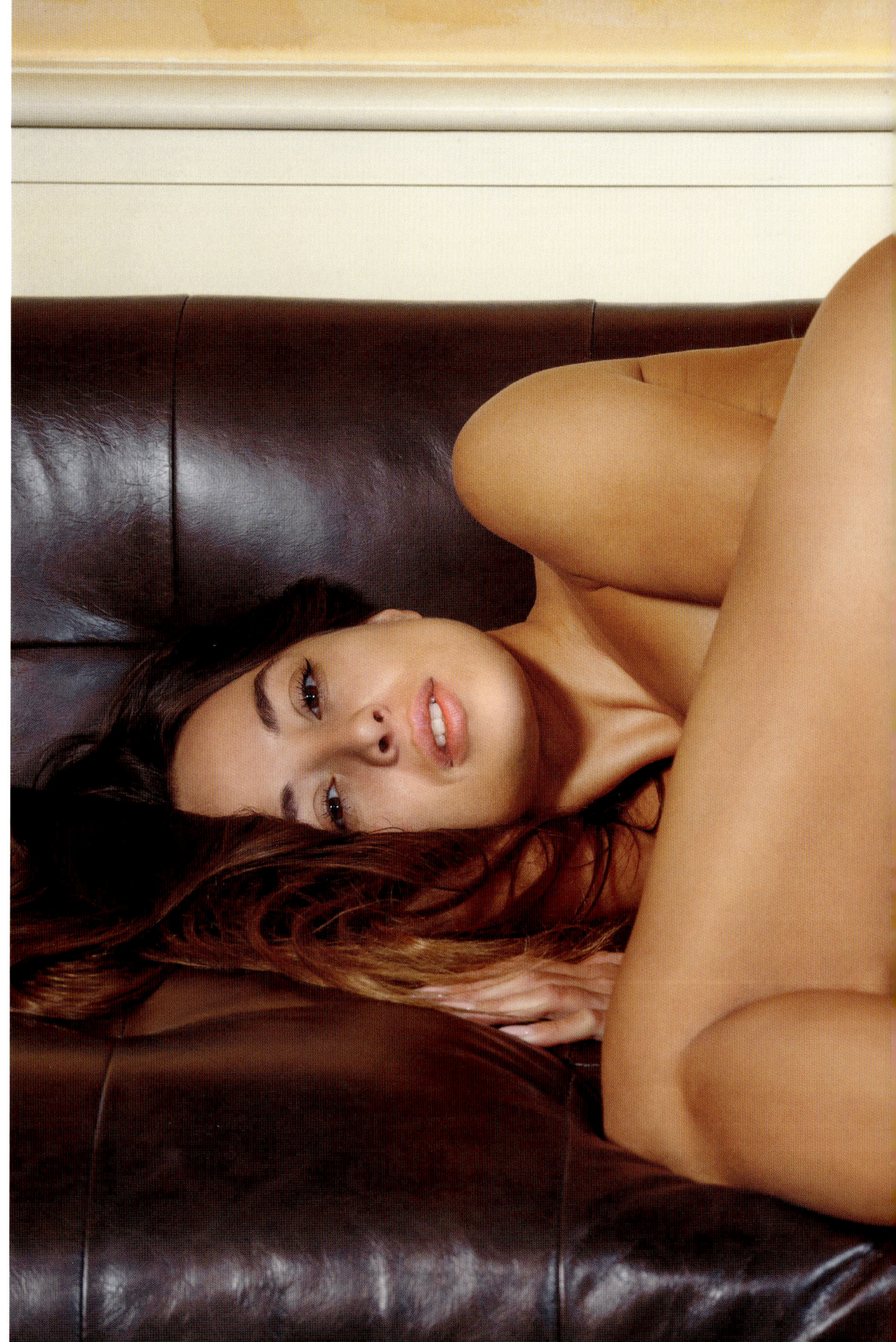

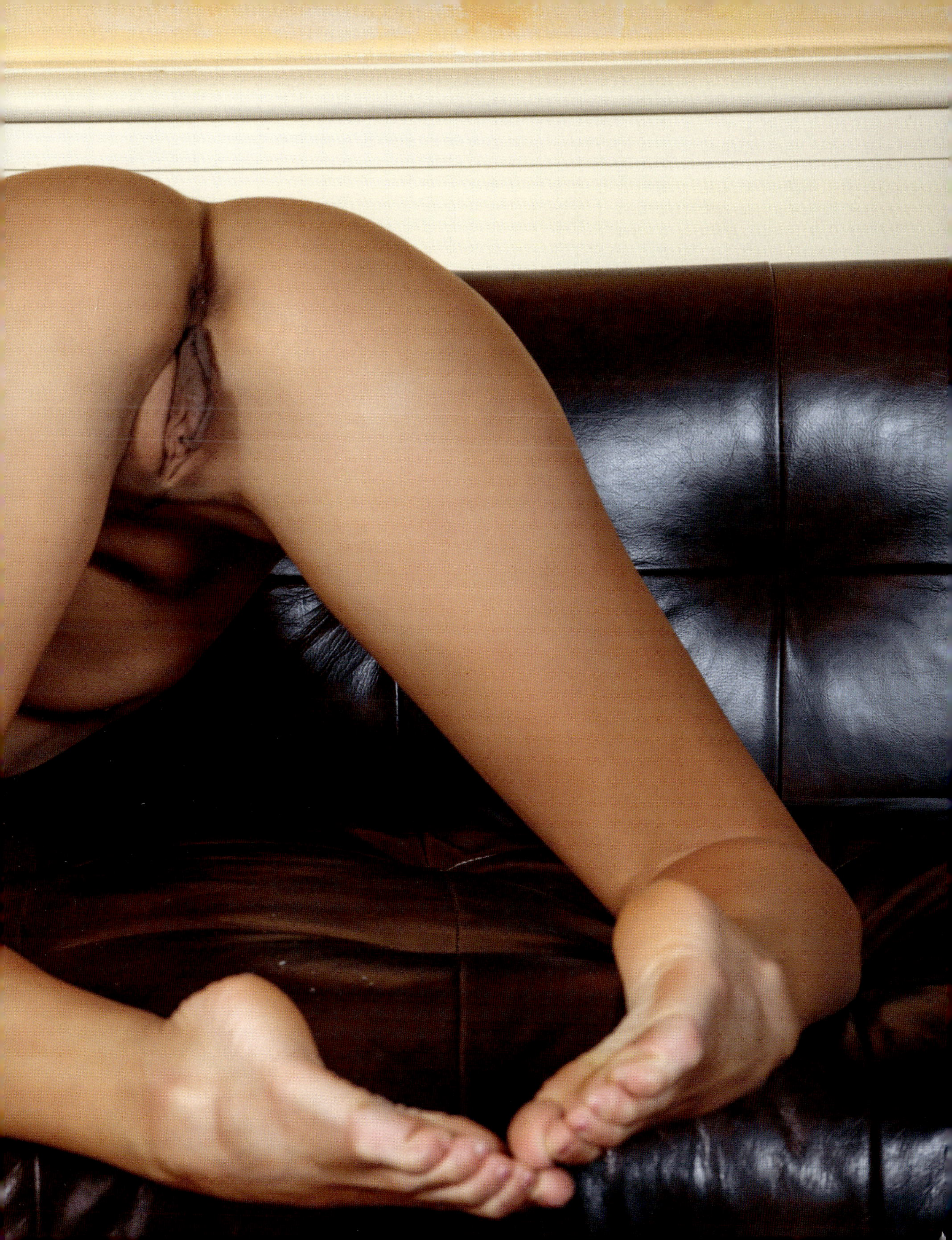

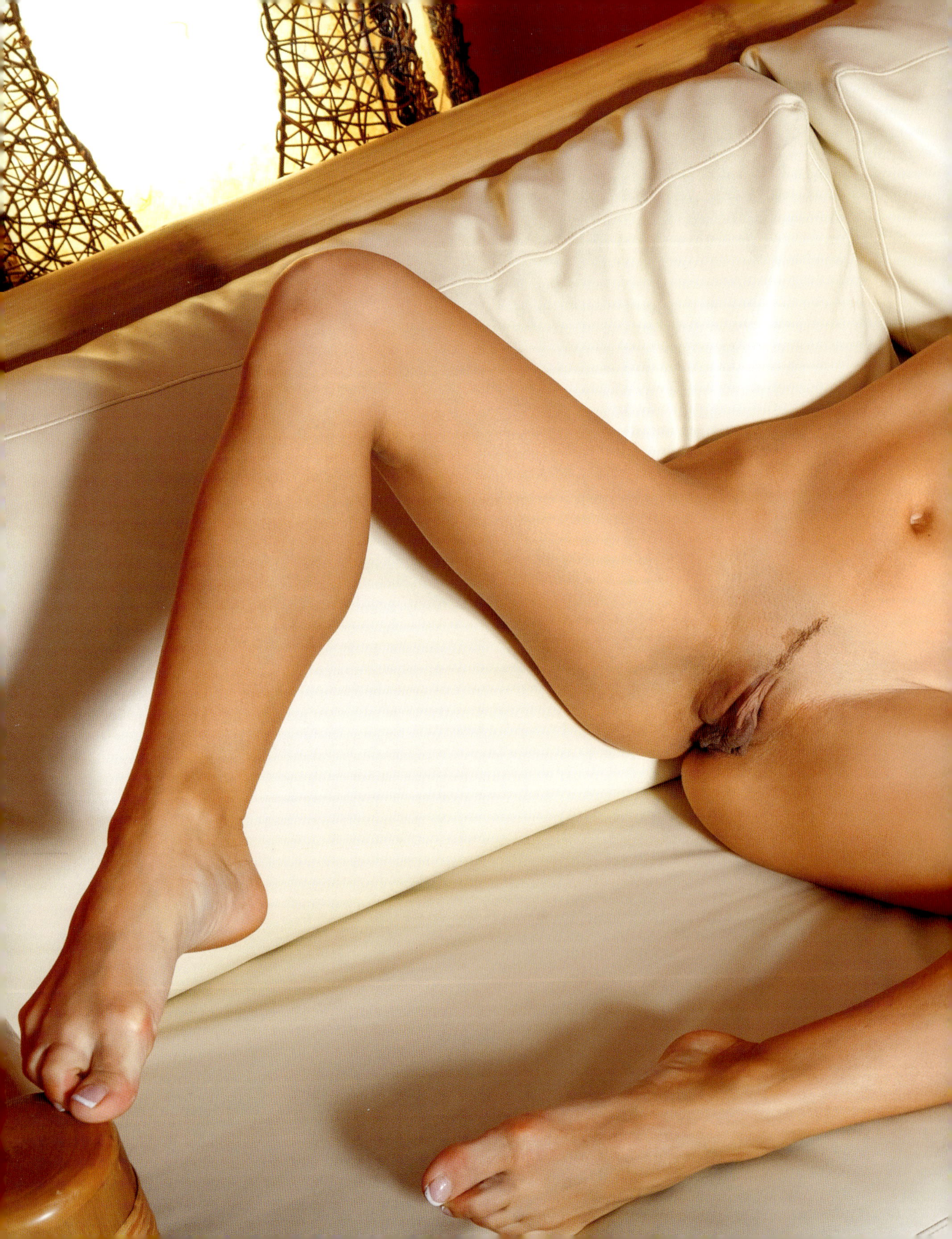

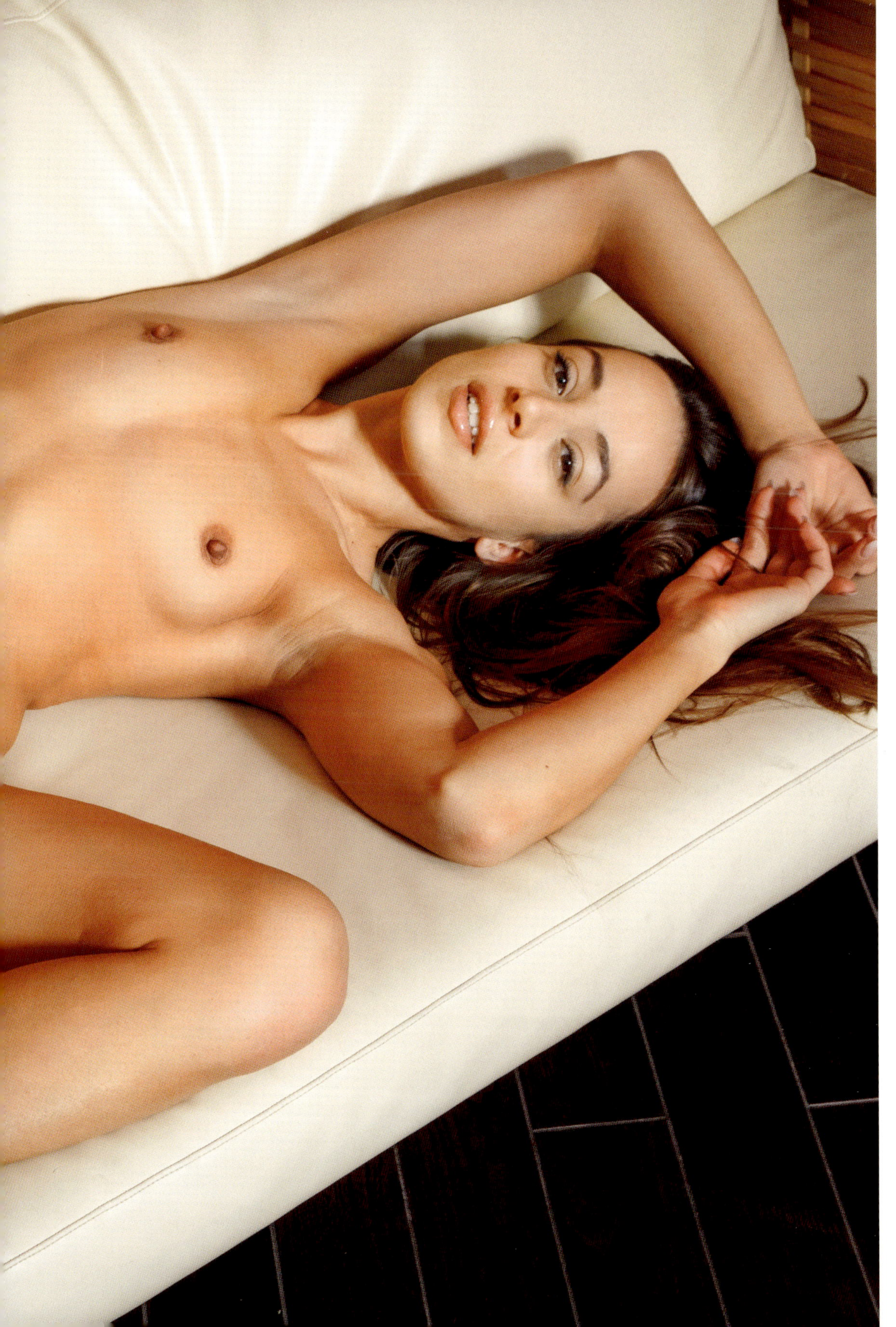

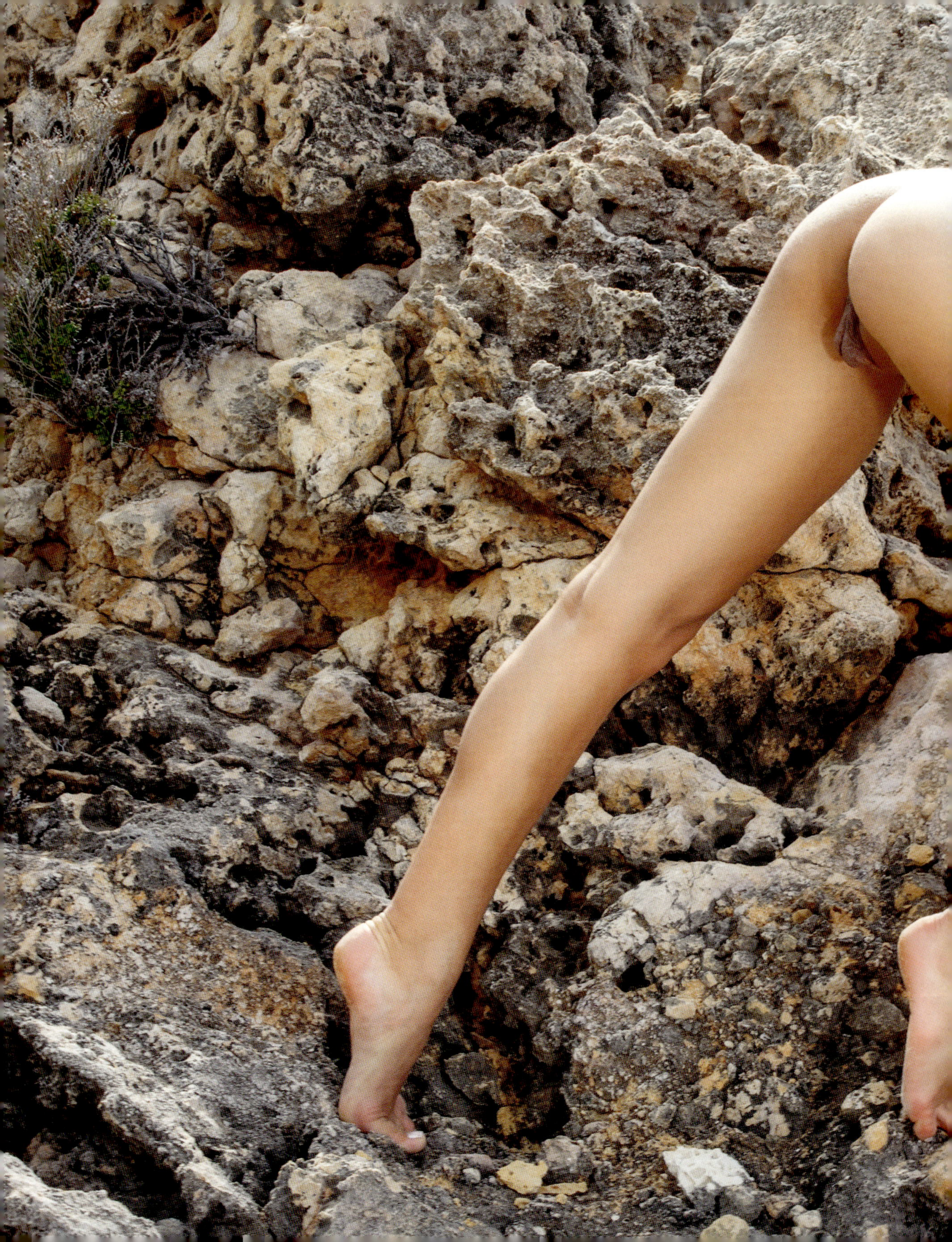

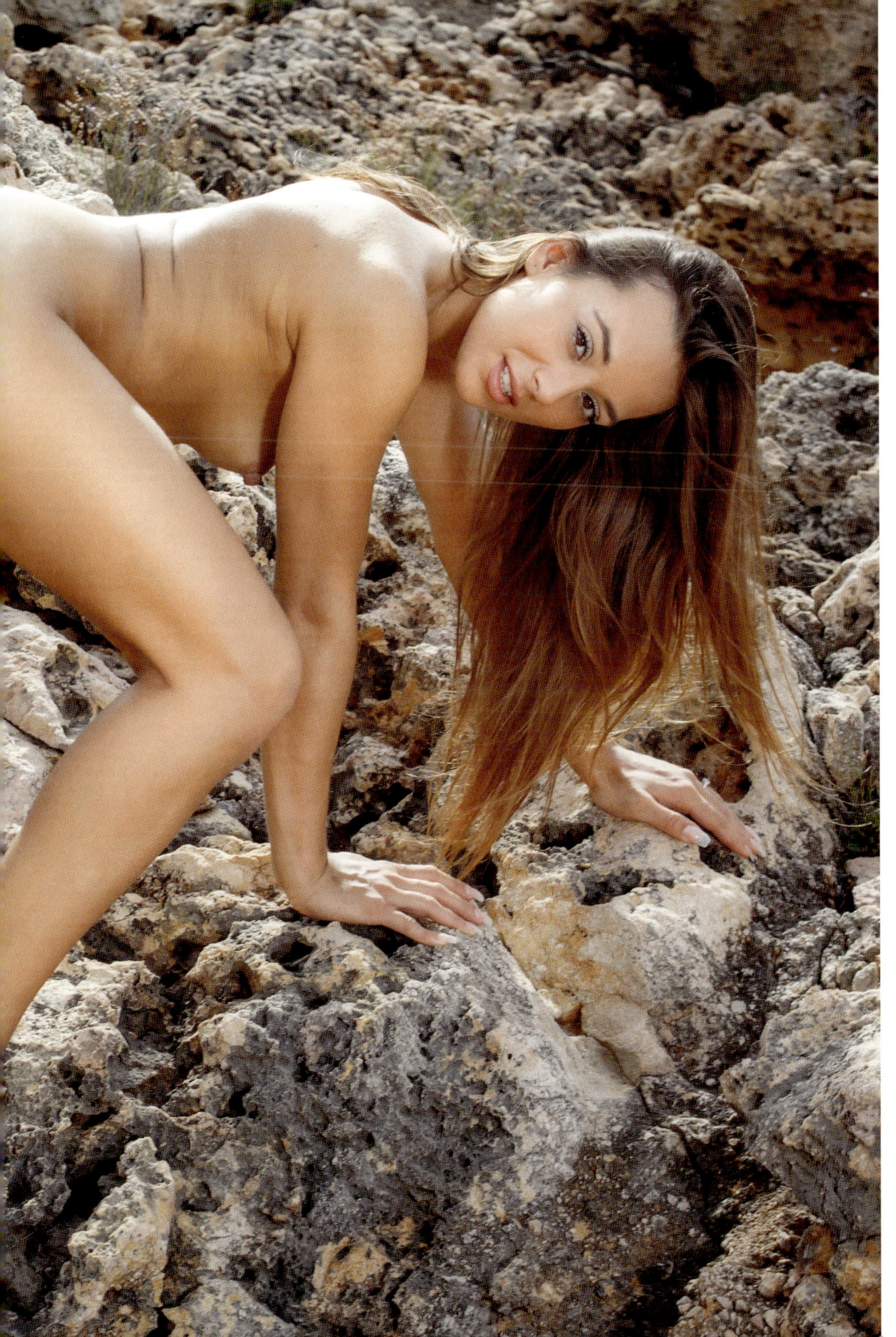

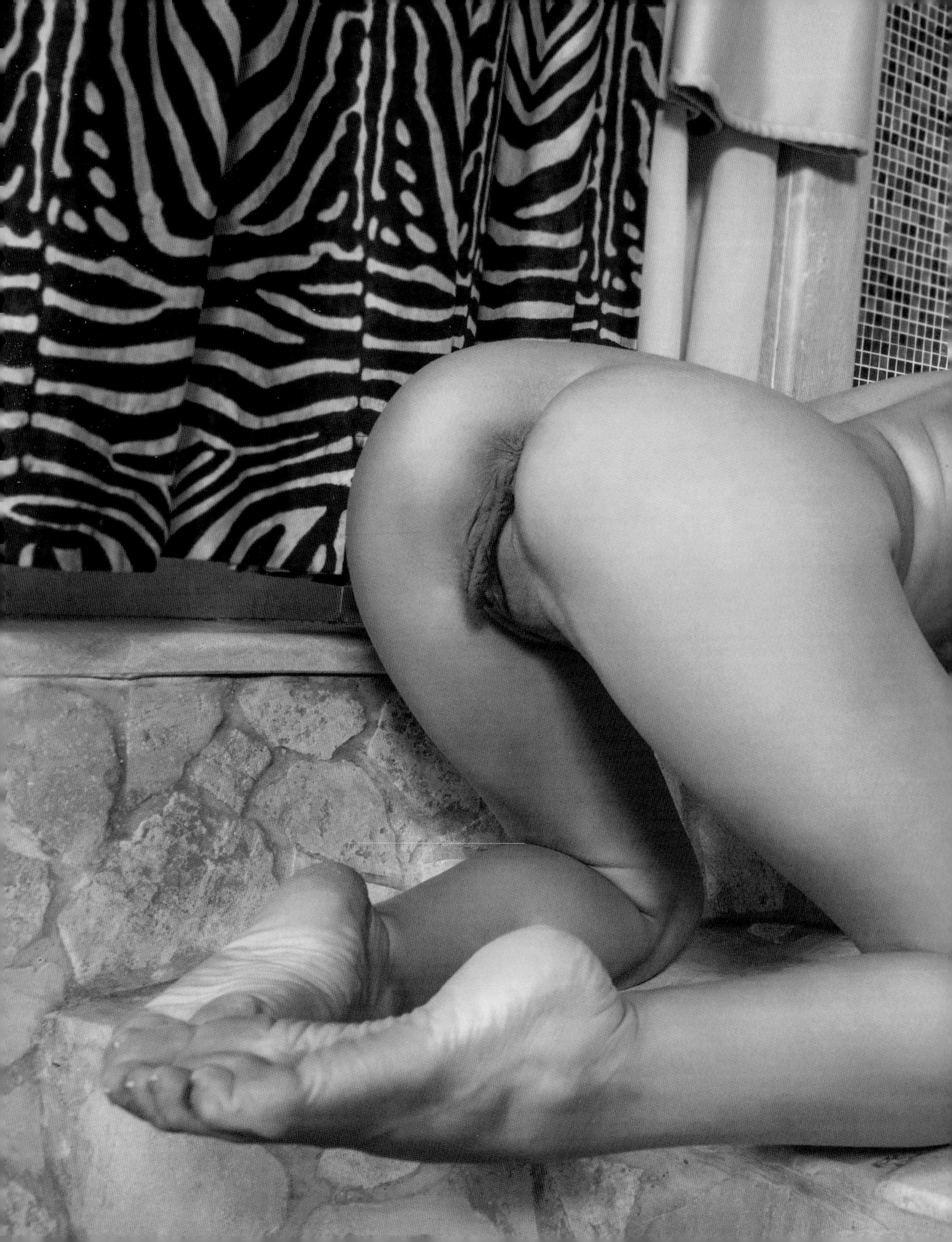

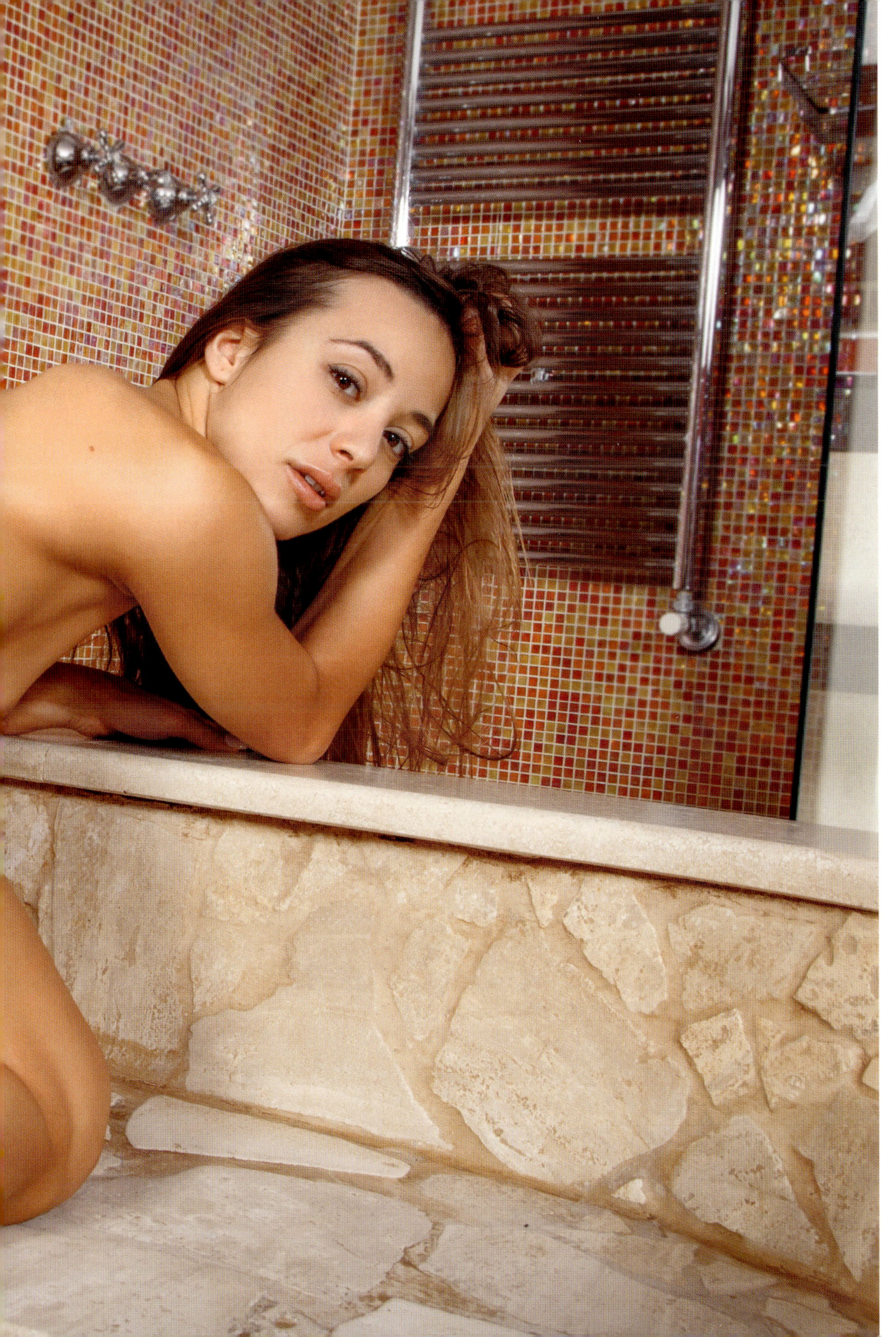

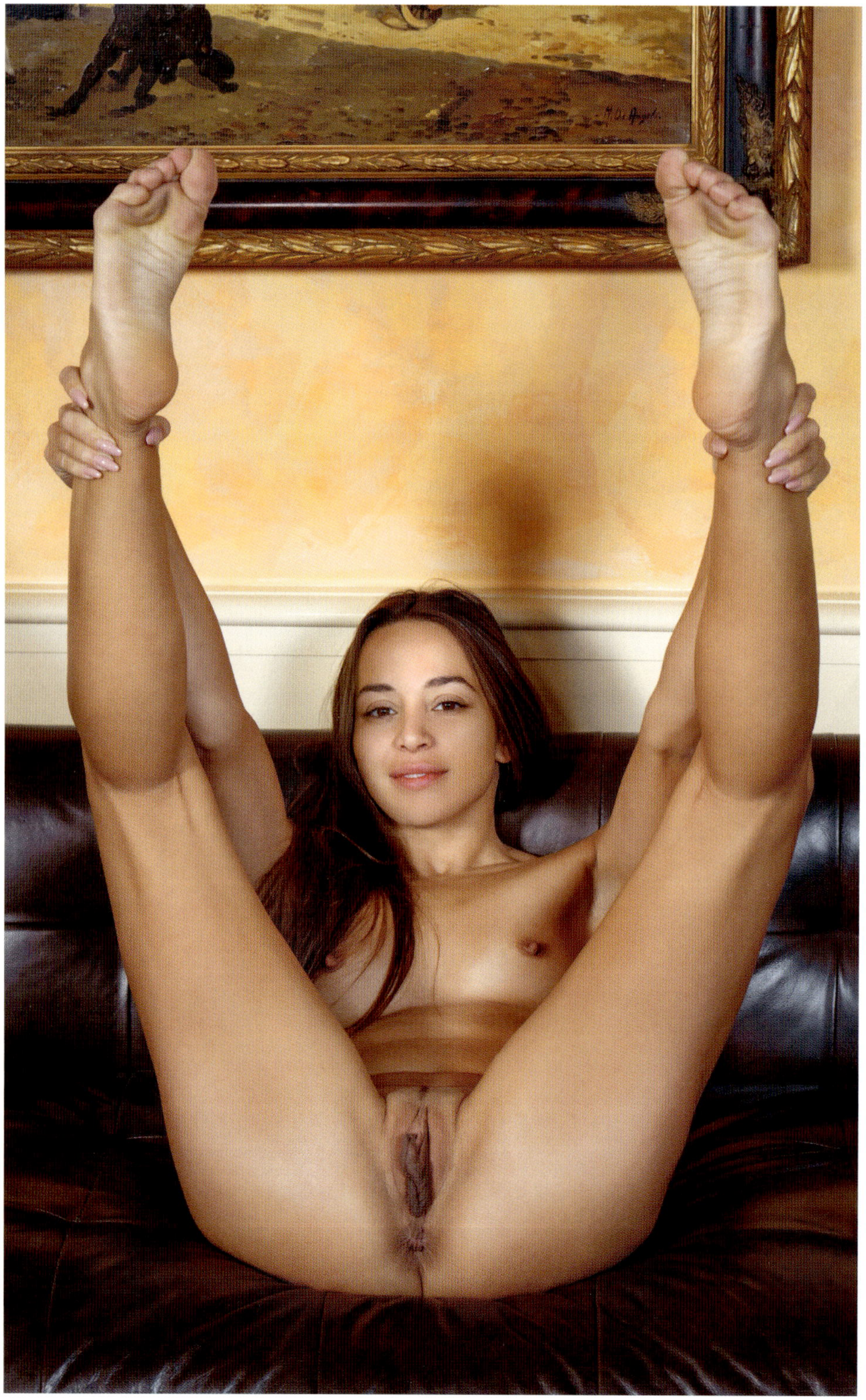

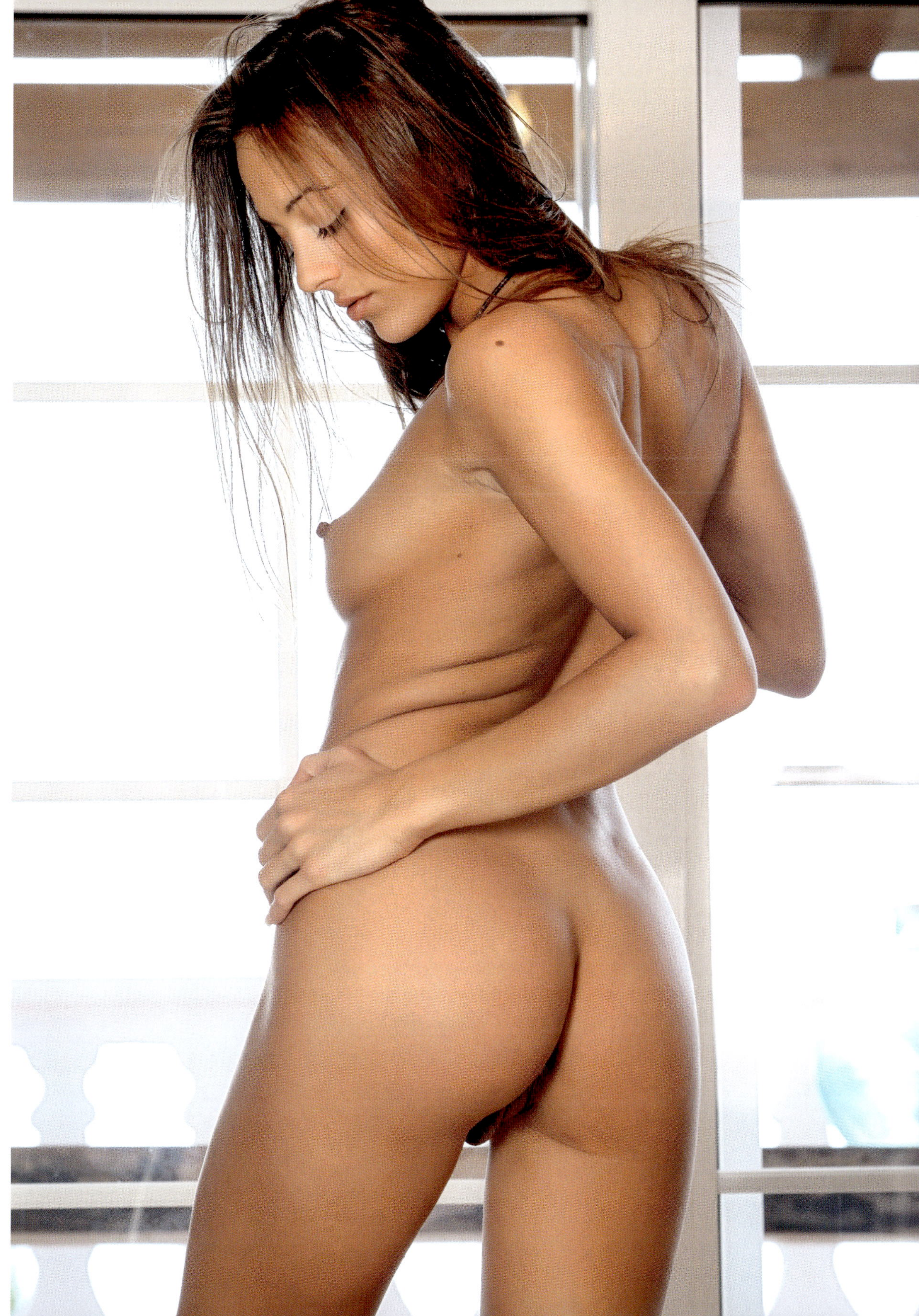

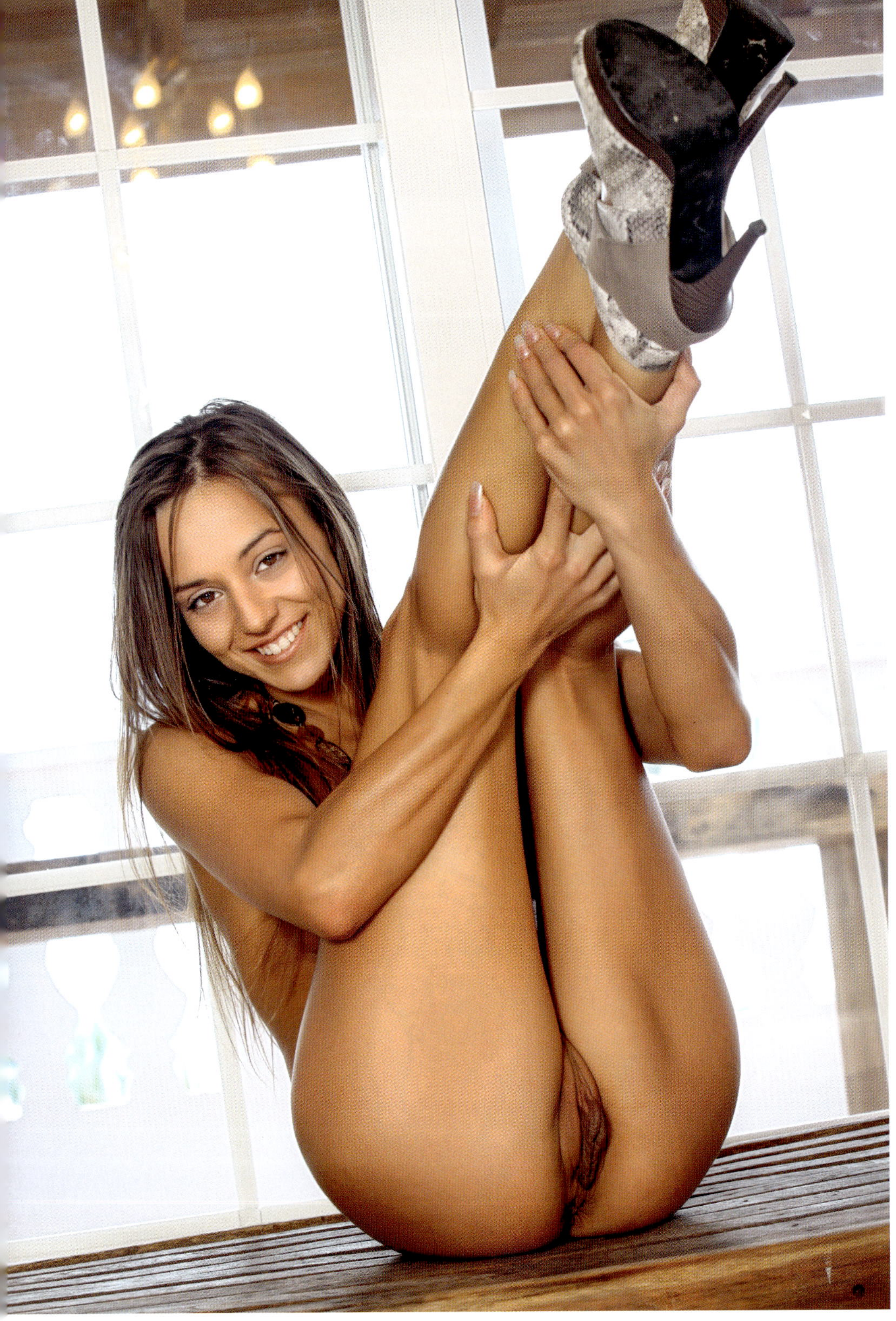

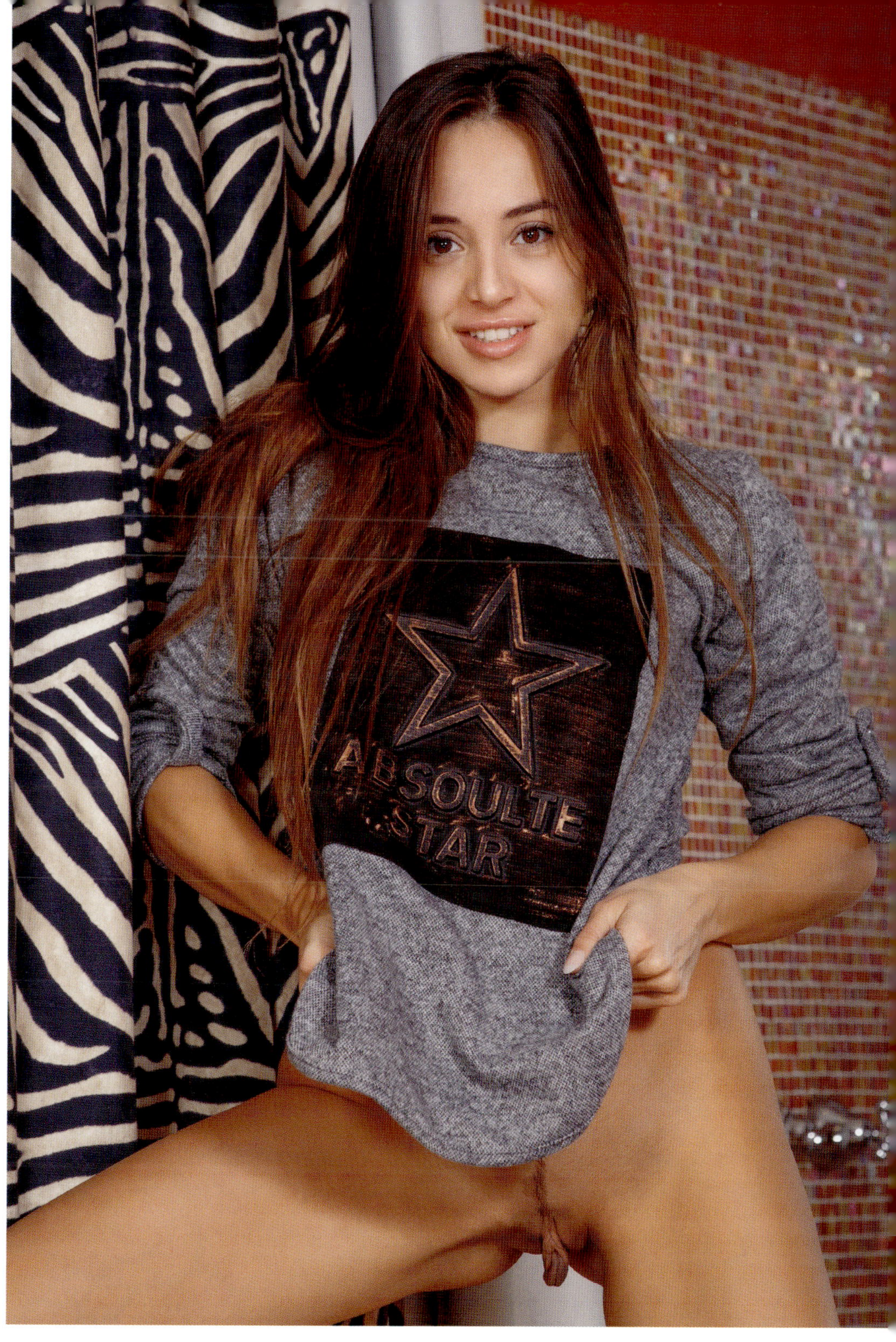
ABSOULTE
STAR

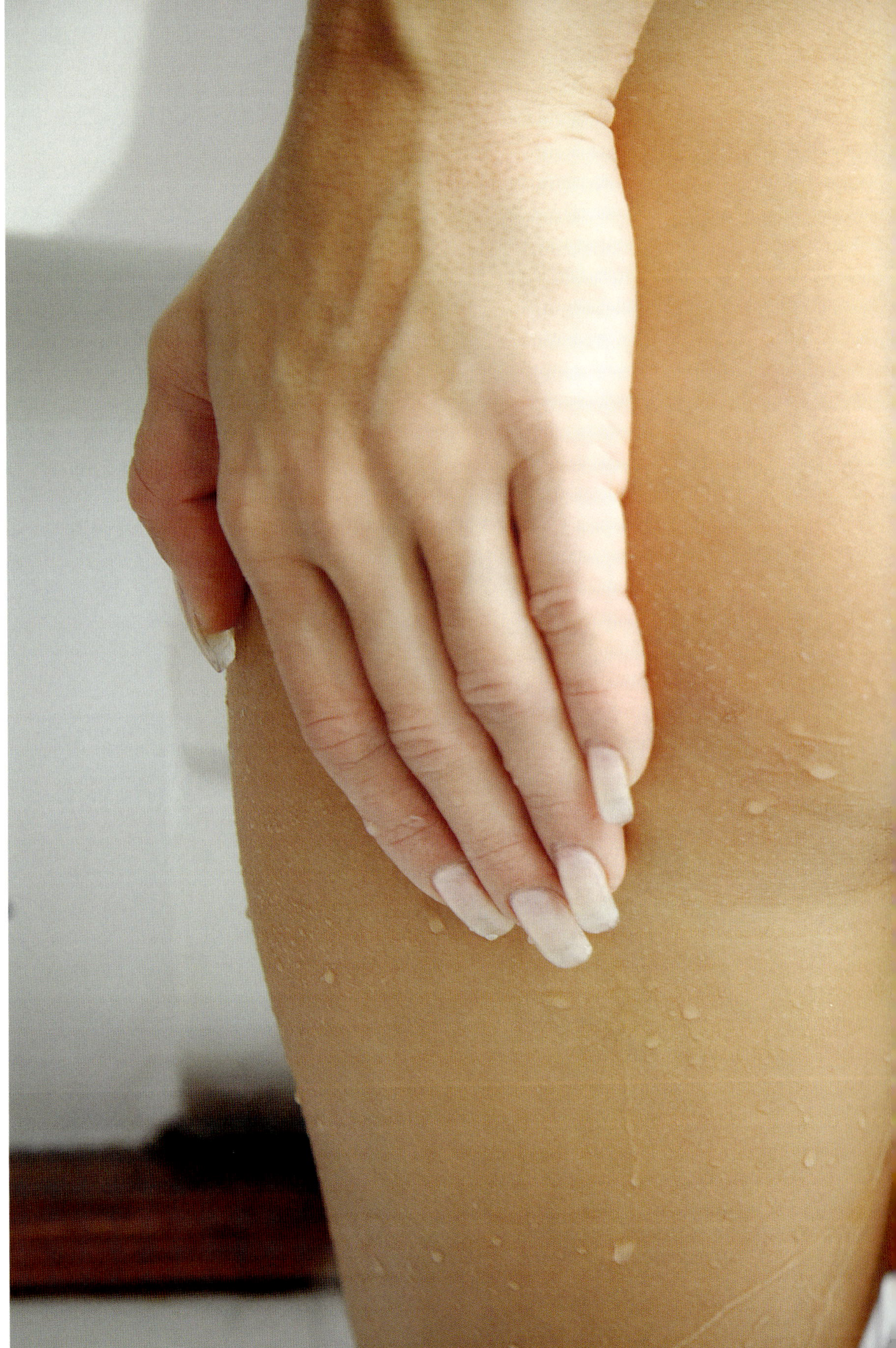

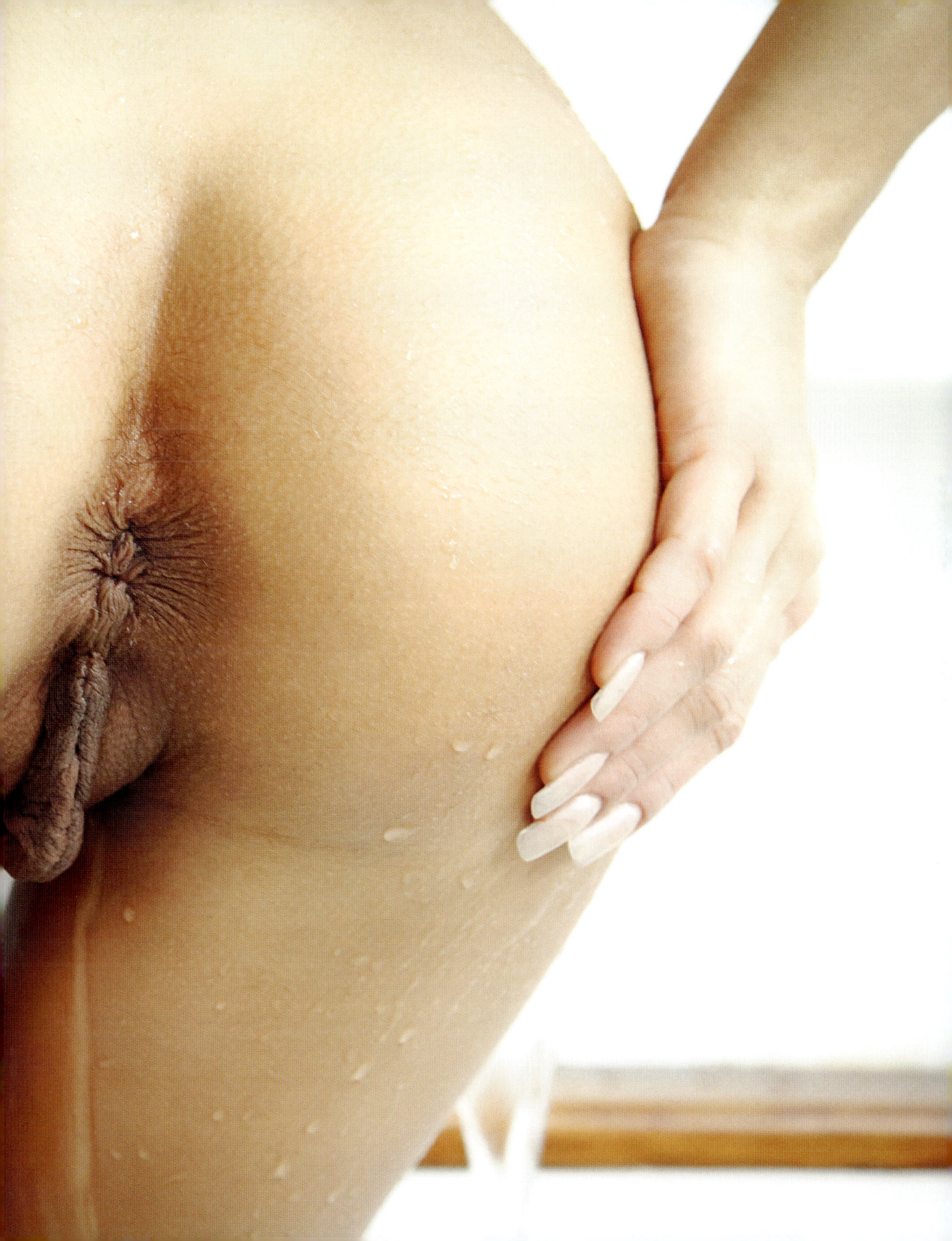

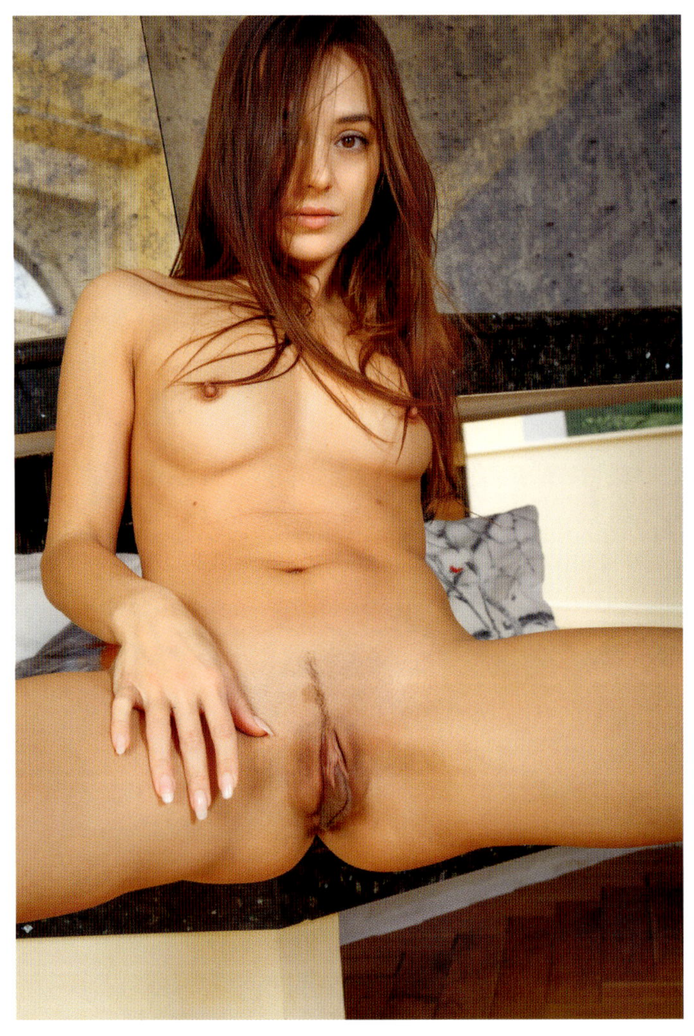

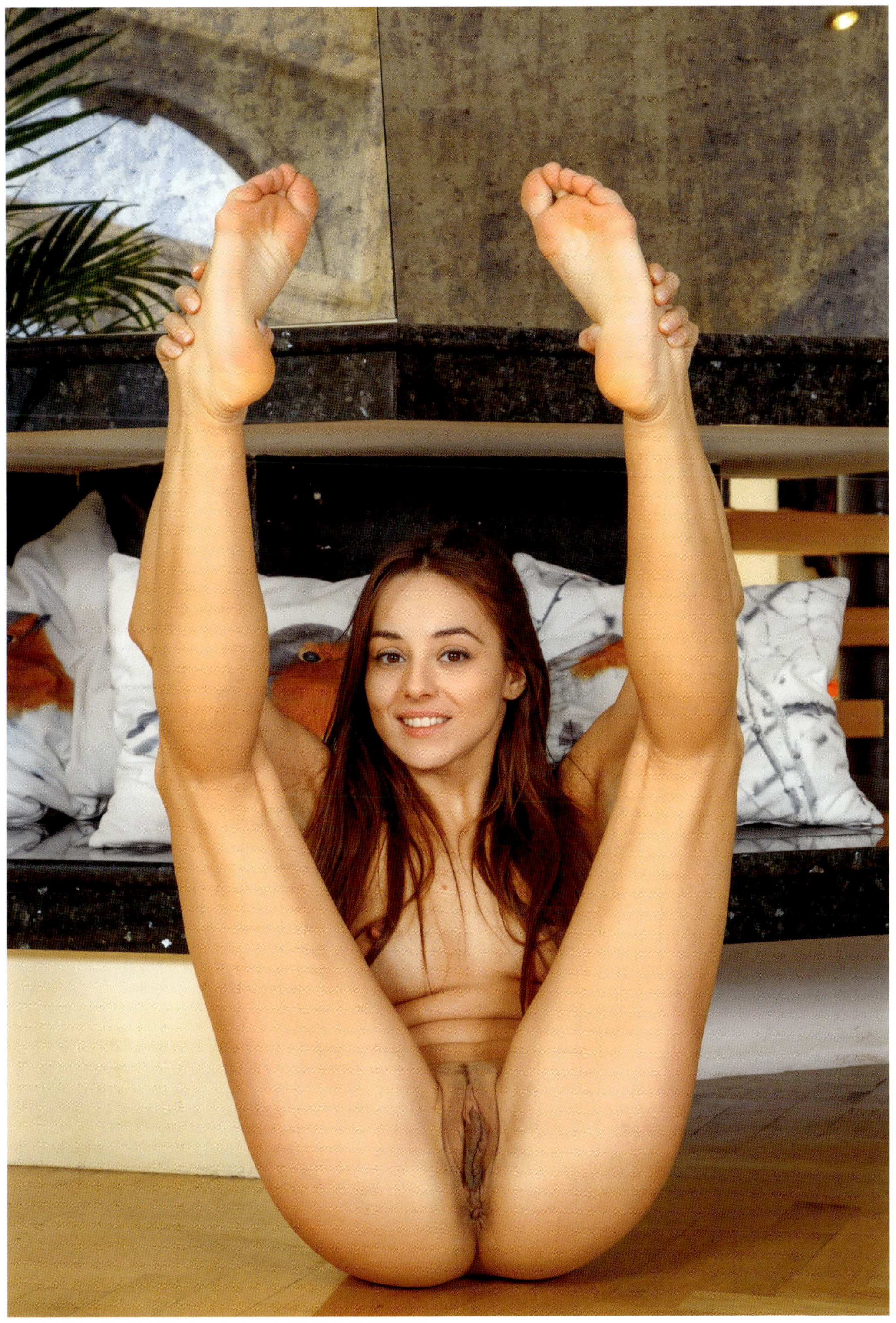

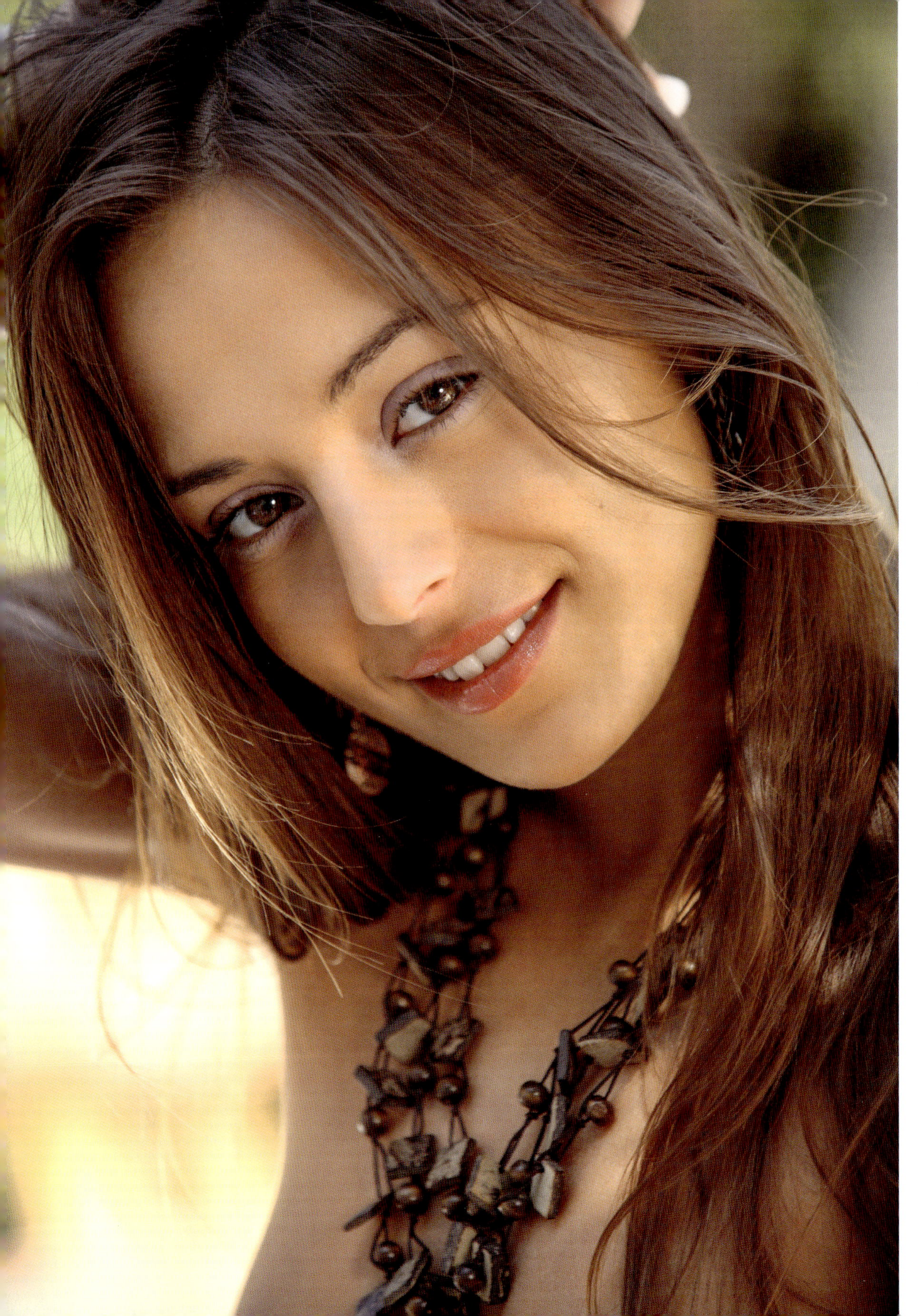

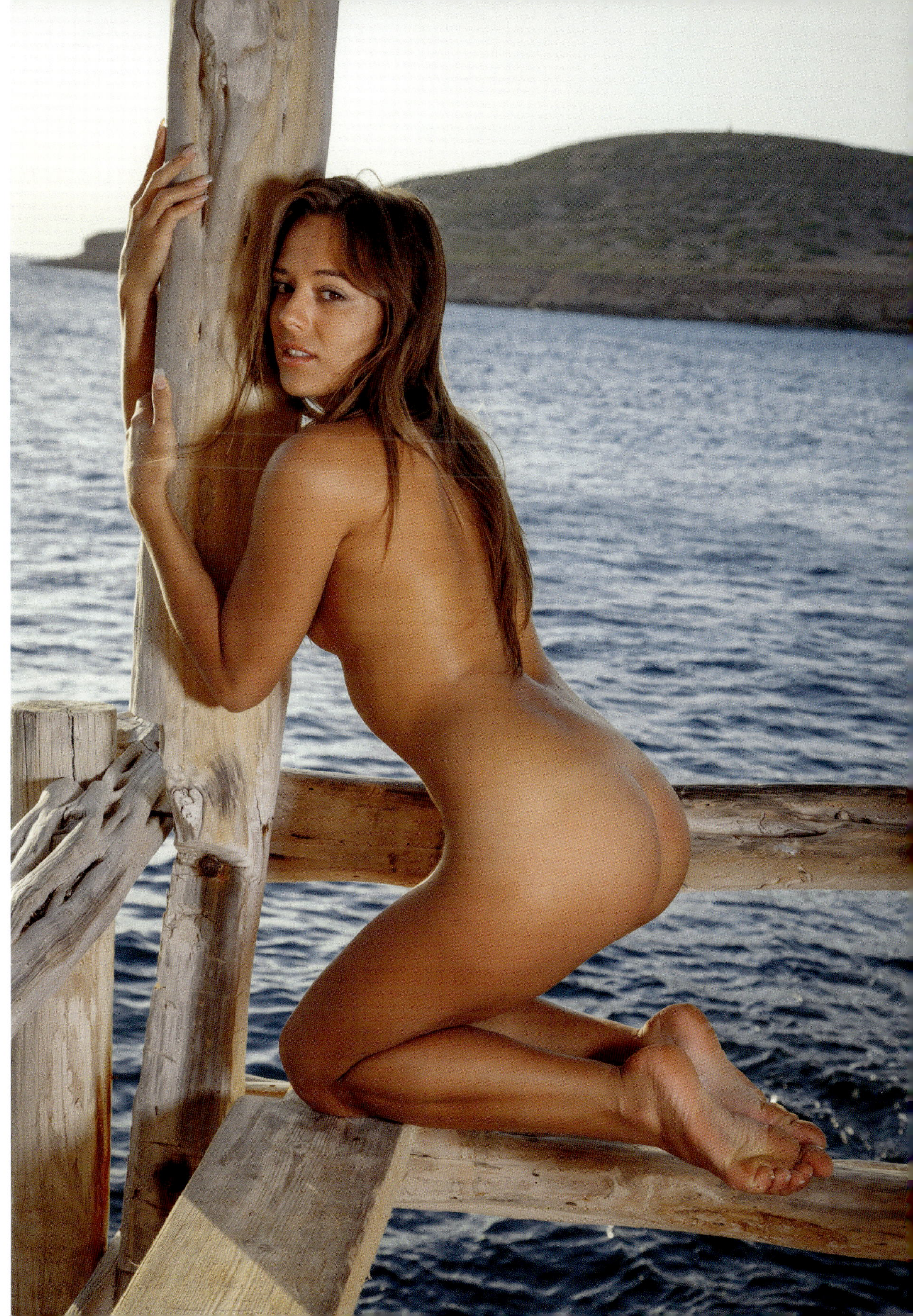

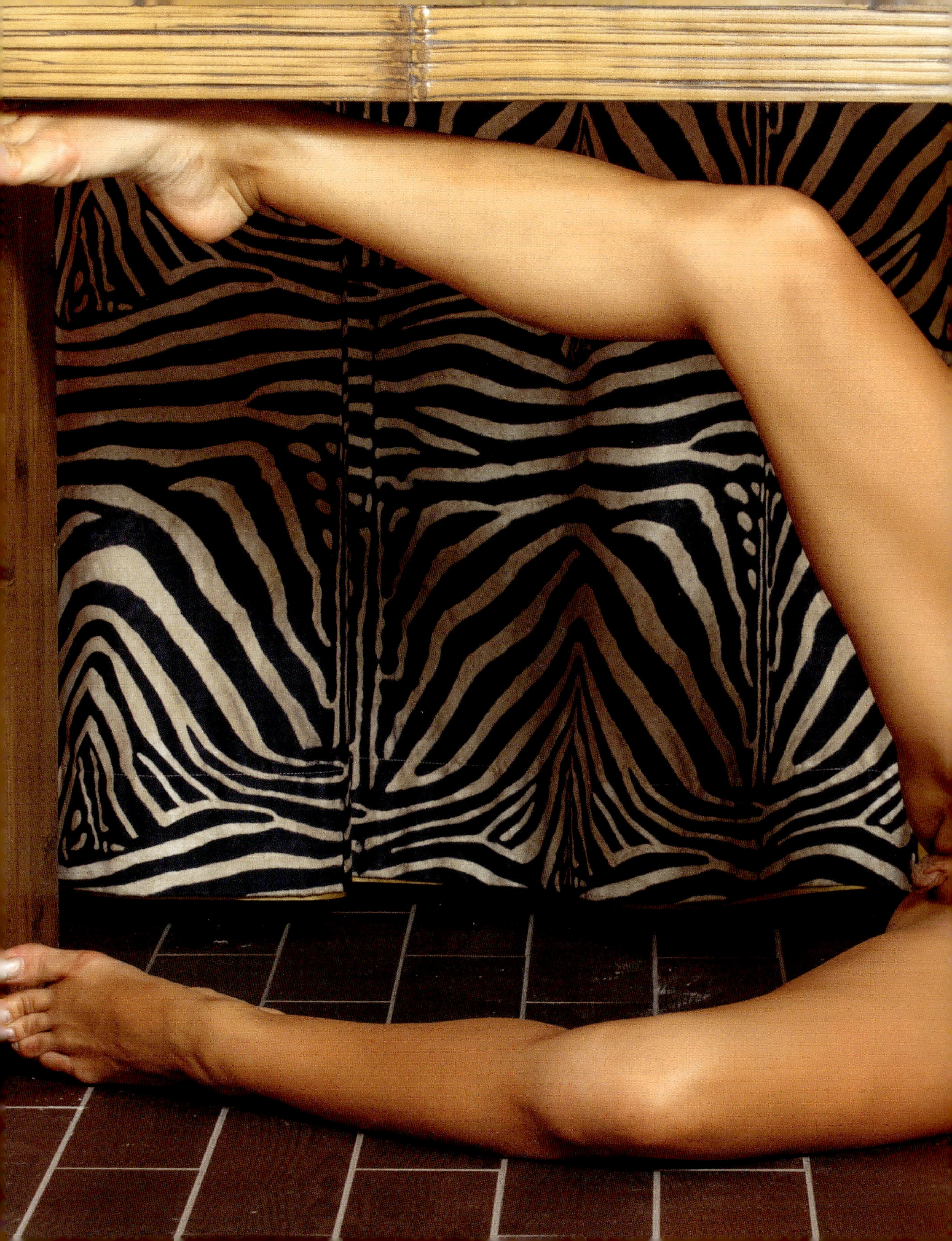

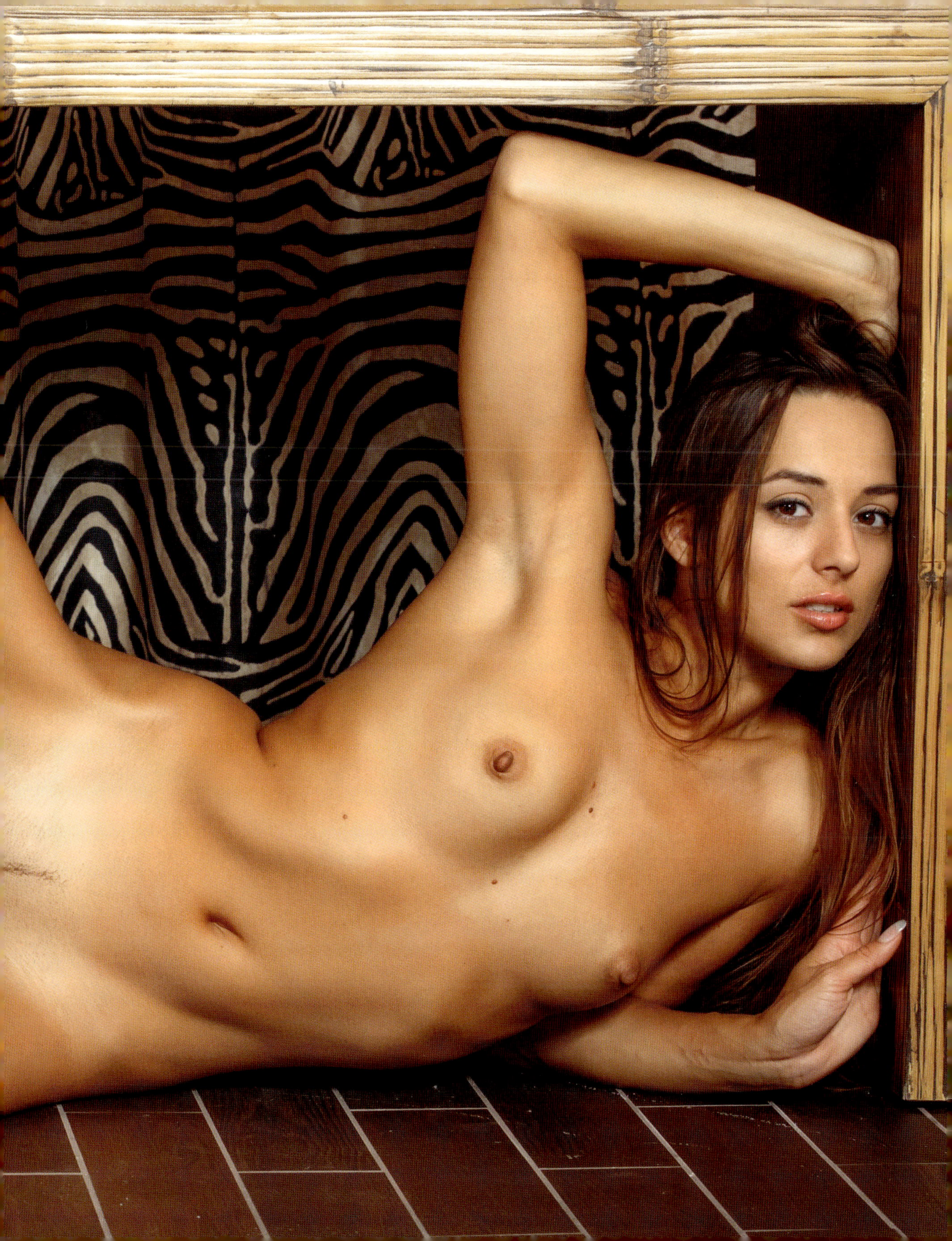

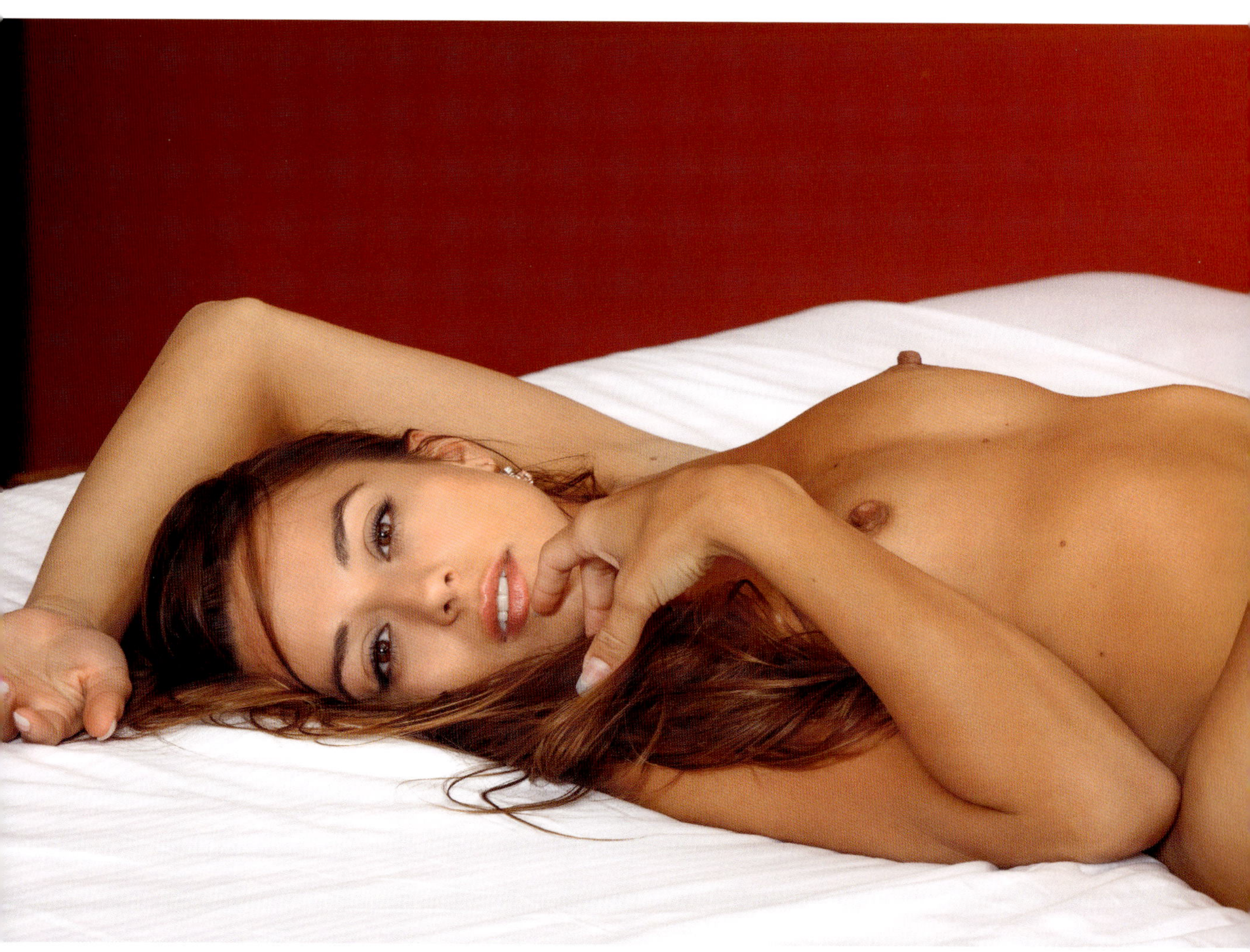

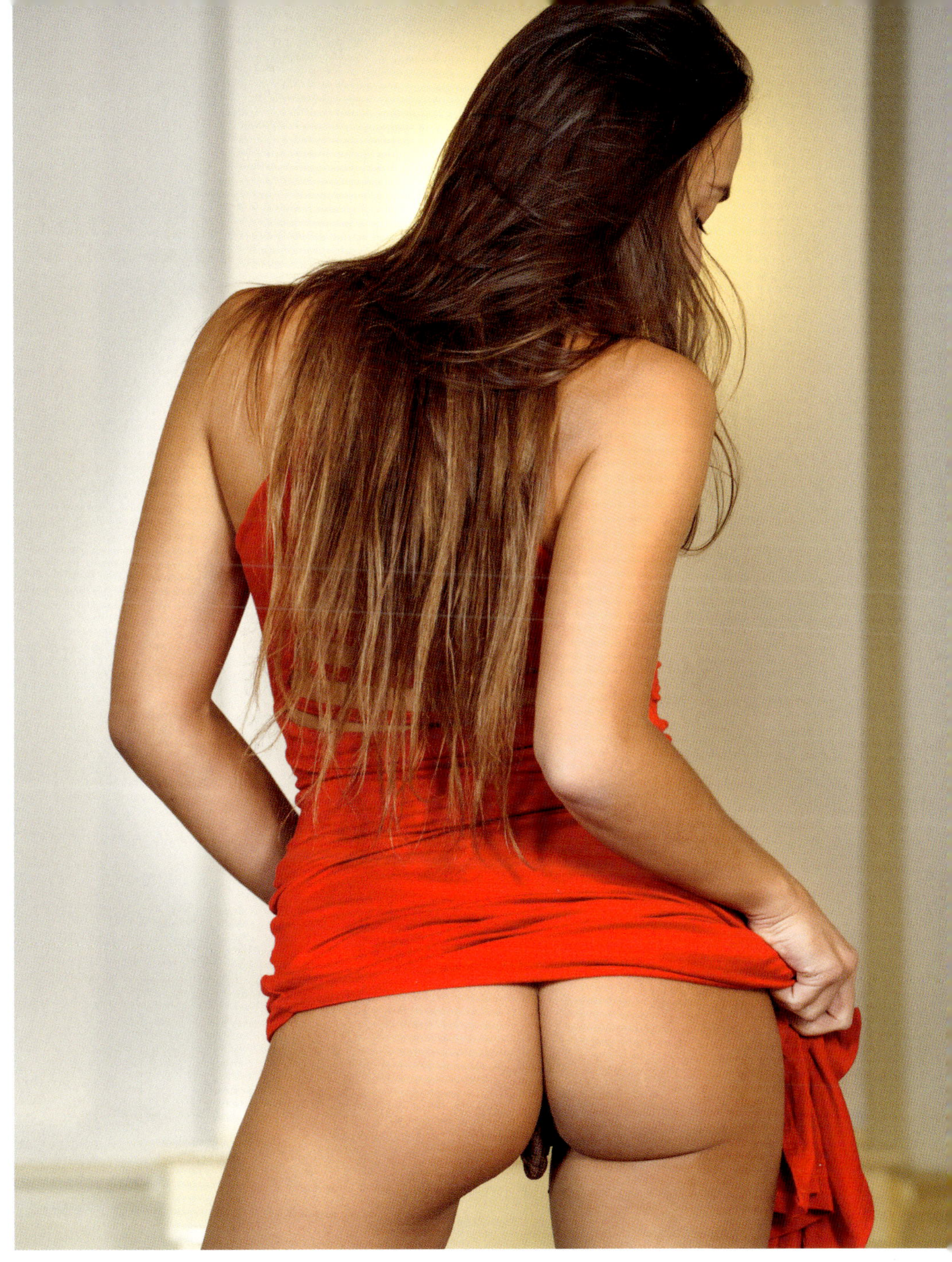

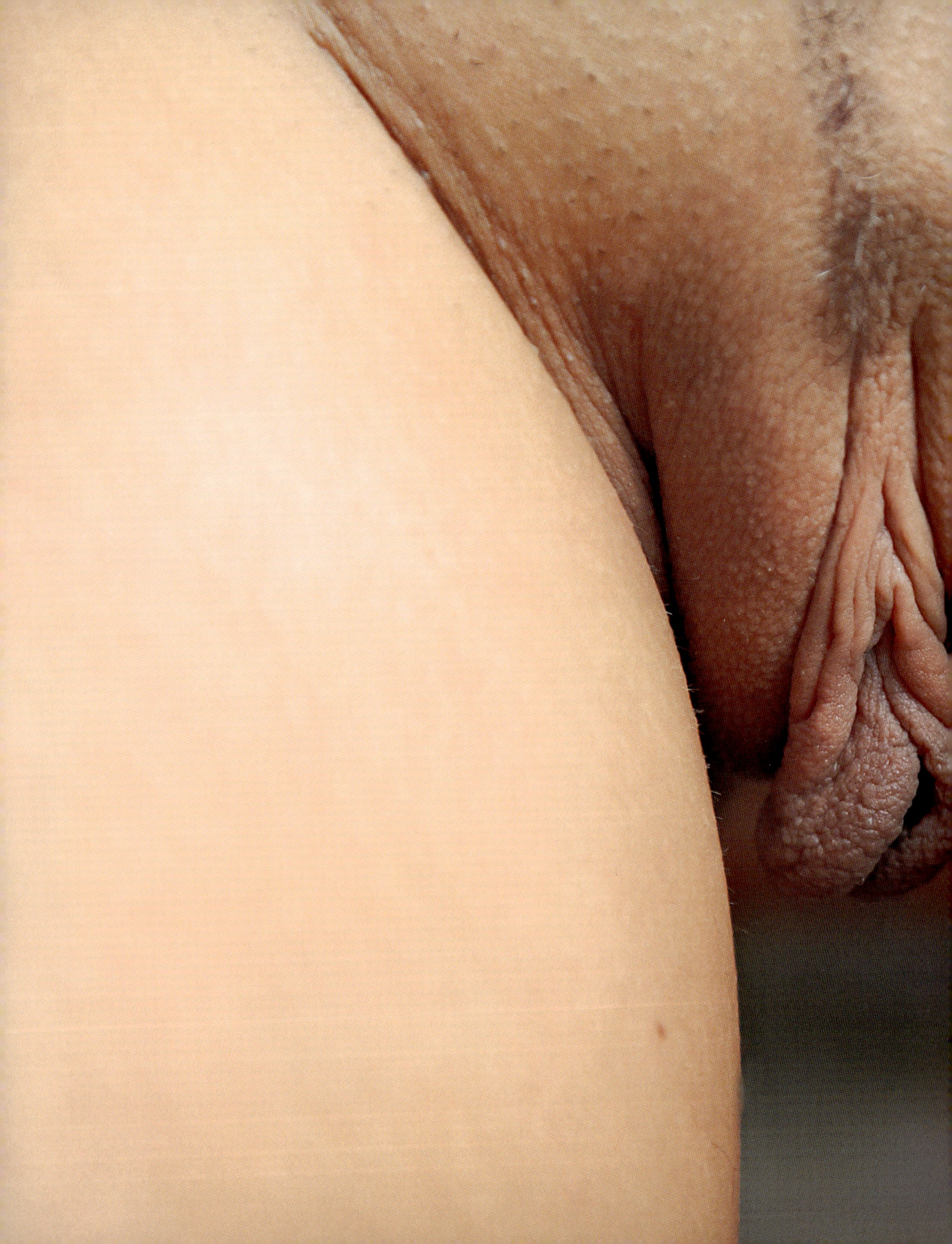

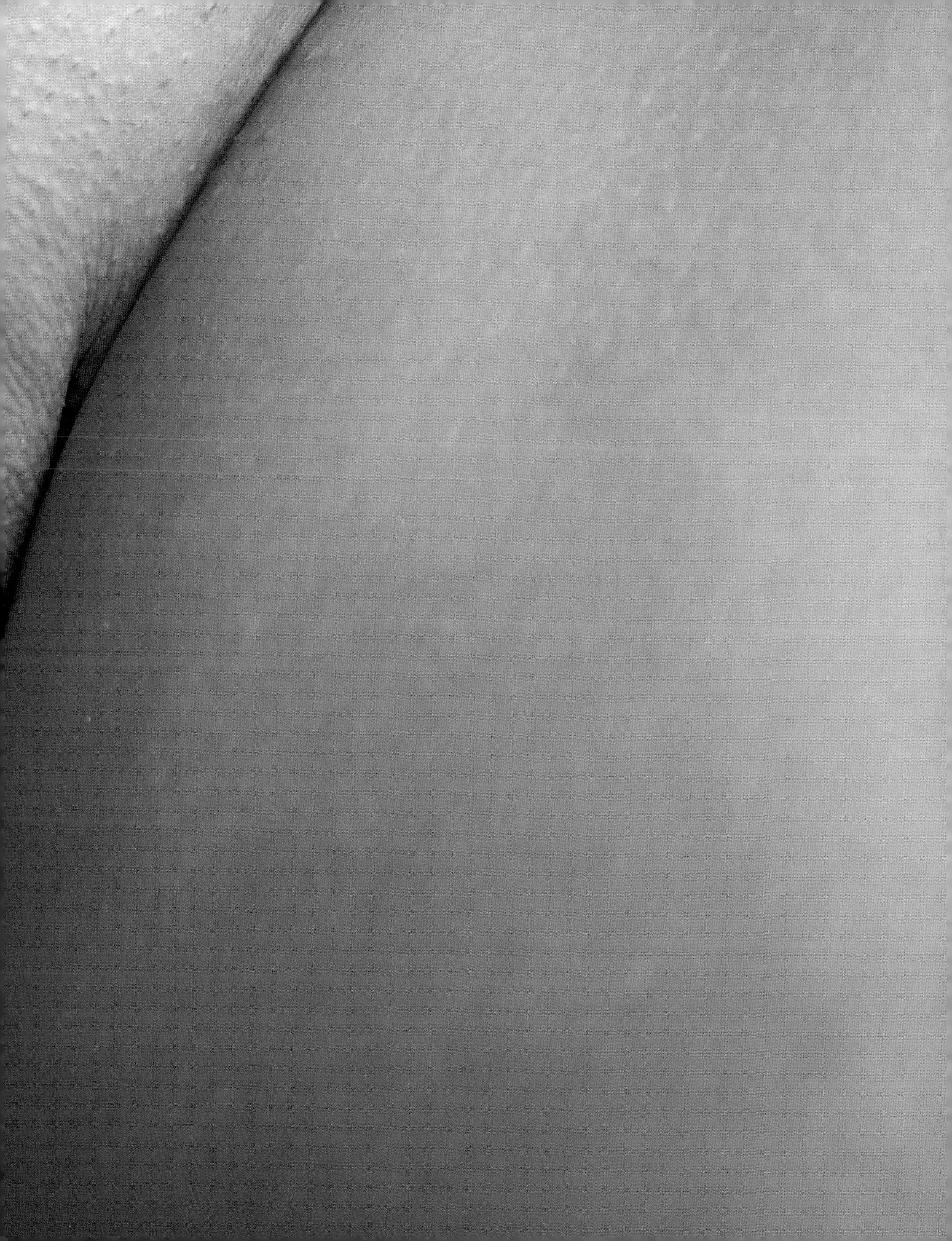

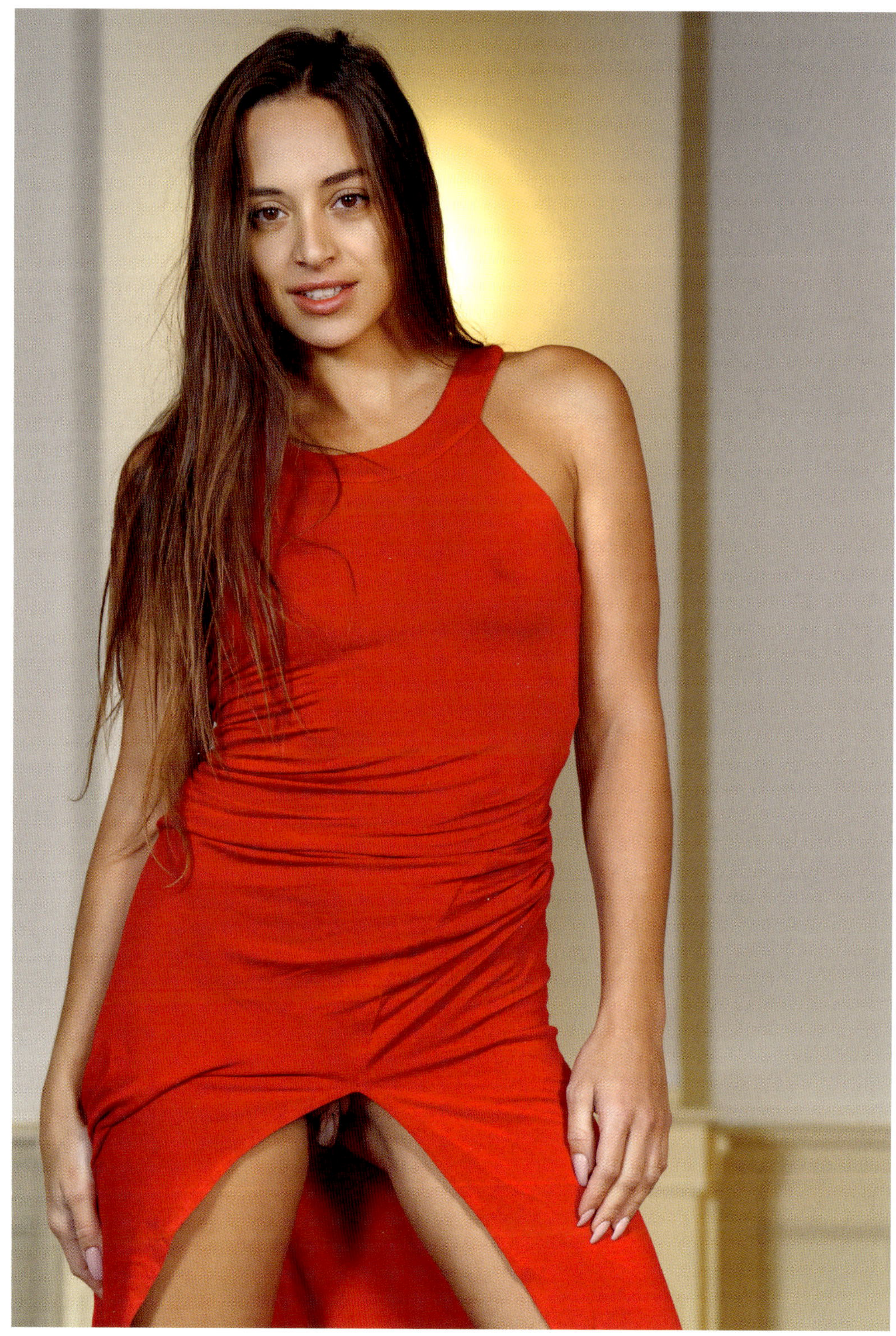

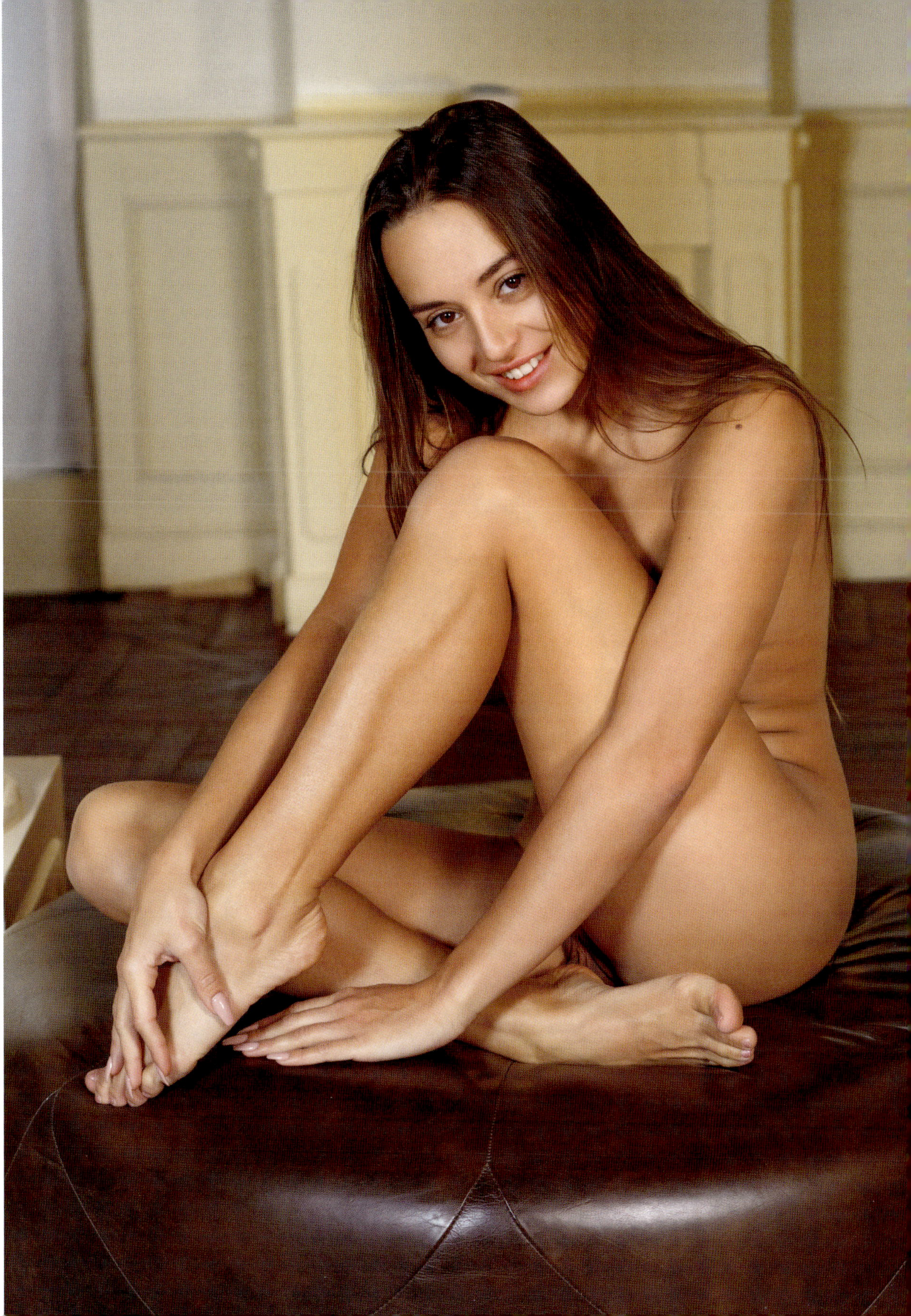

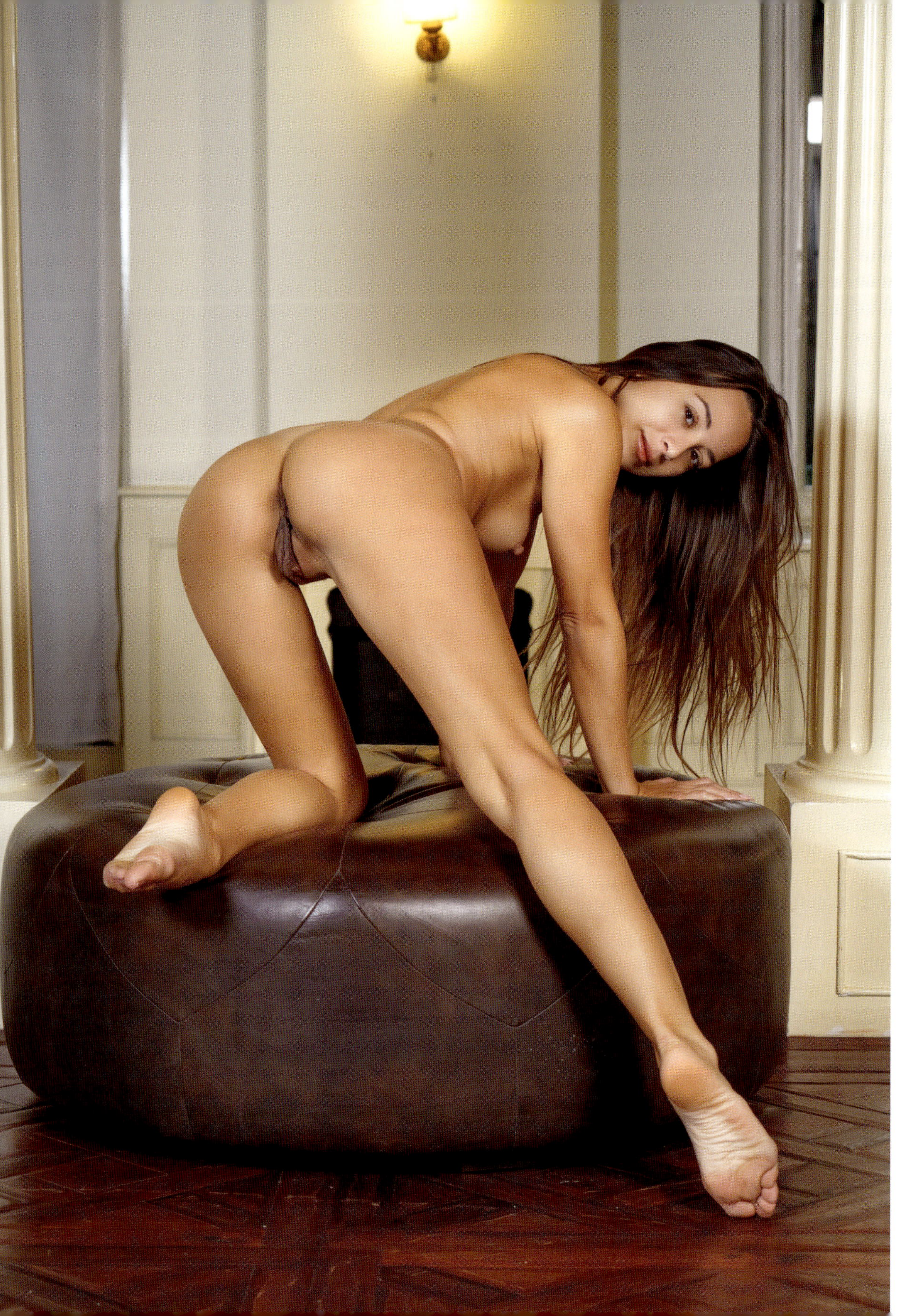

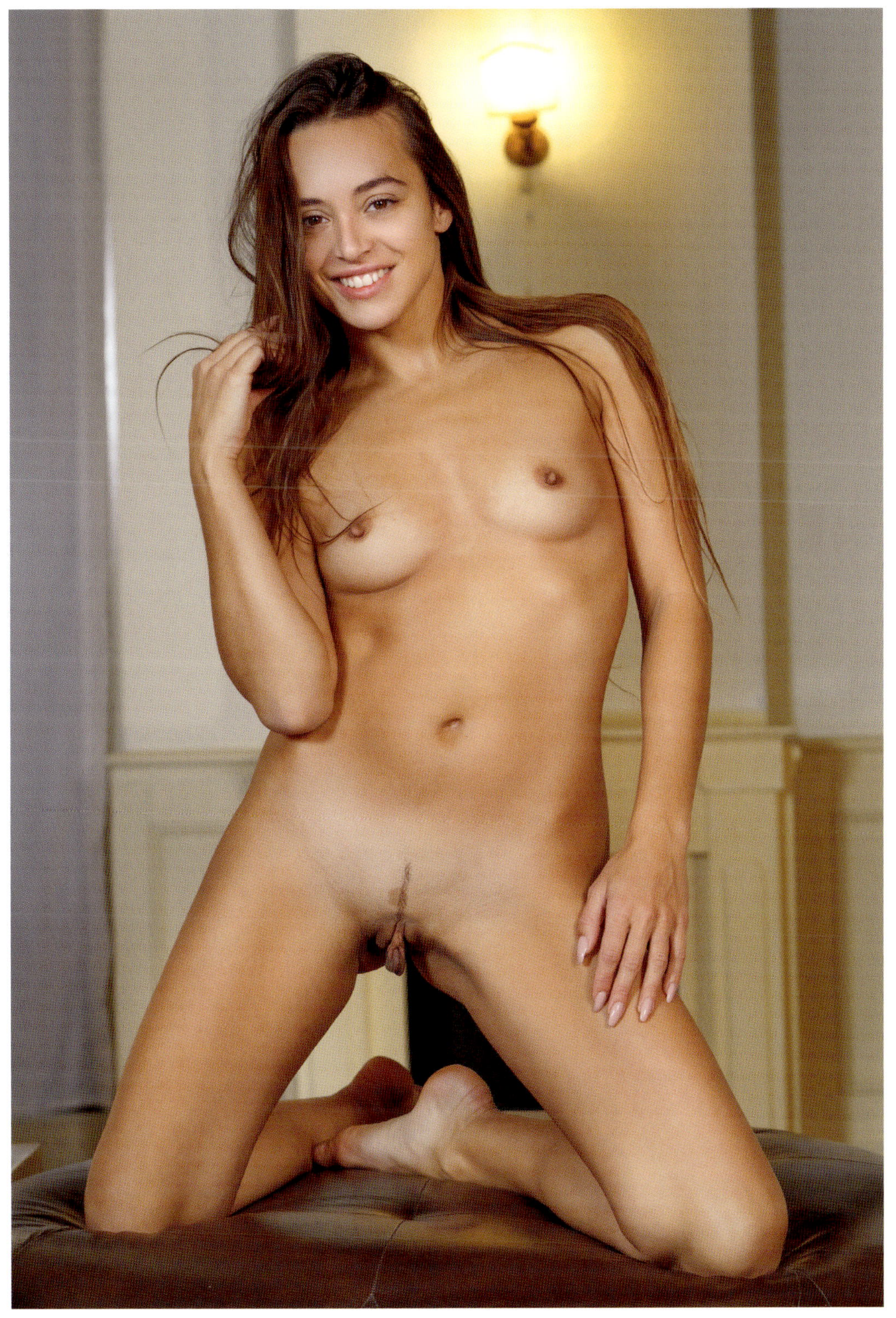

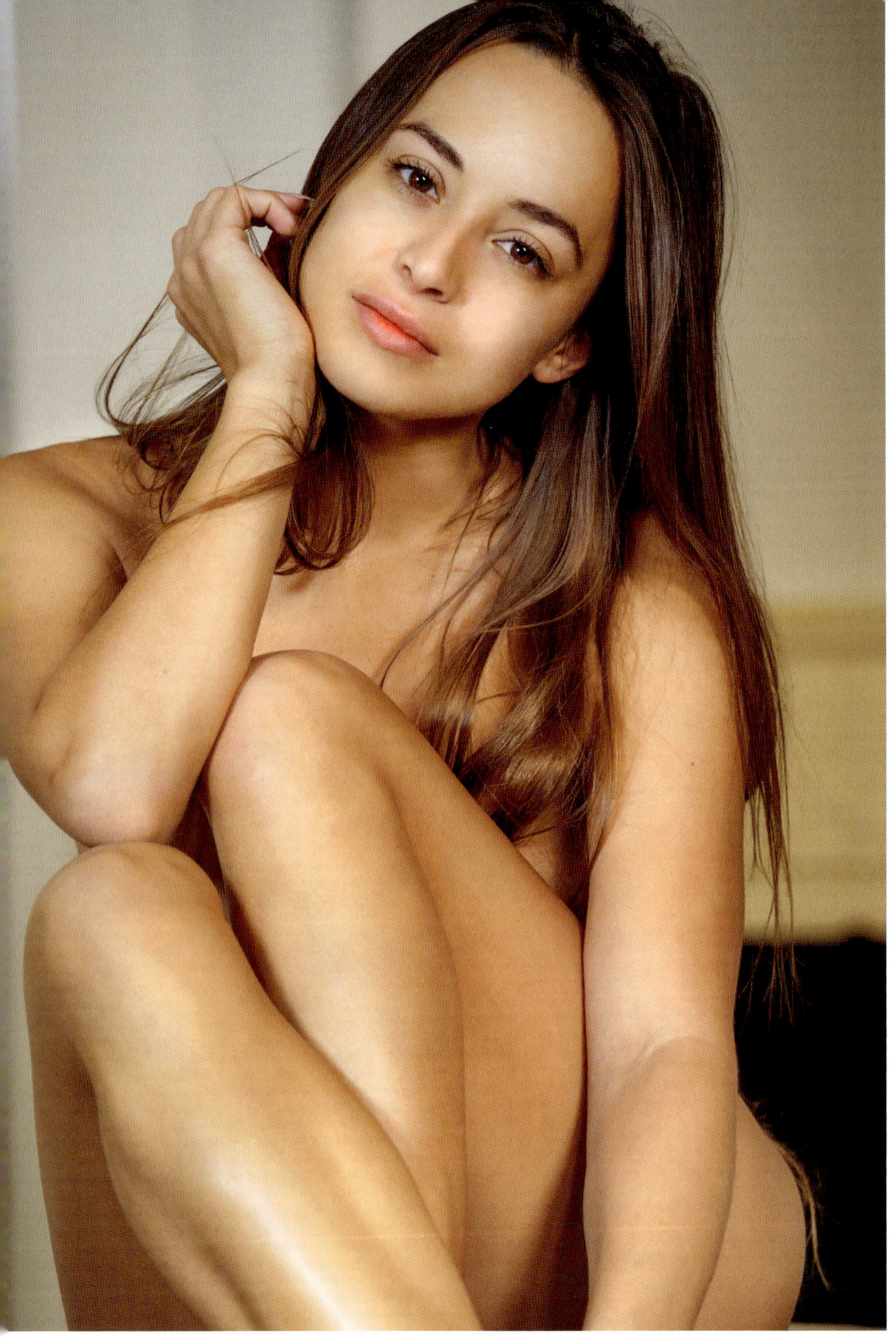

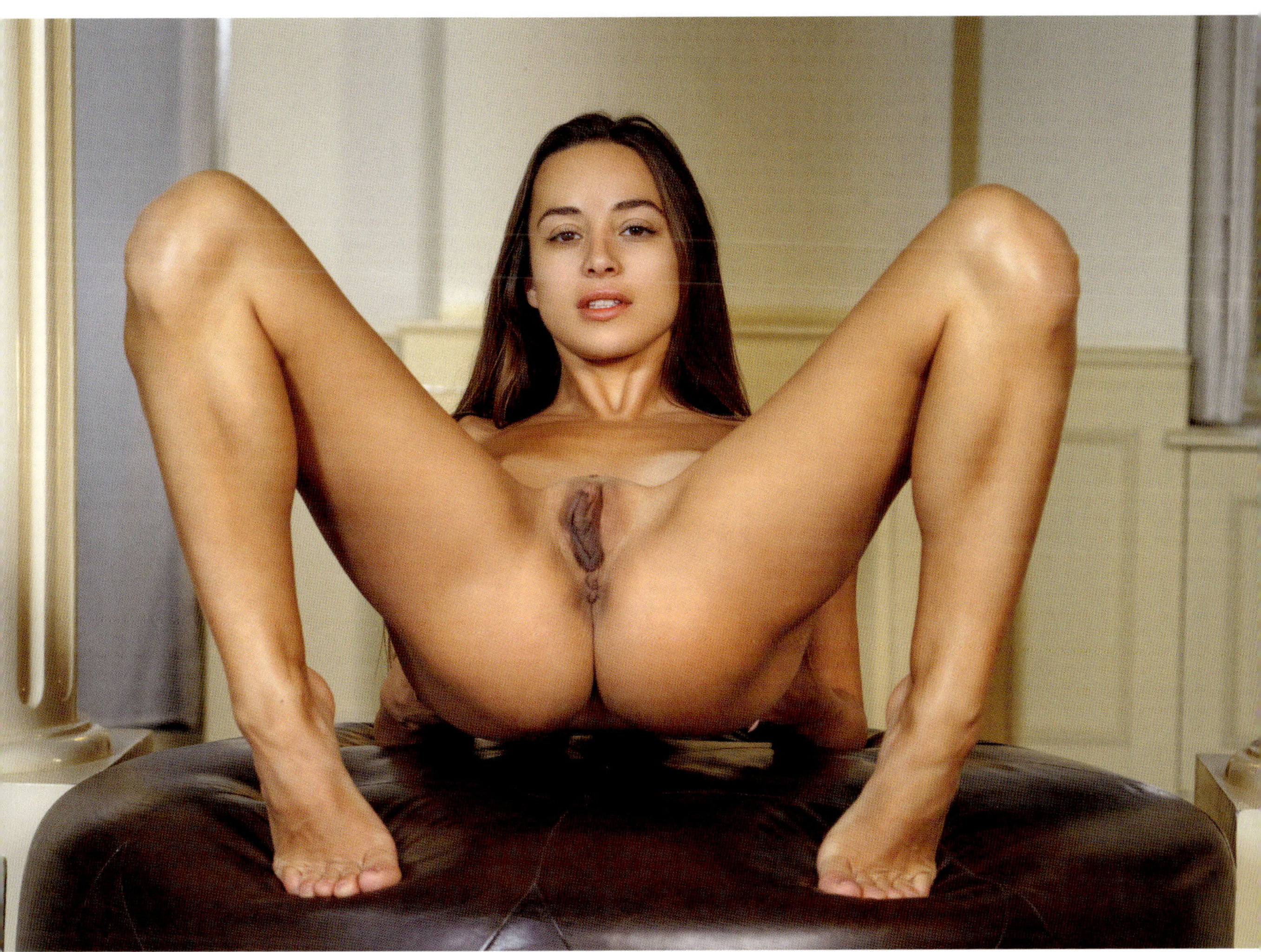

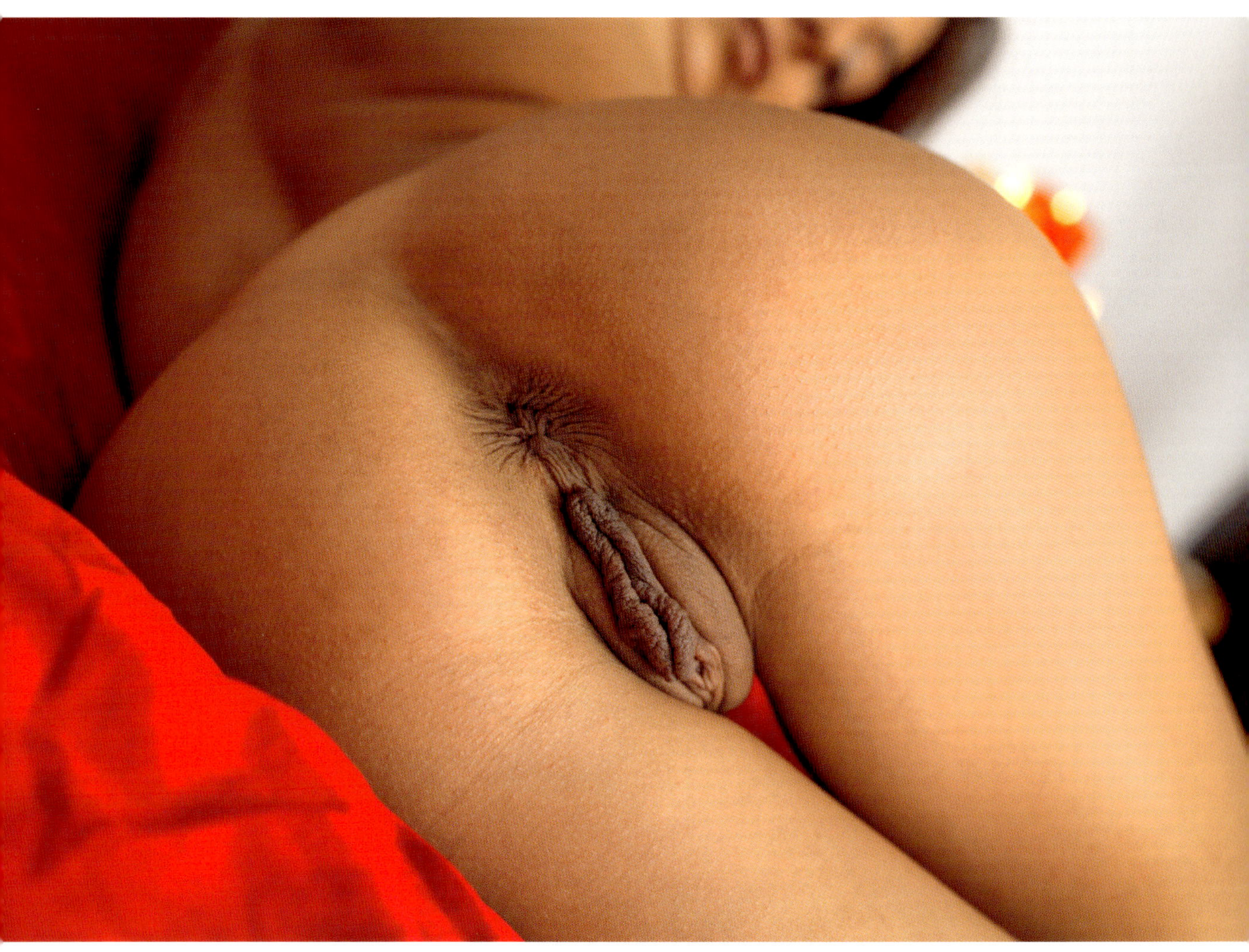

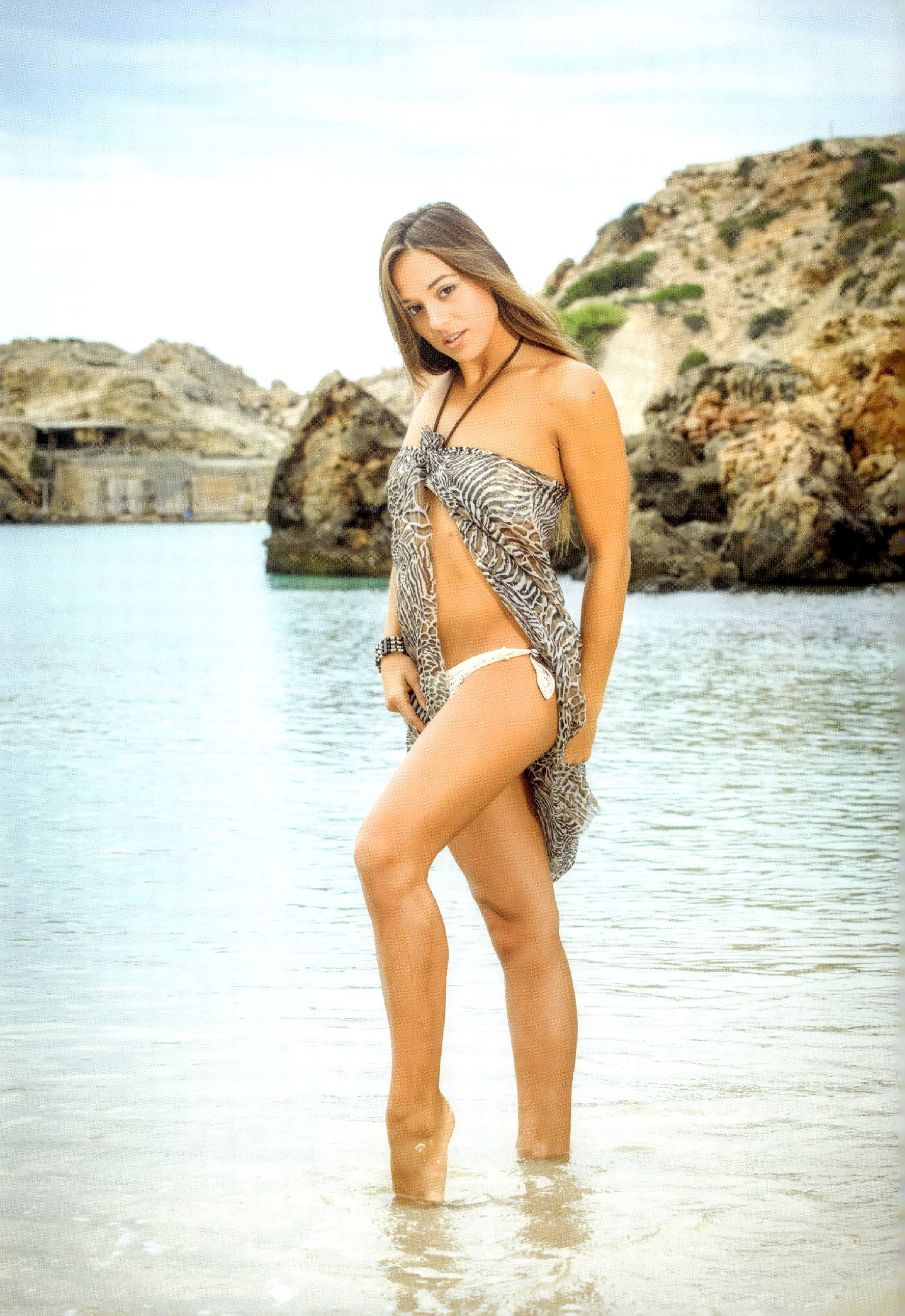

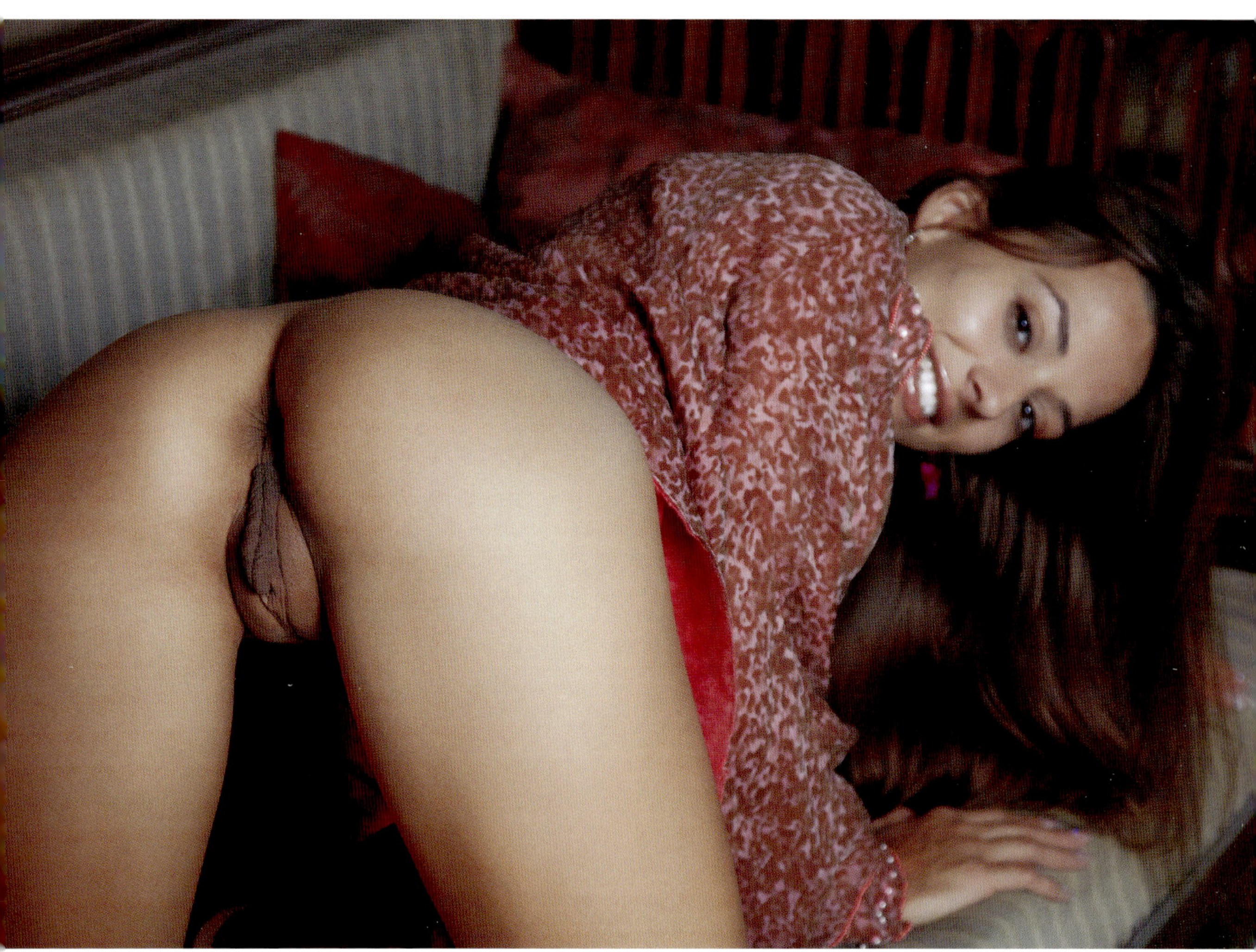

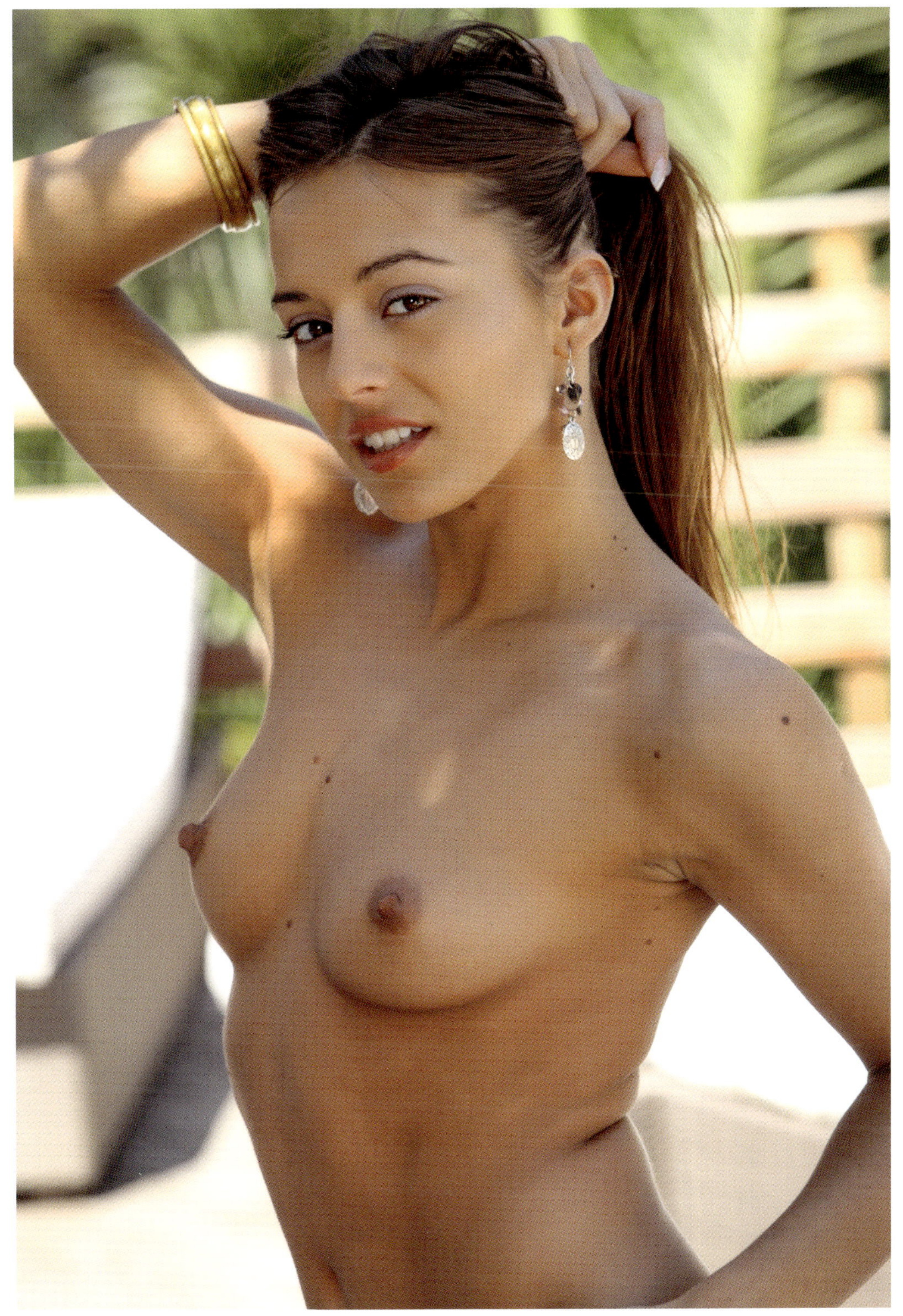

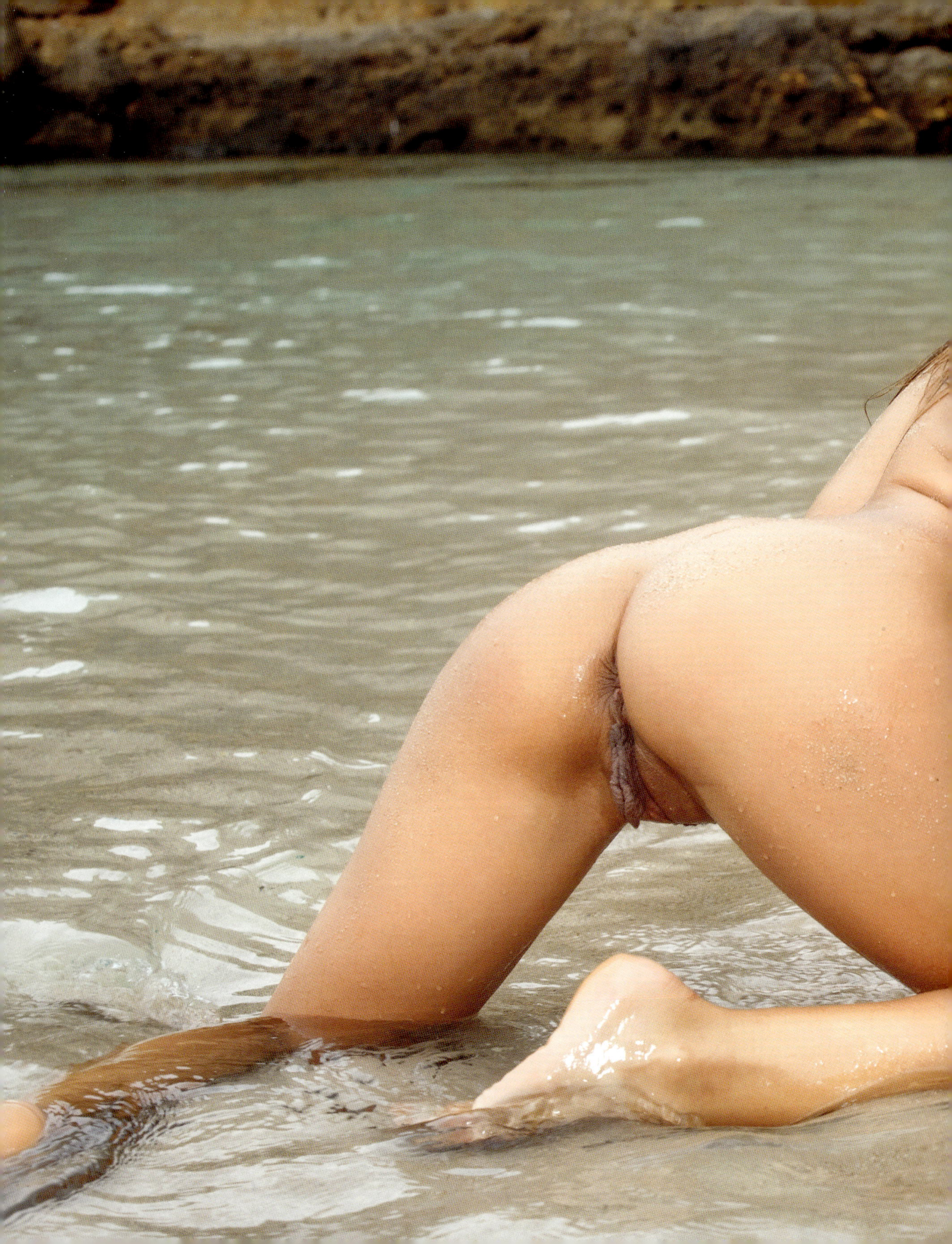

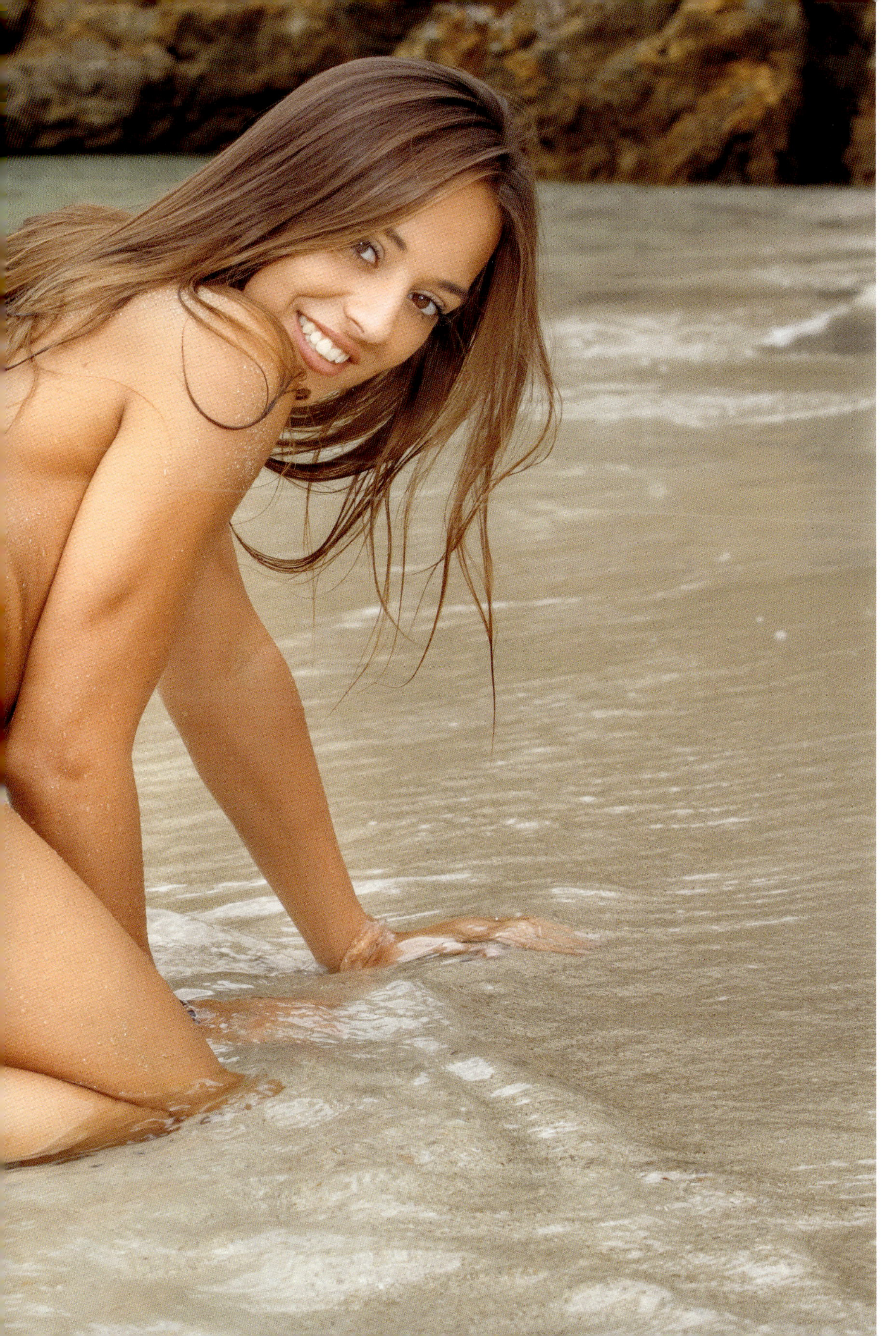

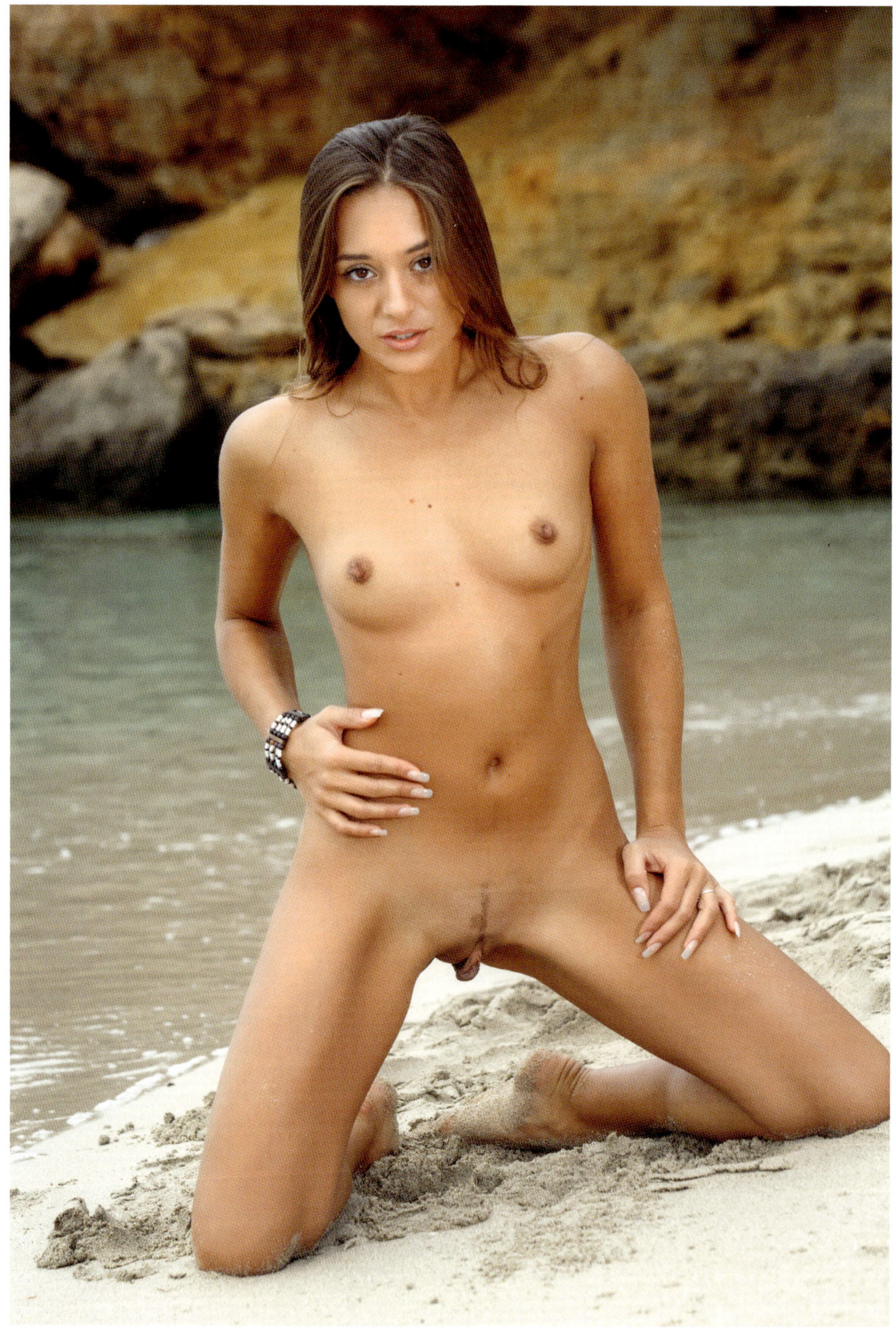

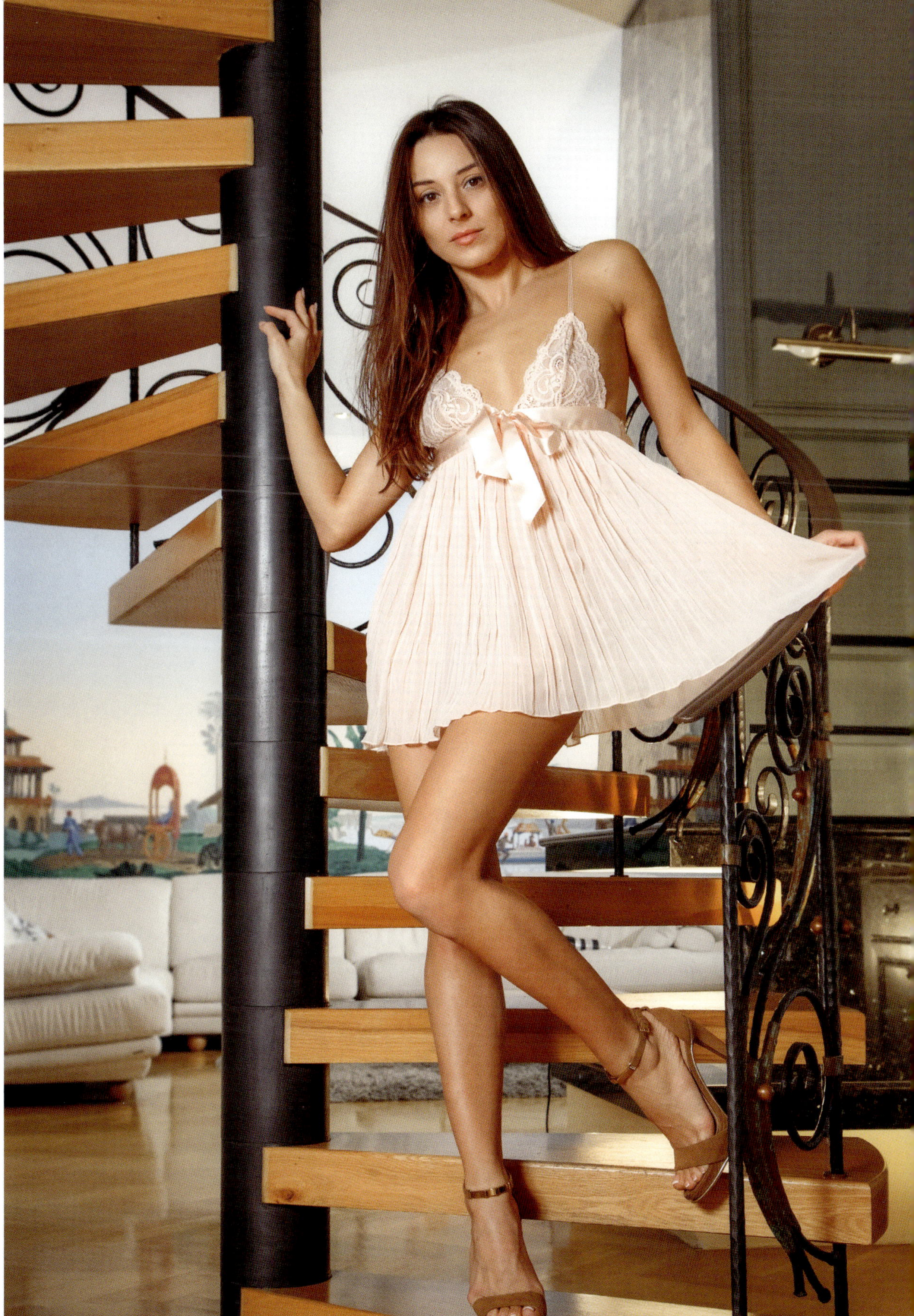

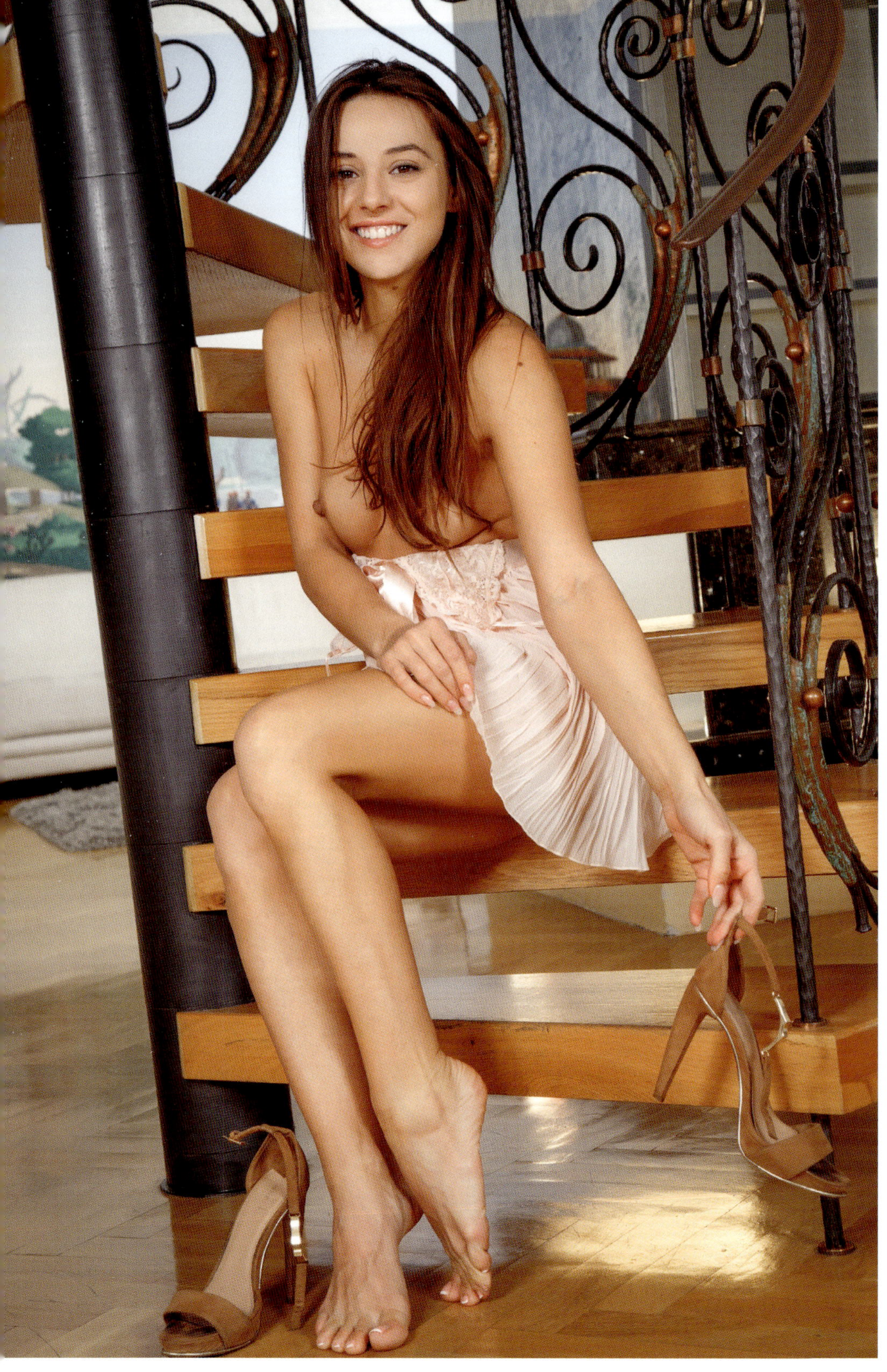

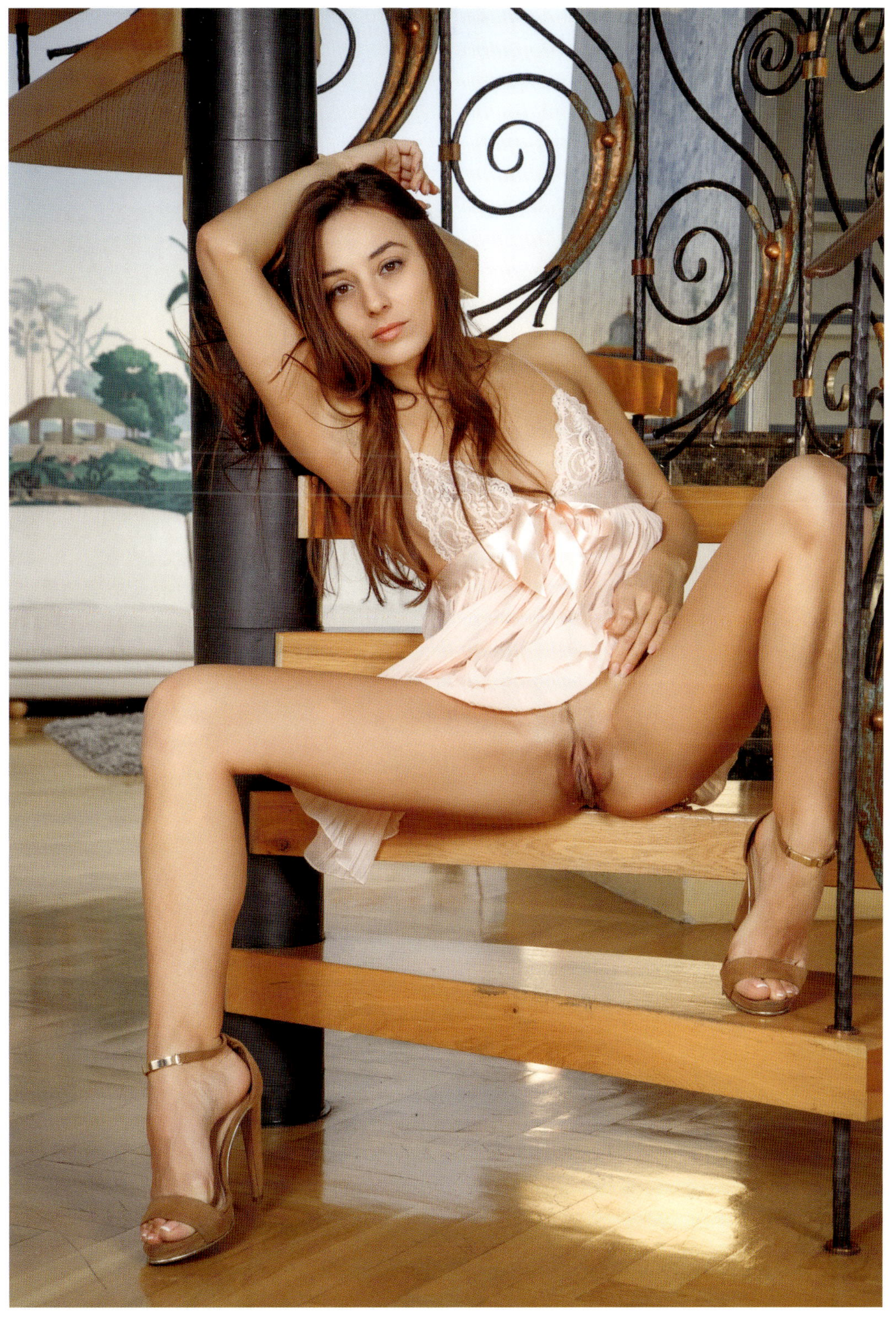

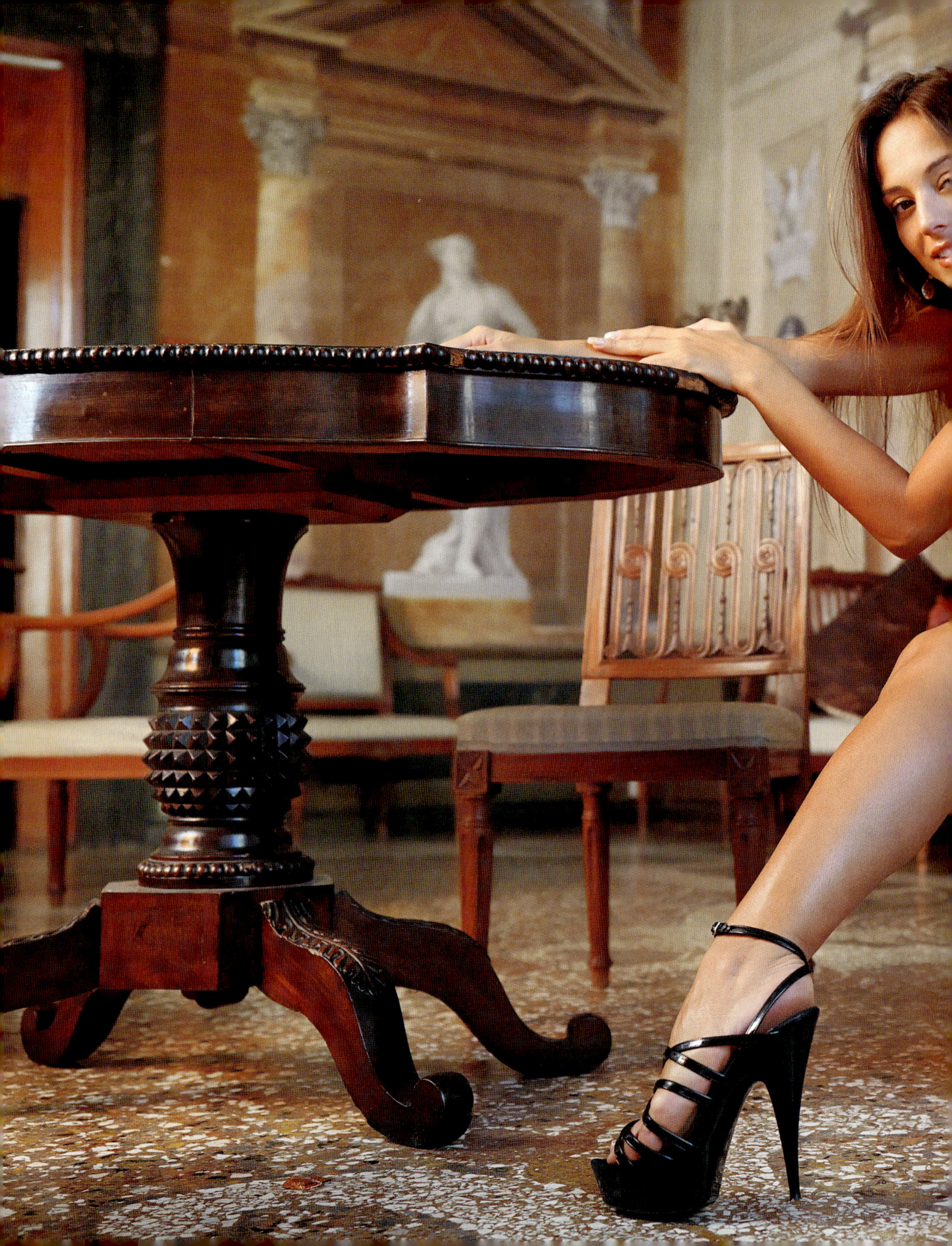

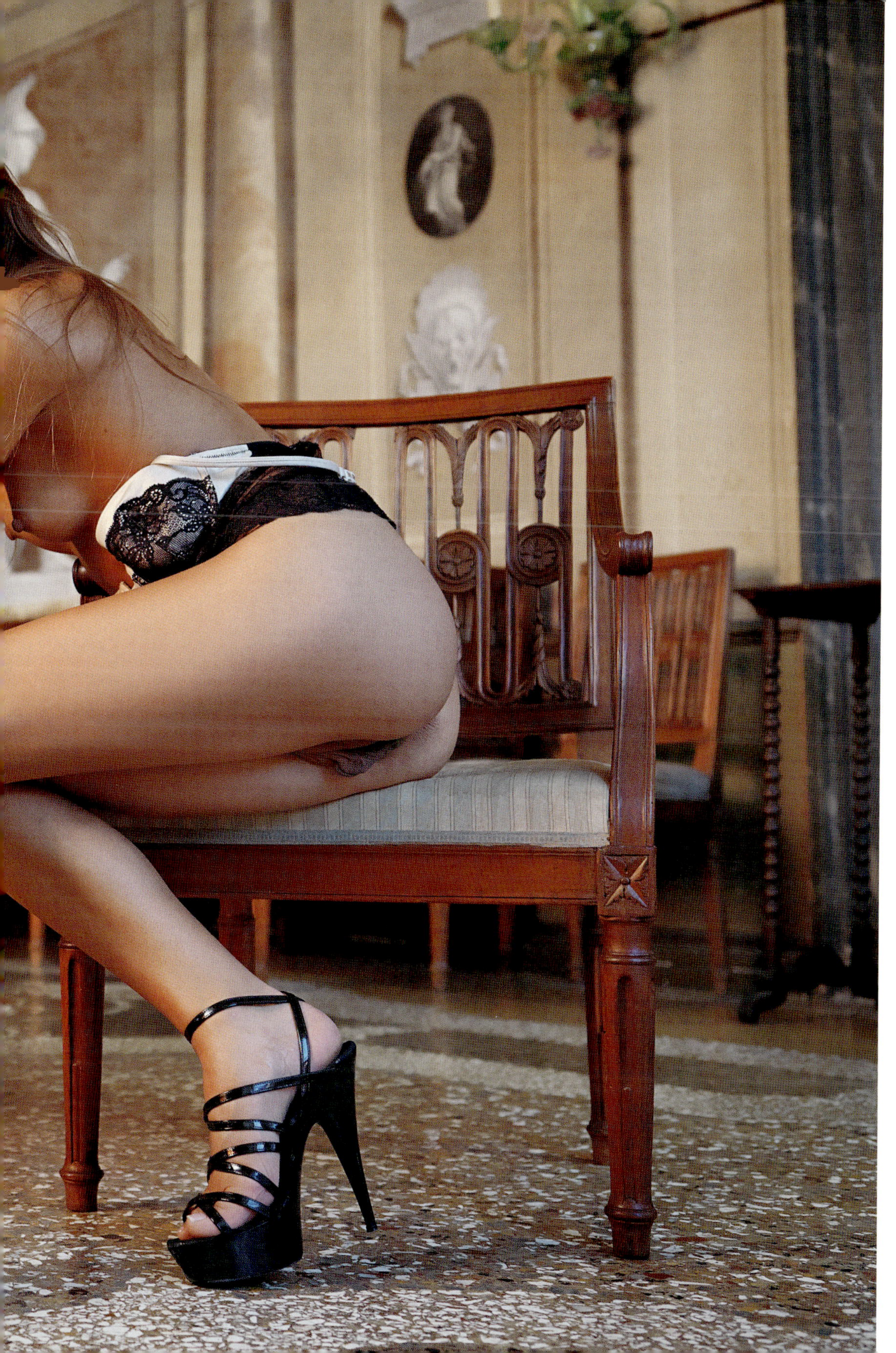

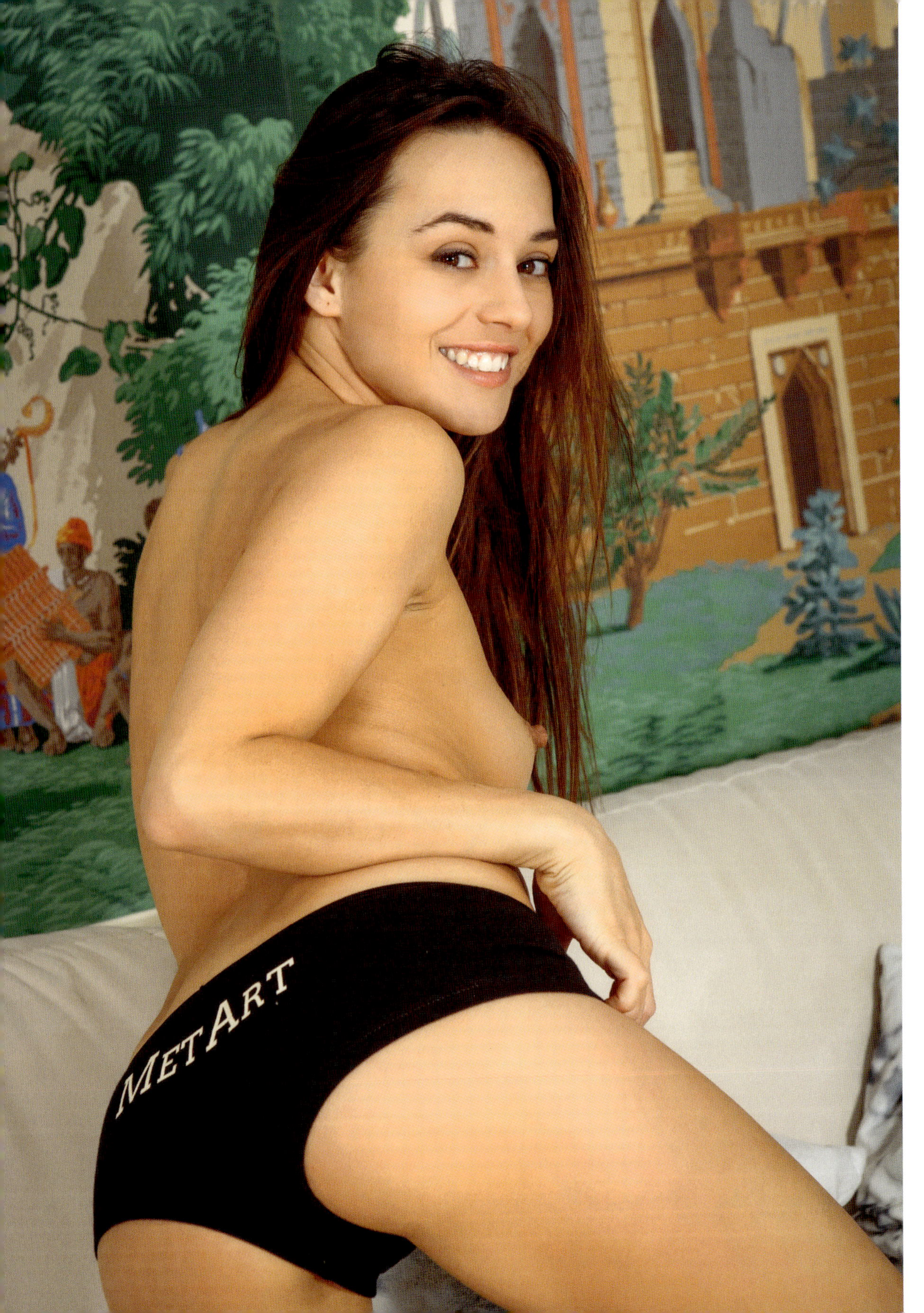
MetArt

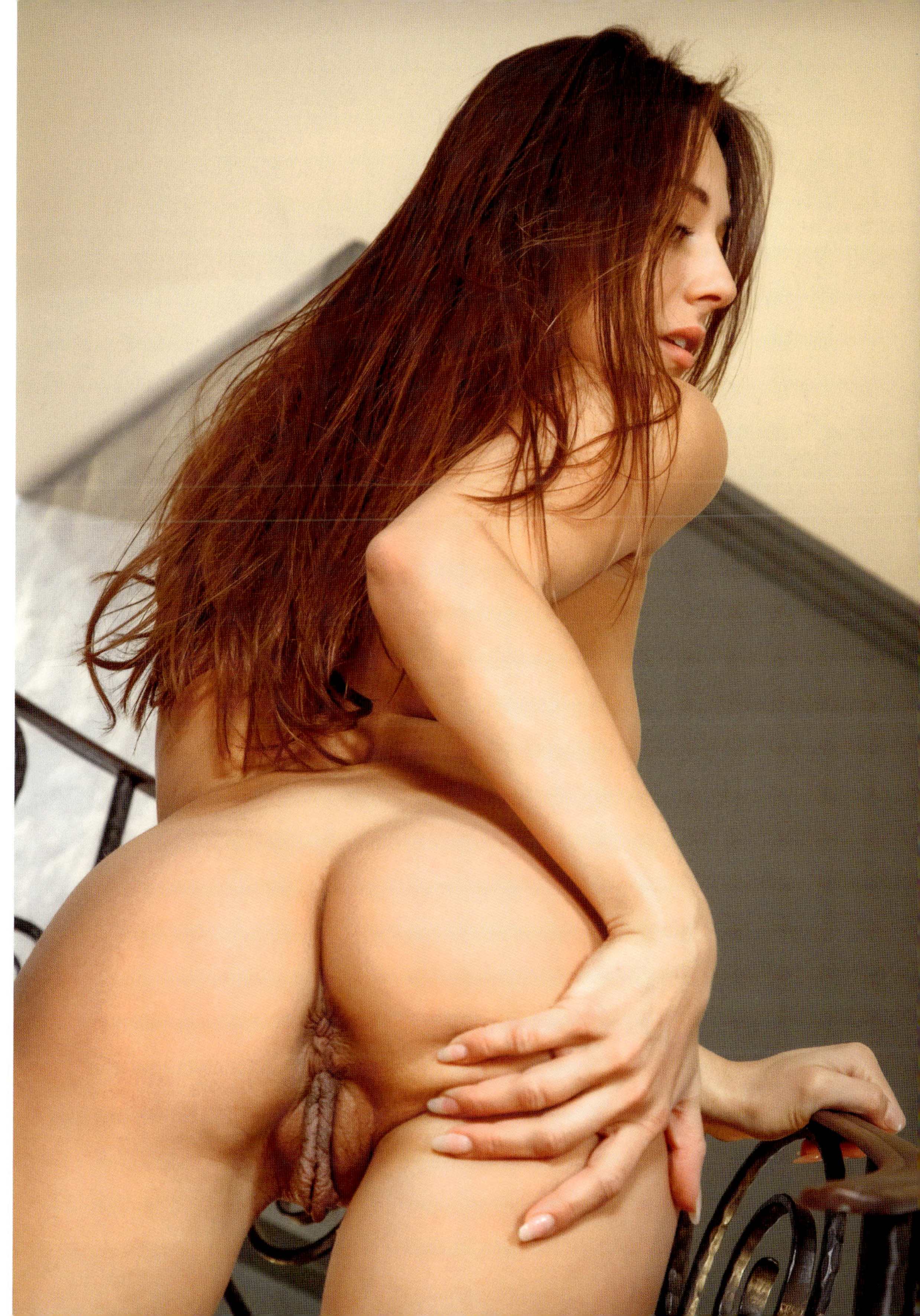

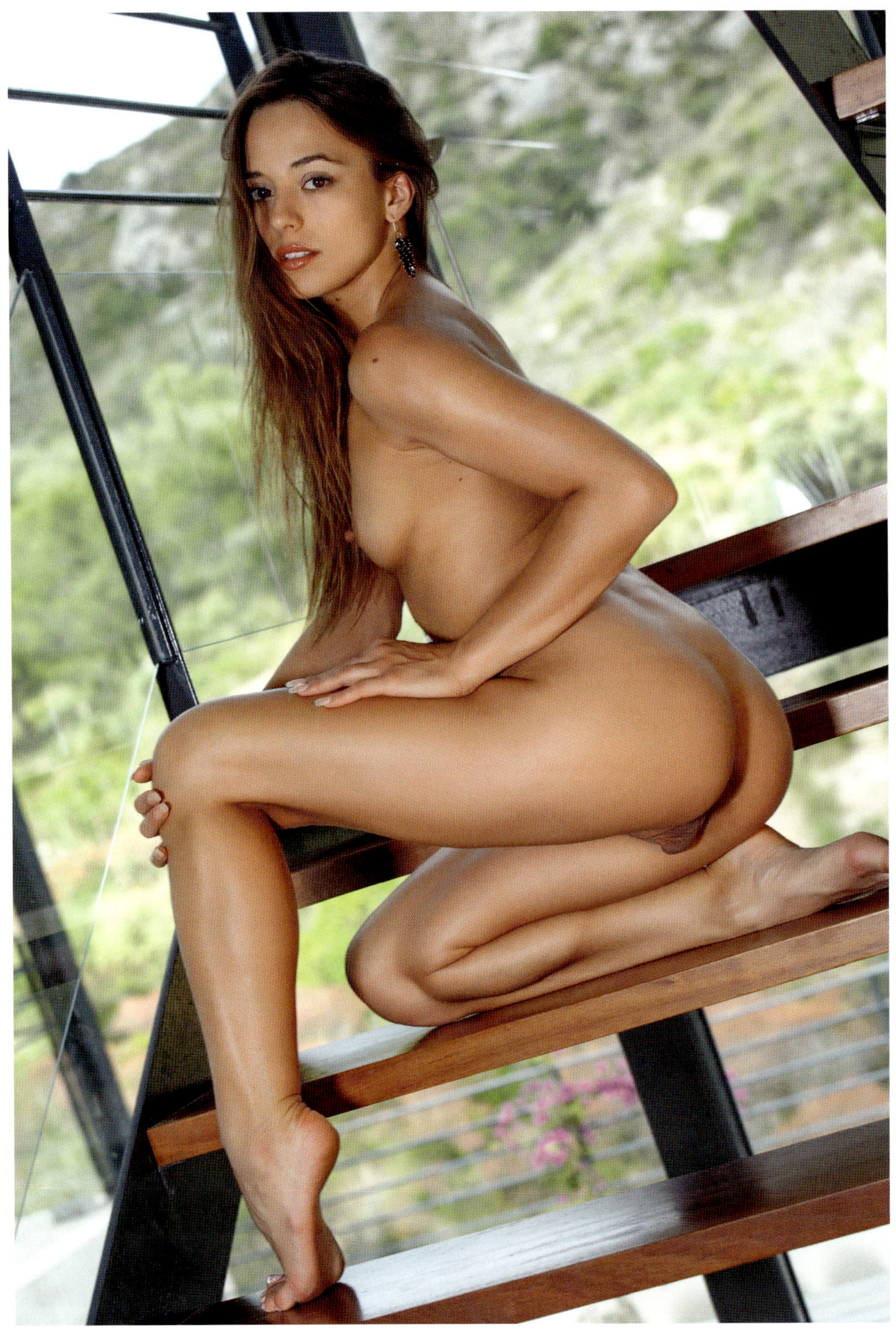

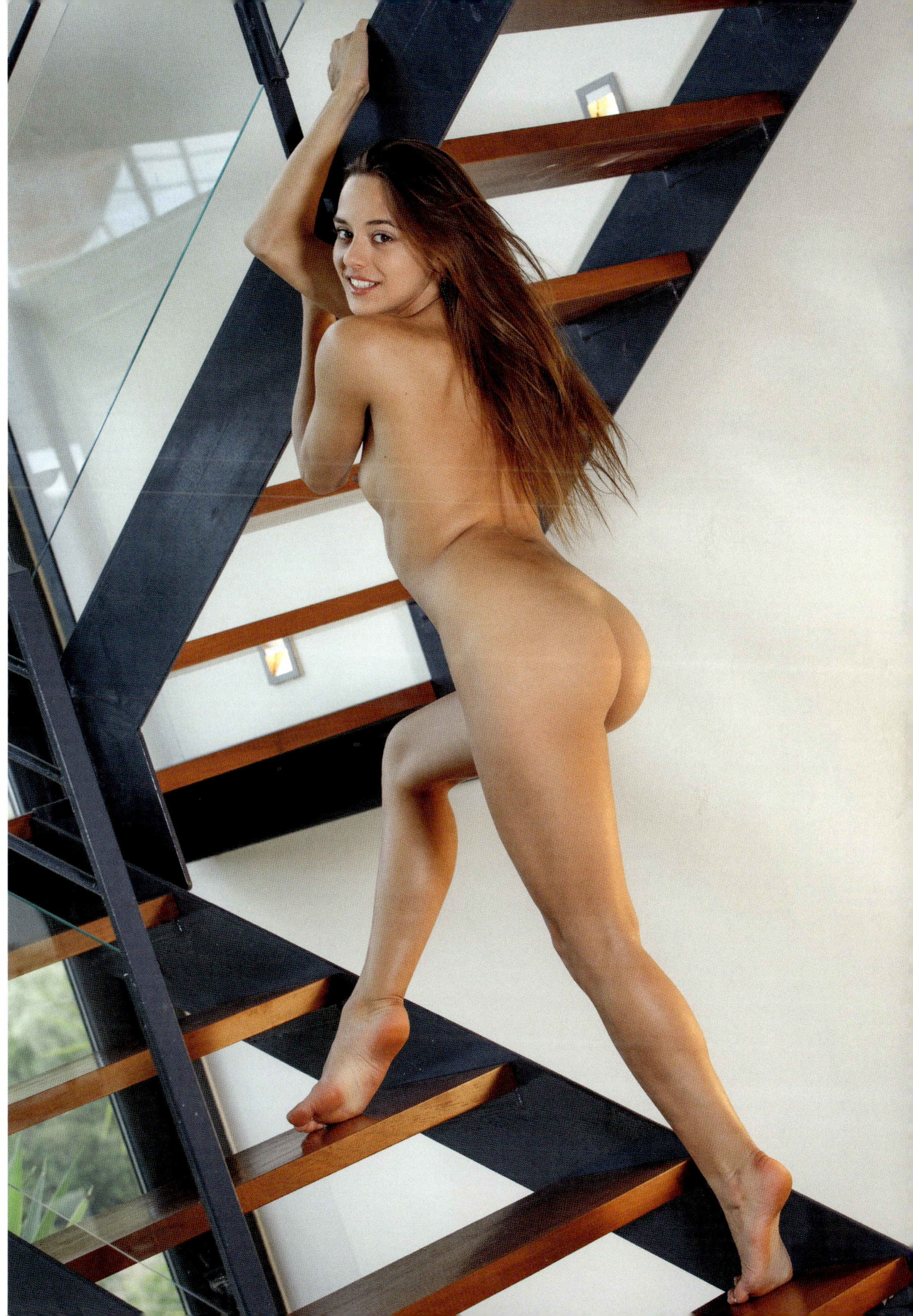

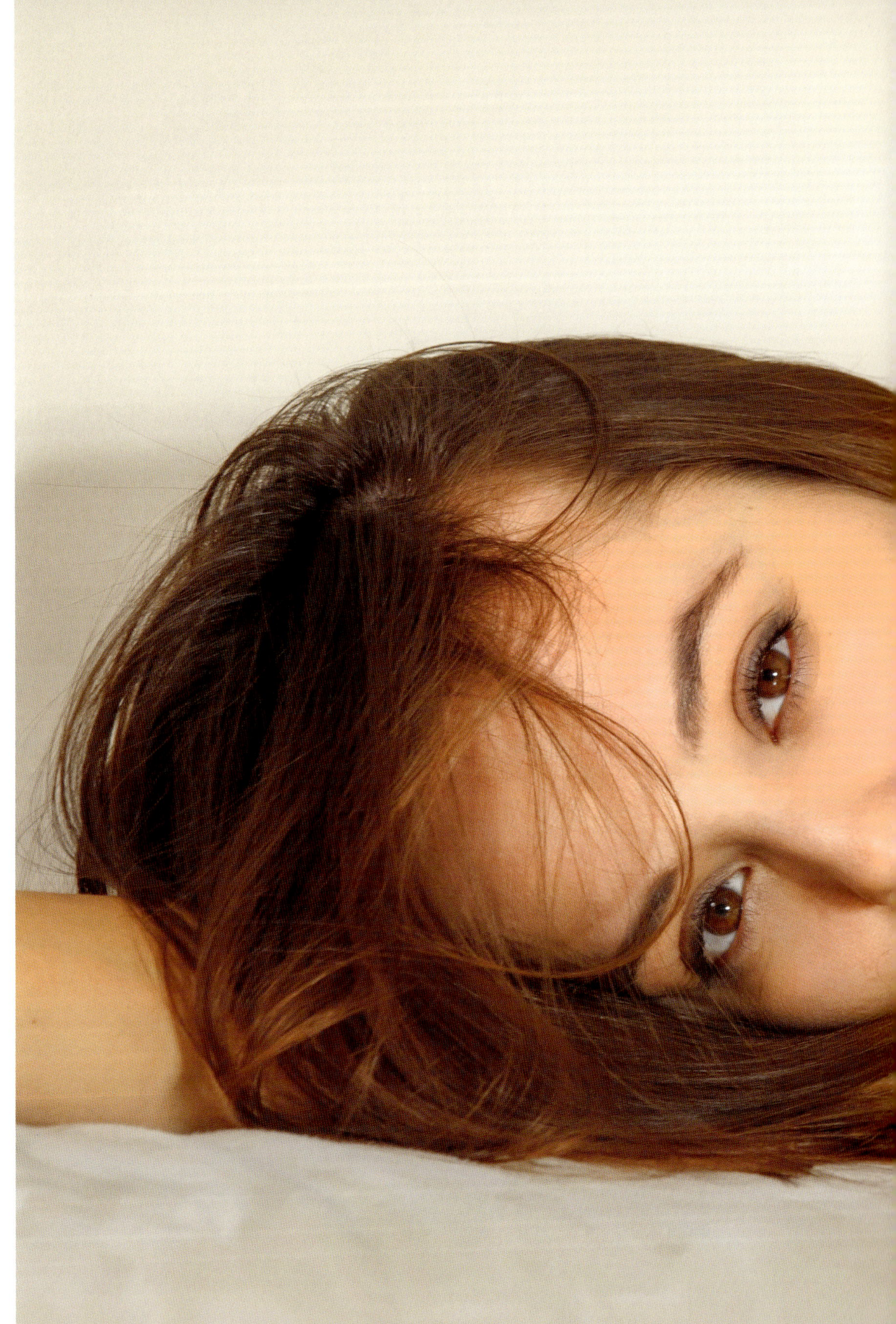

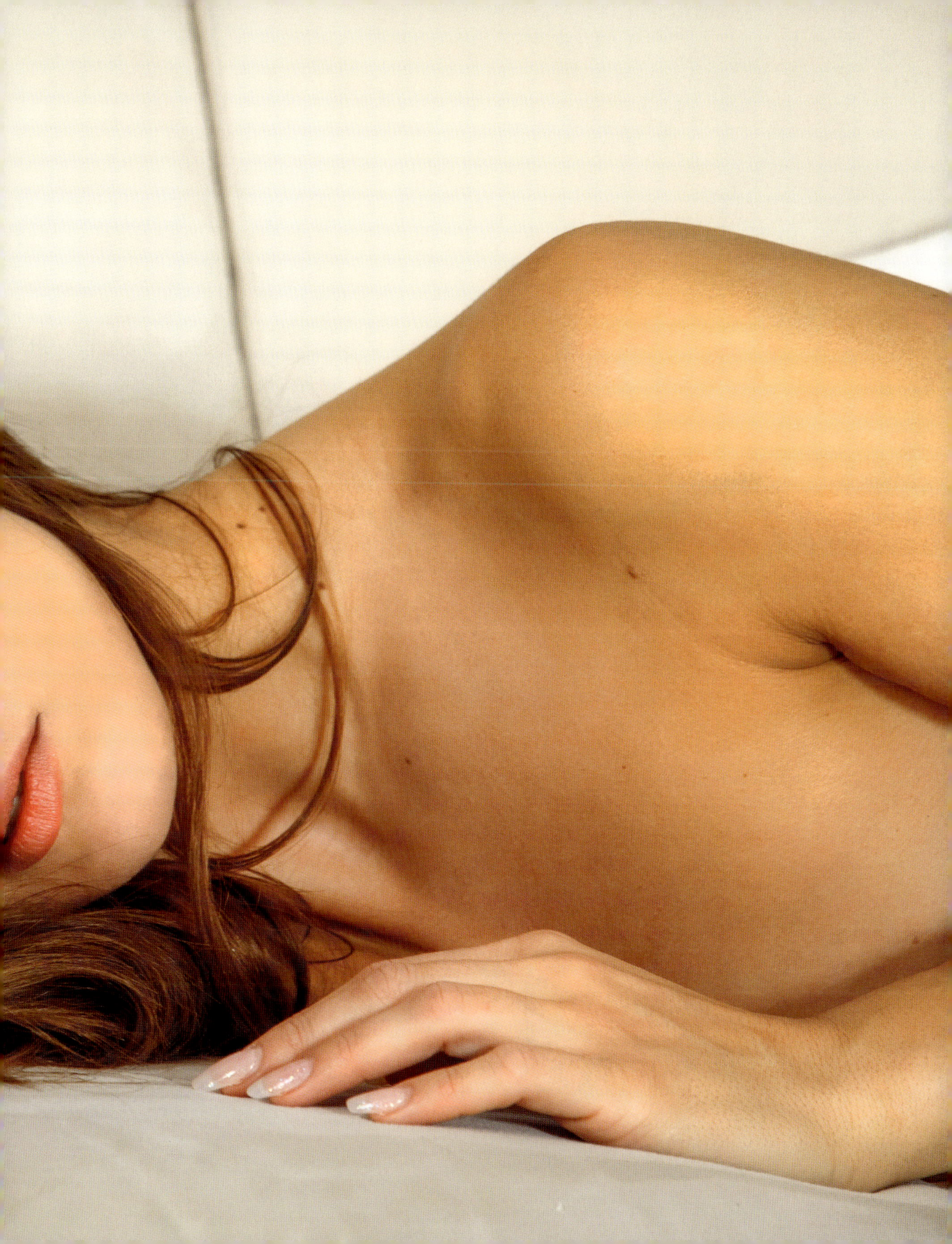

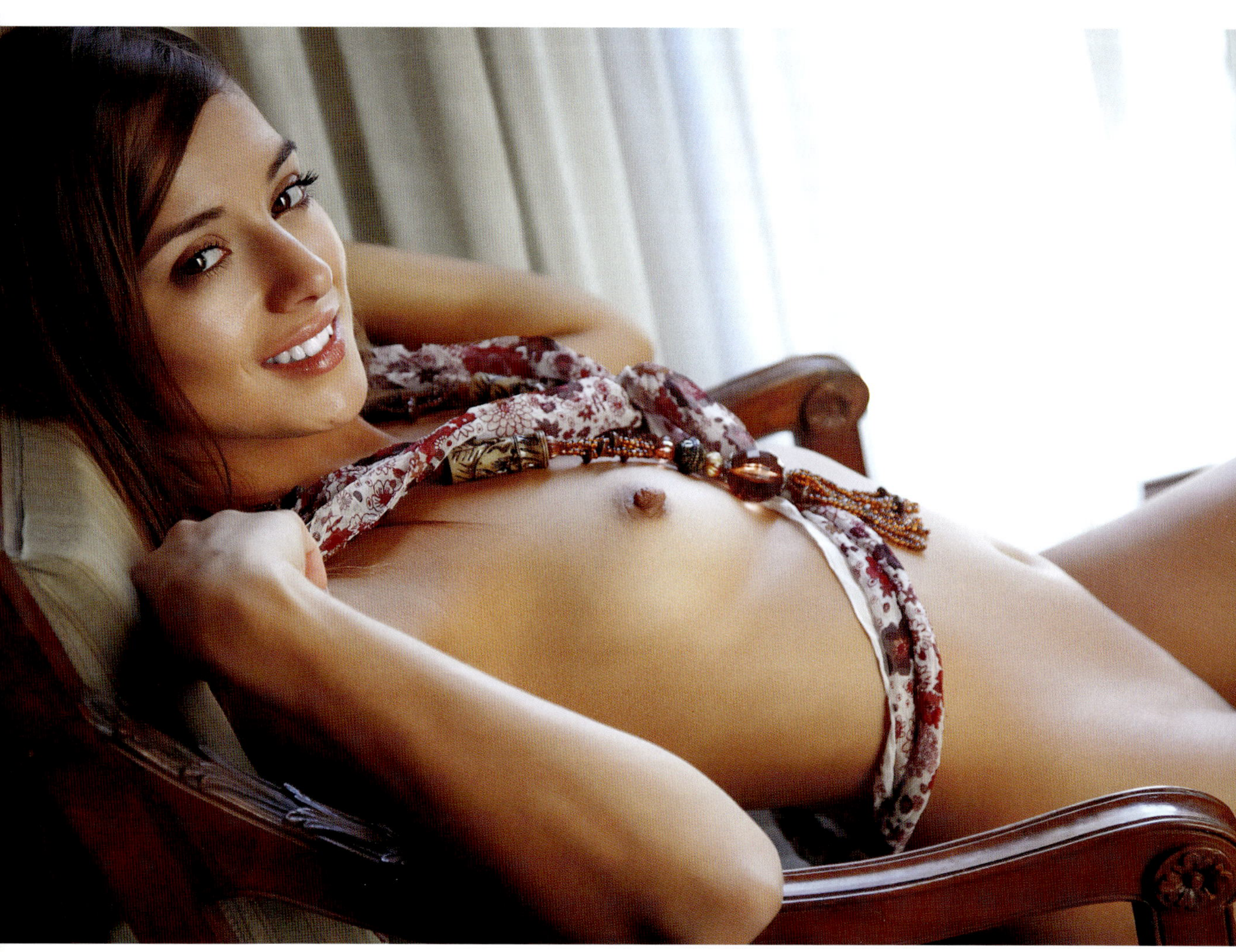

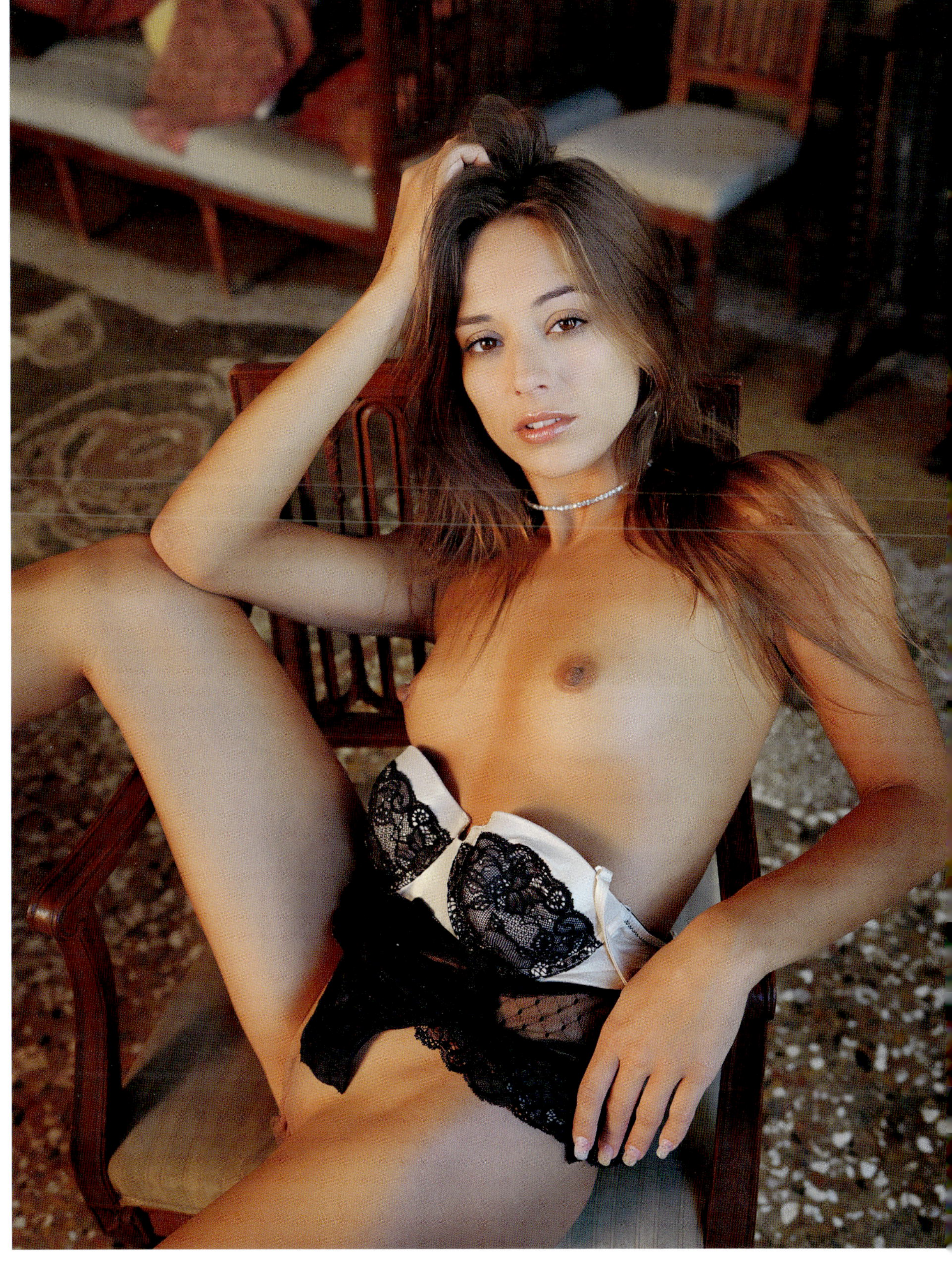

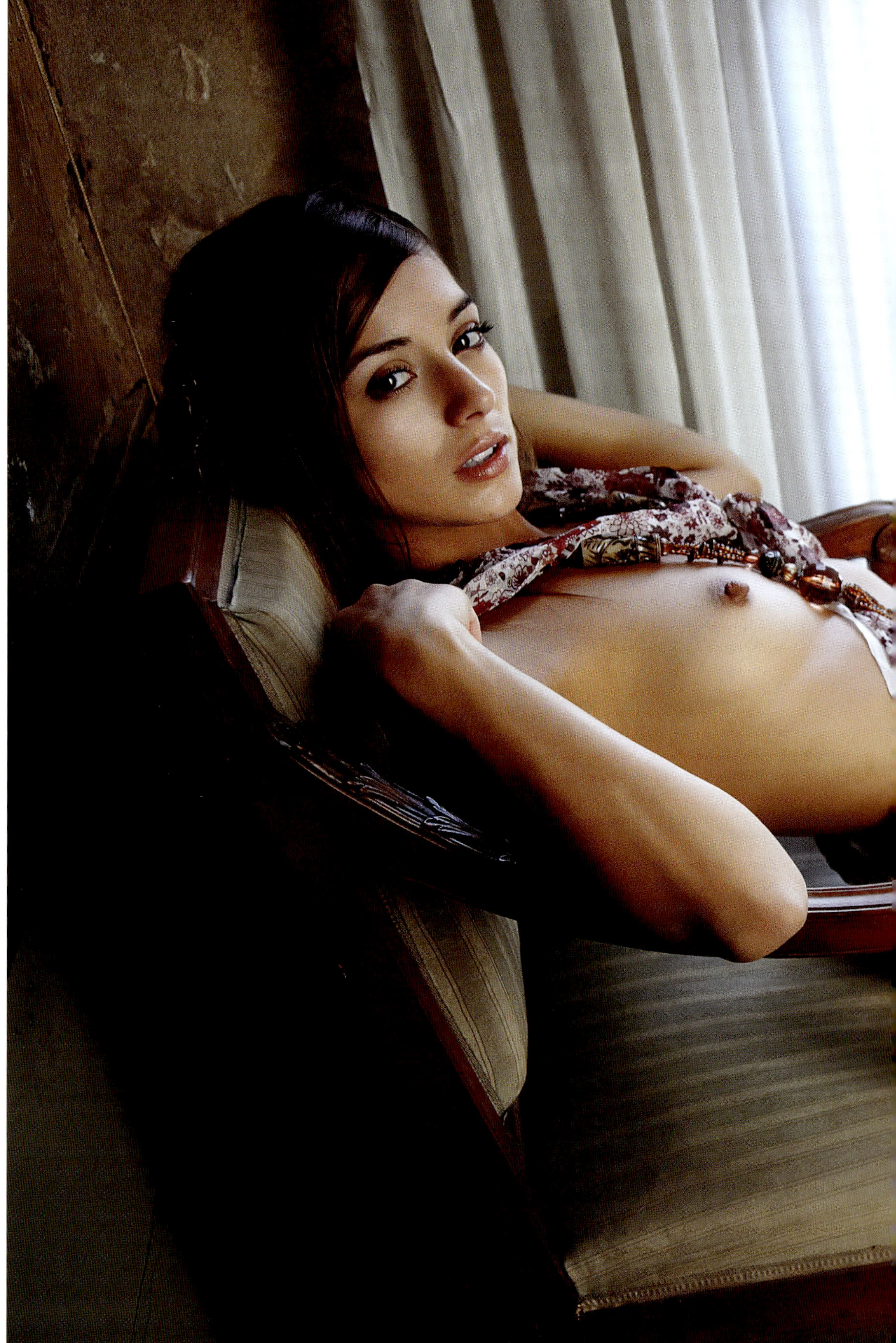

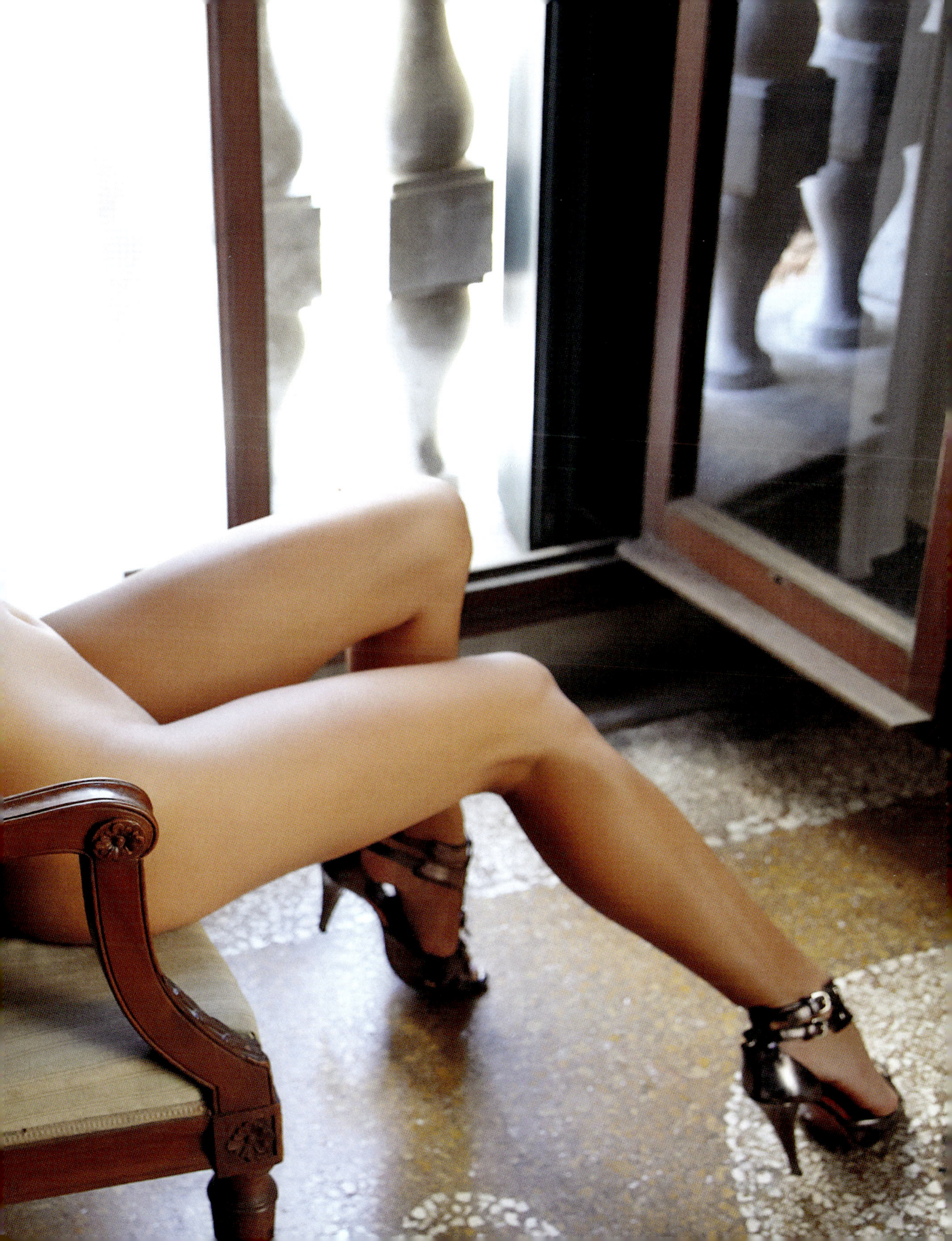

# PHOTOBOOKS ABOUT METART – MODELS

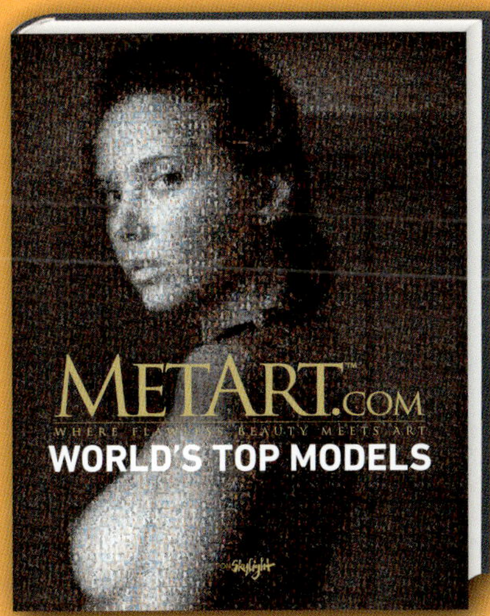


ISBN 978-3-03766-658-6

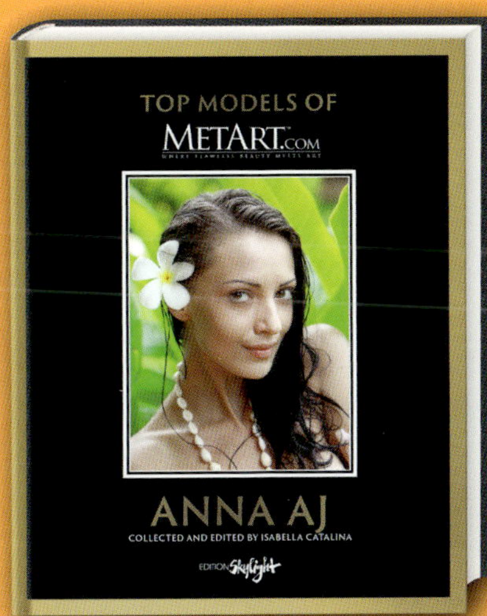


ISBN 978-3-03766-695-1

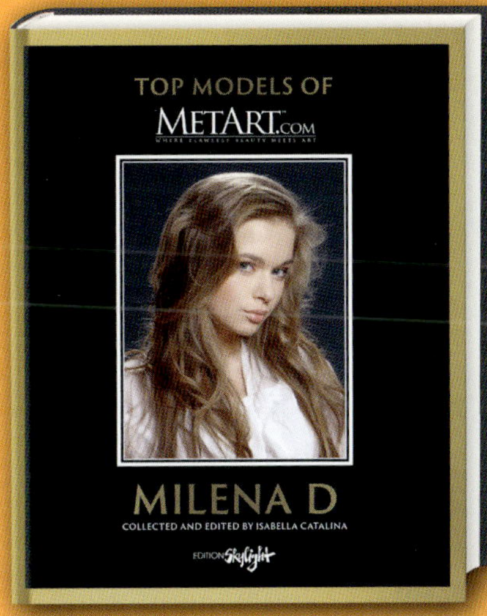


ISBN 978-3-03766-696-8

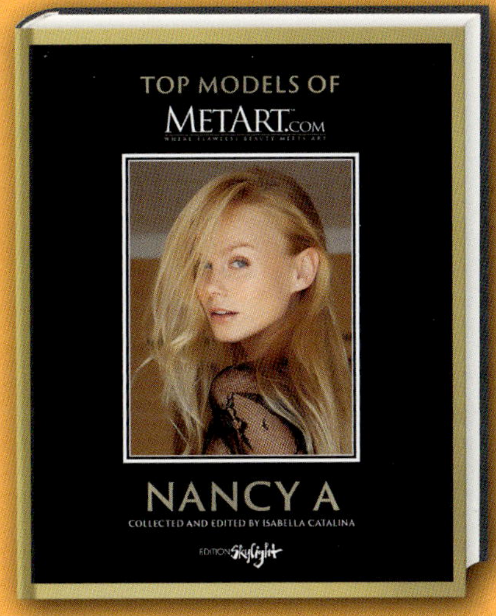


ISBN 978-3-03766-687-6

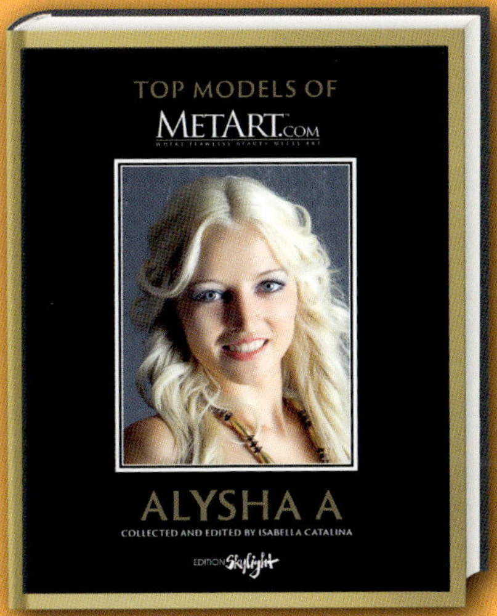


ISBN 978-3-03766-692-0

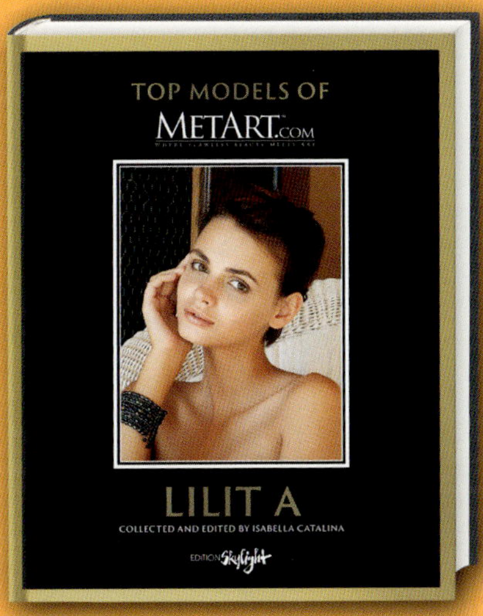


ISBN 978-3-03766-693-7

**WWW.EDITION-SKYLIGHT.COM**

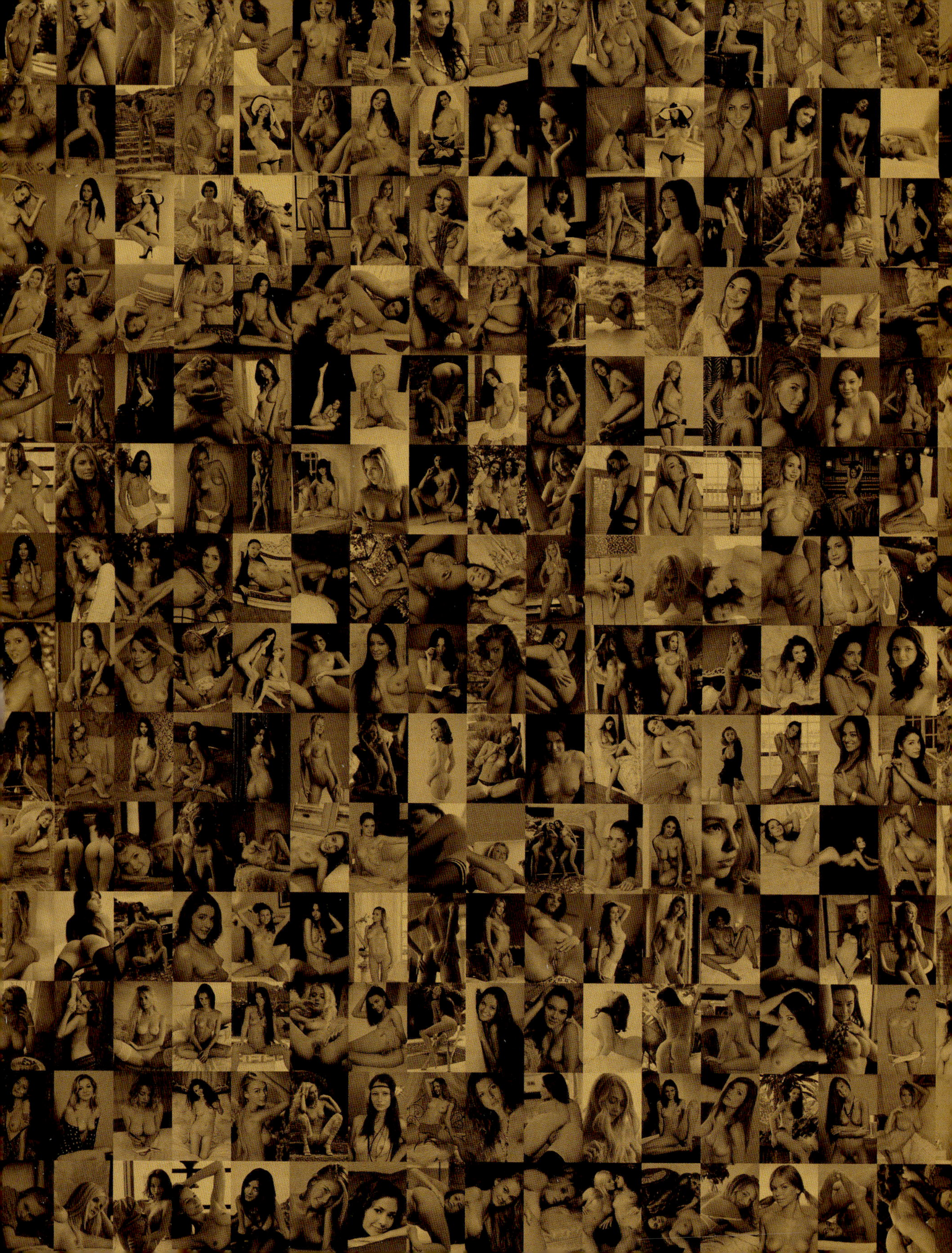